Women, the Family, and Policy

SUNY Series in
Gender and Society

Cornelia Butler Flora, Editor

Women, the Family, and Policy

A Global Perspective

Edited by
Esther Ngan-ling Chow
and
Catherine White Berheide

STATE UNIVERSITY OF NEW YORK PRESS

Production by: Ruth Fisher
Marketing by: Dana E. Yanulavich

Published by
State University of New York Press, Albany

For information, address the State University of New York Press,
State University Plaza, Albany, NY 12246

Library of Congress Cataloging-in-Publication Data

Women, the family, and policy : a global perspective / edited by
    Esther Ngan-ling Chow and Catherine White Berheide.
        p.   cm. — (SUNY series in gender and society)
        Includes index.
        ISBN 0-7914-1785-9. — ISBN 0-7914-1786-7 (pbk.)
        1. Women—Government policy. 2. Family policy. 3. Women in
    development.   I. Chow, Esther Ngan-ling, 1943– II. Berheide,
    Catherine White. III. Series.
    HQ1236.W643   1994
    305.4—dc20   93–847
                                                                              CIP

10 9 8 7 6 5 4 3 2 1

*To our mothers,
to our families,
and to women all over the world.*

Contents

Preface

This book examines how the system of domination created by the interaction of patriarchy, socioeconomic development, and the state transforms women's position within and outside of the family worldwide. The volume celebrates new scholarship generated by feminist critiques and Third World perspectives by challenging conventional thinking and by providing theoretical insights into the linkages between macro-changes and micro-interaction in women's everyday lives.

This book originates from the first editor's transformative experience of growing up in a Third World country, witnessing Hong Kong's industrialization and its enormous effects on women's lives and families, especially among the urban poor. Brought up in a female-headed household for a major part of her life, the first editor has cherished still-searing memories of what it is like to be a Third World woman. Bare survival has motivated the daily struggles of generations of Chinese women. These women have offered hope but encountered despair in the bittersweet mixture of their lives. The first editor's mother, a prime example of these women, made her daughter aware of her Third World existence, planted the seed for her feminist ideals, and ignited her desire to seek intellectual enlightenment.

Like them, the first editor worked as a child laborer in factories, combined housework and schoolwork as a young girl, worked as a seasonal street vendor and as a home-based subcontracting factory worker, fought for low-cost housing as an assistant housing manager, and volunteered monthly in a welfare agency as a case worker. This variety of work experiences provided first-hand insights to the issues this book addresses. These personal experiences, together with those of other contributors, demonstrate that although women's participation in economic development is beneficial to some extent, the system is constructed to intensify male domination, favor capital accumulation, and place women in subordinate positions within class, race, gender, and culture hierarchies.

The first editor's experiences inspired in her a feminist vision of and commitment to translating women's everyday experience into feminist analysis and praxis. As a Third World feminist trained in the United States, she uses her own experience in particular historical, political, and social locations and her interest in culture, consciousness, knowledge, and the politics of empowerment for people in an international context to advance feminist thought.

The editors' collaboration can be traced as far back as 1980, when our paths from the East and the West met. We were both participants in a conference sponsored jointly by Research Committee 32, Women and Society, of the International Sociological Association, and by the Bulgarian Sociological Association and the Committee of the Movement of Bulgarian Women. This meeting cemented feminist connections by building a network for scholars, researchers, policy-makers, and activists from different parts of the world. It provided us an intellectual impetus to relate our research to global concerns. We became cognizant of our shared feminist ideas and research interests, laying the foundation for our subsequent collaborative work over more than a decade.

The conception of this book stems more specifically from our professional experiences while organizing program sessions for two World Congresses sponsored by the International Sociological Association. We first organized and co-chaired a session on "Women and the Family" at the 1986 Congress in New Delhi; later, Marcia Texler Segal and the first editor organized and co-chaired another session on "Women and Development: Variations in Changing Political Economies" at the 1990 Congress in Madrid. These inspiring conferences provided an opportunity to get together with potential contributors and exchange ideas for this book. Our participation in meetings of the International Interdisciplinary Congress on Women and of the Association of Women in Development further exposed us to international feminist scientific communities, broadened our perspectives regarding Third World concerns, and forged feminist coalitions across cultures. We proceeded with scholars in different fields and from various parts of the world.

This anthology represents our efforts to address the interlocking of the economy, the family, and the state that impinges on women's lives globally. We focus on recent debates, feminist critiques, and Third World challenges to mainstream scholarship in three specialized fields—sociology of the family, women and development, and gender and the state. Drawing literature from diverse sources and weaving threads from discussions of theory in these different fields, we use an analytical framework that places women at its center in order to examine their lives from both feminist and Third World perspectives.

Studies in this book represent an intellectual collaboration of internationally committed scholars. Their chapters contain both theoretical models and empirical evidence for understanding global linkages between macro- and micro-forces, the dialectics of material and ideological circumstances, and intimate connections between objective conditions and human subjectivity in the lives of women and their families.

We hope that offering diverse viewpoints and cross-cultural studies to illustrate the main themes of this book will stimulate provocative analyses. We also hope that this volume will inspire those who share our commitment to translating feminist thought into collective action for the liberation, empowerment, equality, and humanity of all people.

E.N.L.C.
C.W.B.

Acknowledgments

First, we thank all the women and their families worldwide who contributed to this volume, either as segments of aggregated data or as individual foci for analysis. They form the soul of this book; without them, the spirit of global feminism and Third World struggle could not be fully understood. We are indebted to the chapter authors for their generosity, dedication, and commitment to this project. Their scholarly work articulates the voices of many invisible women globally and raises our intellectual horizons.

Rachel Kahn-Hut, Irene Tinker, and Mounira Charrad especially provided helpful critical review of and constructive suggestions concerning the introduction. They, along with Marcia Texler Segal, Joan Acker, Montserrat Sagot, Chin-Chun Yi, and Susan Tiano, offered solid support and encouragement throughout this project.

We particularly want to acknowledge support received from both the American University and Skidmore College. At the former, Betty T. Bennett, Dean of the College of Arts and Sciences, and Austin Barron, Associate Dean for Curriculum/Faculty Development, provided initial funding. Helen Koustenis, Johanna Foster, Heather Alderman, Lisa Silverberg, and Ke Bin Wu helped as needed with administrative tasks, proofreading, and research assistance. The first editor's bright graduate students in the Gender and the Family Seminar provided insightful suggestions on some chapters.

Skidmore College provided a faculty research grant, generous travel funds, and clerical assistance. David Seligman, former Associate Dean of Faculty, and David Burrows, Associate Dean of Faculty, were instrumental in obtaining research and travel monies. Deborah Sutherland, Georgia Boothe, and Geraldine Retizos offered cheerful and timely administrative support. The second editor's brother and sister-in-law, Andrew and Jane White, and her student assistants, Sangki Kwon and Kerry Gemmett, helped with the proofreading.

Numerous other people provided spirited support throughout the years it took to bring this project to fruition. Bonnie Thorton Dill and many colleagues from our feminist network within Sociologists for Women in Society (Margaret Andersen in particular) shared their experience and wisdom in academic publishing. Carla Howery energized us when the project seemed to make slow progress. Elaine Stahl Leo spent numerous hours and endless effort rendering valuable editorial services on demand, even on short notice. Luciante Li, Lauri Christiansen, Fu Liu, Helen Moy, and Peggy Dennis, who have devoted their lives to homemaking, occasionally helped the first editor with childcare and have put up with her when she was totally immersed in the exciting, yet tiring, process of producing this volume.

We also owe a great deal to Rosalie Robertson, our SUNY Press editor, who has given us her expert guidance. Her seemingly endless patience in answering our questions is deeply appreciated. In addition, we would like to thank the anonymous reviewers for SUNY Press who provided critical readings of the manuscript and valuable suggestions.

Last but not least, our thanks to our beloved children—Paul, Jennifer, Daniel, and Sarah—for allowing us to take precious family time for our professional work, and to our spouses, Norman and Bruce, who enthusiastically gave us unwavering support, sharing our hope and love for a better world. This book has been a testing ground for our friendship, which has deepened as we have shared our feminist vision and scholarship, transforming our ways of thinking as well as ways of living.

❧ Introduction ❧

Studying Women, Families, and Policies Globally

Esther Ngan-ling Chow and Catherine White Berheide

The global persistence of gender inequality and concern regarding the future of the family in a rapidly changing world have inspired in scholars and lay people alike a new interest in how state policies affect the status of women and families during the process of economic development. To explore this issue, one must address several central questions: How do particular political economies around the world transform gender and household relations? How do state policies attempt to deal with these political economic realities? How do women and their households both initiate and respond to state policies? What are the policy implications of women's and households' survival strategies?

This book explores the intricate relationships among changes in women's positions, family structures, socioeconomic development, and social policies from a global perspective. By focusing on the interconnections among gender, the economy, the family, and the state, it examines how state policies affect gender and household relationships in countries with various types of political economies and under different historical and cultural contexts. The state operates differently in socialist or capitalist economies and in democratic or authoritarian regimes, as well as at various stages of economic development. The state as a form of public patriarchy is intimately related to the family as a form of private patriarchy. Both interact with the economy to produce policies that have significant effects on women and families. As a result, state policies differ in their degree of sensitivity to women's

1

issues and have produced (directly or indirectly, intentionally or unintentionally) mixed outcomes for women and their families. In turn, the ways in which individuals and their families respond to particular state policies may transform them.

For example, Sweden is the only society in the world that has as an official goal the equal participation of fathers and mothers in childcare (Hass 1992). It also has the oldest and most generous paid parental leave policy. Yet Acker shows how some of these same progressive Swedish policies which have women's interests at their center, while benefitting women to some extent, still reinforce gender inequality in both private and public contexts. Sagot shows how low-income women in Costa Rica reacted to the limited government policy by becoming politically active, which resulted not only in helping to meet their families' basic housing needs, but also empowered these women and eventually altered state policies on housing.

We also examine the interaction of the family, the economy, and the state with gender, as these multiple forces (the "quadruple overlap" as Blumberg puts it) affect policy formation and household relationships in countries at various stages of political and economic development. We neither subscribe to a particular theory nor a typology of developmental stages. To enhance our understanding of the diversity of social life, we do not classify countries according to a hegemonic hierarchy such as the world system to study variations in their political economies. Instead, we seek to understand how gender and household relationships are socially constructed as they are shaped by a multiplicity of macro- and micro-forces at different times and places. We do offer a general analytical framework by delineating different arguments from the studies presented in this book and by highlighting the common threads that link various theoretical analyses into an integrated whole.

Our analytical framework is inspired by and derived from feminist and Third World perspectives in three specialized fields of study—sociology of the family, women and development, and gender and the state. Rather than treating feminist thought as a monolithic approach or seeing the Third World as a homogeneous group, we have recognized contributions of various feminist perspectives from different parts of the world.[1] The collection of studies that we include here reflects a broad spectrum of Third World experiences and contexts.[2] Before we delineate the linkages in our analytical framework, we first discuss the development of these three specialized fields and highlight the major ideas in each that have led to their theoretical convergence.

The Convergence of the Sociology of the Family,
Women and Development, and Gender and the State

As the women's movement has expanded throughout the world, feminists have challenged mainstream scholarship in many different disci-
plines by legitimizing gender as a distinct principle of social
organization and by critiquing conventional theories. Sociology of the
family, women and development, and gender and the state have
developed independently of each other. In contrast to the relatively
long historical tradition of family studies, studies of women and
development and of gender and the state emerged in the 1970s and
1980s as changes in the global political economy unfolded. These
changes had particularly wrenching consequences for women,
although the consequences were ignored in both the mainstream
development and political economy literatures.

The women and development field has given exclusive attention
to the effect of economic development on women's changing status. A
recent theoretical shift redefines development to incorporate its social
dimensions, paying more heed to micro-level gender relations and
household analysis while at the same time addressing broader questions about gender inequality (Beneria and Roldan 1987; Dwyer and
Bruce 1988; Tinker 1990). In the early 1980s, renewed interest in "bringing the state back in" led scholars to reconsider the state, the role of
policy in economic development, and its subsequent effects on women
and their households (Charlton, Everett, and Staudt 1989; Staudt 1990).
Studies on gender and comparative politics in the past few years have
revealed how the politicization and empowerment of women, individually and collectively, have shaped state policies (Bunch and Carrillo
1990; Everett 1989; Mohanty, Russo, and Torres 1991).

This book celebrates the contribution of feminist thought,
method, and praxis by integrating studies, especially those from the
Third World, in these three specialized fields. Their theoretical convergence shapes the analytical framework of this book, which examines
the interlocking effects of patriarchy, economic development, and the
state in transforming gender relations in the family as well as in the
larger society. Thus, we begin by examining how these fields have
developed and intersected.

Sociology of the Family: From Micro- to Macro-levels

Sociologists approach the family analytically as an important institution in society. In documenting the historical development of the field,

Adams (1986) divides scientific family studies into four major periods; we add a fifth. During the "Social Darwinist" period, from 1860–1890, scholars such as Marx and Engels, using historical and cross-cultural approaches, attempted to discover the origin of the family and how it evolved into its current form. During the "Social Reform" period, from 1890–1920, scholars concerned with problems families faced as a result of industrialization and urbanization, particularly in the United States and Western Europe, produced policy-oriented family research. The "Scientific Study" period, from 1920–1950, saw a proliferation of research on family behavior, resulting in a large body of empirical data. During the "Attention to Family Theory" period, from 1950–1970, Adams (1986) and Christensen (1964) both argue that family scholars engaged in systematic theory building, while at the same time continuing to produce a considerable amount of empirical research. Some of the new theories, especially the more macro-sociological ones, demanded a return to comparative research.

From the early 1970s to the present, family studies has entered what we call the "Family Diversity" period. Although scholars have often considered the family as women's domain, feminists have criticized the sociology of the family for its androcentric nature reflecting primarily a white, male, and middle-class bias (Bernard 1987; Thorne and Yalom 1992). These critics argue for making women the central focus of analysis to explicate both their objective social conditions and their subjective experience (Hartsock 1987; Smith 1979 and 1987). Recent studies that look at families from the standpoint of women have brought to public attention new issues, such as control of sexuality and reproduction, housework as unpaid labor, and several forms of the victimization of women, revealing hidden problems and providing new insight into old issues about the family as a social institution.

Feminist critiques also point to the ethnocentric nature of family sociology, which tends to ignore the diversity of family patterns in the United States as well as in other countries (Beneria and Roldan 1987; Collins 1991; Baca Zinn 1990). Challenging sexist, racist, and class-biased assumptions, women of color scholars unravelled the myths of monolithic, static, undifferentiated, and consensus-based family patterns (Baca Zinn and Eitzen 1988; Dill 1988; Jones 1985; Thorne and Yalom 1992). By incorporating race, class, gender, and culture into the study of families, these scholars provide a fuller understanding of the diversity of family forms, of the historical and cross-cultural development of these variations, and of their close linkage to forms of social inequality. Systematically integrating hierarchies of race and class into the reconstruction of a more inclusive family theory remains a challenge faced by scholars today.

Feminists relate diversity in family patterns to macro-social forces, leading scholars to look outside the boundaries of the family as a social institution. First, the interconnectedness between the family and other social institutions needs to be studied from a historical perspective. As Tilly and Scott (1978) have argued, the United States' shift from a subsistence-agriculture, family-based economy to an industrial, family-wage and family-consumer economy has had profound effects on family structure and women's work, which belie the general belief that the spheres of family and work are separate ones. Feminists, after scrutinizing the nature of women's work, have redefined the concept of work to include unpaid household labor, volunteer work, and emotional labor. They are also reexamining the nature of home-based production and uncovering other "hidden" work (Bose, Feldberg, and Sokoloff 1987; Christensen 1987; Daniels 1987; Hochschild 1983). These analyses relate both the visible and invisible work associated in the family to gender stratification and the capitalist mode of production outside the family.

Scholars have begun to develop analyses that transcend divisions such as "family and work" and "private and public spheres." We have identified three theoretical models which describe the relationship between family and work: a "separate sphere" model, a "spillover effects" model, and a "system interdependence" model (Chow and Berheide 1988). The separate sphere model regards family and work as separate systems, seeing the family as a domestic haven in which women are primarily homemakers who provide expressive and emotional support and work as a public arena in which men are the primary breadwinners who fulfill material family needs (Parsons and Bales 1955). Recognizing permeability between the work and family systems and the simultaneous membership of individuals in both, the spillover effects model often stresses asymmetrically the effects of work on family life rather than the reverse influence of family on work life, especially in the case of employed women (Crouter 1984).

The third model emphasizes the mutual interdependence of the family and work systems, viewing each system as having independent as well as joint effects, directly and indirectly, on the other and its members (Ferree 1990; Gerstel and Gross 1987; Jones 1985; Kanter 1977; Pleck 1977; Sokoloff 1980). Failure to see this interconnectedness results from "functionalist fixation" reflected in the separate sphere and spillover effects models, which clearly translate gender into two distinct terrains, roles, and sets of sex-typed characteristics, one for men and one for women. A "separate but not equal" principle implicit in these two models gives primacy to work over family, to production over reproduction, and to instrumentality over expressiveness; consequently, both models serve as ideological supports maintaining the existing patriarchal system. Overall family research and theory has moved away from the separate sphere and spillover models to the system interdependence model for it offers a more profound understanding of the complexity of social realities in the United States as well as in the Third World.

Critical of family sociology at both the individual and the societal levels, feminist analyses underscore the importance of understanding linkages between micro-interaction within families and macro-structural forces by showing how both relate to social inequality. Feminists question various forms of inequalities between men and women, such as: the distribution of power and resources; control of sexuality and reproduction; and responsibility for household labor, childcare, and productive activities in the formal and informal economies. Rather than taking such inequalities for granted, recent feminist analyses challenge traditional family theories by explaining how social institutions (including the family, the economy, the state, education, and religion) maintain the ideological and material bases for patriarchy, thereby perpetuating gender inequality (Andersen 1993; Chafetz 1990; Hartmann 1981; Lengermann and Niebrugge-Brantley 1988).

The desire to eliminate barriers to all forms of equality leads feminists to translate their theories into collective action. Except in the welfare and poverty fields, policy research in the United States has just begun to focus on the role of the state and its relation to gender and the family (Diamond 1983; Hyde and Essex 1991; Piven 1984). Recent research in the United States has examined the role of the government in collaboration with corporations in shaping family policies such as the Child Care and Development Block Grant legislation that Congress finally passed in 1990, as well as the Family and Medical Leave Act that Congress passed and President Clinton signed in 1993 after President Bush vetoed it twice. This book examines the implications of family research for social policy.

Women and Development: From Macro- to Micro-levels

At the outset, women and development focused on changing the priorities and practices of development assistance agencies and gradually became incorporated into research and university curricula (Tinker 1990). After two decades, this field now encompasses the ideas and goals of advocates, practitioners, and scholars from the developing countries of the South and the industrialized countries of the North, who work together to influence government policies, to design programs, and to advance knowledge that benefits women world-wide.[3]

Fernandez Kelly (1989) identified several major perspectives in economic development. Based on neo-classical economics and mainstream sociology, modernization theorists argue that poor countries need to adopt the economic, political, and cultural patterns of the industrialized countries to become "developed." This theory was attacked in the 1960s for implying Third World "backwardness" and for failing to indicate the deleterious effects of colonialism and imperialism. Neo-Marxist critics, among others, denounced modernization for ignoring the exploitation of "less developed" countries by industrialized ones.

The proponents of "dependency" theory articulate the "longstanding 'unequal exchanges' between advanced and less-developed nations" (Fernandez Kelly 1989, p. 614). Its critics point out that it tends to see Third World countries as homogeneous entities without much differentiation in economic growth and standards of living among and within them. This theory also tends to view these countries as influenced by a monolith of imperialist and advanced industrialized nations. World-system theorists tend to over-simplify the positions of countries in the global economy by using the taxonomic divisions of "core," "periphery," and "semi-periphery." Finally, the latest approach to development focuses on the new international division of labor, examining the movement of capital investments of multinational corporations throughout the global economy.

Feminist critiques have made specific contributions to the field of women and development. First, their analyses question the concept of development itself as one shaped by the primary value Western thought places on rationality and by the capitalist notion of linear progress in economic development. Boserup (1970) challenges the assumption that societies following the path of Western industrialization will improve their standards of living and thus benefit women.

Various studies have documented how the gendered nature of the development process and practices limits their positive effects on women's lives. The issue, as Rogers (1983) explains, involves "problems of perception" when Western male experts regard women as merely mothers/wives and fail to see them as participants in economic sectors, thus excluding them from the development process. "While [women] represent 50 percent of the world population and one-third of the official labor force, they [account] for nearly two-thirds of all working hours, receive only one-tenth of the world income and own less than one percent of world property" (United Nations 1980, p. 5). Women throughout the world consistently work harder and longer hours than men (United Nations 1991).

Studies document the marginalization of women's position from conditions inherent in colonialism and in capitalism (Mies 1986; Mohanty et al. 1991; Ollenburger and Moore 1992). For example, Boserup (1970) points out how the expansion of cash cropping and the use of agricultural technology tends to benefit men rather than women, who often shoulder a greater burden in the family and in production as casual or seasonal workers. Other research, including Acosta-Belen and Bose (1990), Beneria (1982), Berheide and Segal (this volume), and Kandiyoti (1985), also show how the division of labor by gender increases as men move into technologically advanced production, leaving labor-intensive work in the subsistence economy to women.

Furthermore, development theory and policies tend to overemphasize economic growth, with the expectation that this growth will eventually trickle down to the poor. This theory tends to measure societal progress only in economic terms, ignoring the importance of other human needs. Since women's economic activities are often invisible, feminist researchers challenge this theory's definition of work and its methods of gathering data on women's work. They point out that women's labor is still not considered crucial for the maintenance of society in a purely economic sense.

In addition, women's informal micro-enterprises and home-based industries are largely regarded as family or individual activities that are an extension of domestic responsibilities rather than as contributions to the economy. Tinker (1987) is particularly critical of the U.N.'s International Labor Office (ILO) and others who dismiss micro-entrepreneurs such as street vendors and market sellers as unworthy of support simply because they do not reinvest or generate employment. Tinker (1990, p. 97) argues ardently for the practice of human economy, saying that "investing money in an enterprise instead of one's children is not an overriding priority for most women entrepreneurs. . . . Women should not be penalized for questioning the primacy of the profit motive; rather programs should be redesigned to accommodate this different world view."

In attempting to broaden development theories, feminist thought has analyzed how capitalism and patriarchy interact to ensure men's control of economic resources and of women's labor both in the wage economy and in the household. Like family sociologists, scholars in women and development are critical of the public–private sphere theory, arguing that these spheres should not be treated as dichotomies but rather as interpenetrating points along a continuum (Tiano 1984).

On the one hand, a growing body of literature has recognized the value of women's work, the pervasiveness of labor segregation by gender, and how wage differentials between men and women workers relate to macro-economic policies. As multinational corporations have increasingly set up factories in developing countries for offshore production, the processes of global capitalist accumulation, industrial restructuring, and the new international division of labor have had substantial effects on women's work. While some scholars point out that the new international division of labor has exploited women as a source of cheap labor (Leacock and Safa 1986; Nash and Fernandez Kelly 1983), others argue that it has expanded their job opportunities (Lim 1983). On the other hand, recent studies resemble family sociology in emphasizing intrahousehold dynamics (such as division of labor by gender, social relations within the family, and survival strategies by class) and their connection with wider socioeconomic processes (Blumberg this volume; Rogers 1983; Tinker 1987). In-depth analyses of who controls economic resources (Blumberg 1991; Dwyer and Bruce 1988) focus on intrahousehold dynamics, where women and development scholars clearly cross theoretical paths with family sociologists.

Finally, feminist analyses in women and development, like those in family sociology, see gender inequality as deeply rooted in the division of labor and perpetuated by structural domination based on class, gender, and race/ethnicity. Those three bases are "irreducible categories that designate specific relations of economic, political, and ideological domination" (Fernandez Kelly 1989, p. 624). Other scholars have added the dimensions of culture and nationality to this triple oppression (Mohanty et al. 1991; Sen and Grown 1987). Understanding the interlocking of race, class, gender, culture, and nation is central to dismantling all forms of inequality.

To eliminate all forms of inequality, to combat male dominance in patriarchal systems, and to build egalitarian societies, scholars, practitioners, and advocates in the women and development field are attempting to influence policy formation and project development. Women and development critically examines the relationship between theory and practice by studying the impact of state policies, by reassessing the efficiency of development programs and projects (e.g., in credit, training, technology, employment, housing, nutrition, and family planning), and by transforming feminist thought into action. Hence, convergence of the two fields has occurred as family sociologists have paid increasing attention to relating micro family issues to macro forces and as researchers in women and development have begun to study gender and intrahousehold dynamics in economic development and their implications for state policy.

Gender and the State:
The Top-Down Approach vs. the Bottom-Up Approach

Clearly, the state has great power to control the shape of policies that eventually affect the lives of women and their families. Generally speaking, policy analyses tend to employ a top-down approach in examining the role of the state, the relevance of its development policies to women's needs, its sensitivity toward women's interests, its placement of women in specific development projects, and its subsequent effects on women's lives. Recent feminist analyses indicate that development assistance programs, even those directly targeted to benefit women, tend to isolate and marginalize them. Therefore, researchers advise that "new projects for women should be embedded in regular sectoral programs organizationally and should be part of the original design, not added on as a `women's component'" (Tinker 1990, p. 43). Although some programs seeking to respond to women's basic needs may have helped them to survive, even those programs have done very little to change the structural conditions that perpetuate women's subordination and gender inequality (Everett 1989).

Debt crises that crippled economies in many world regions during the 1980s resulted in a policy de-emphasizing basic needs in favor of "structural adjustment" programs designed by the International Monetary Fund and the World Bank. These policies had devastating effects on the world's poor, especially women (Sen and Grown 1987). Militarization diverted resources that could have been used to meet basic needs. In view of the adverse effects on women, most recent feminist critiques focus on how sensitive the state is toward the strategic and practical interests of women in the formation of development policies (Afshar 1987; Charlton et al. 1989; Molyneux 1985; Staudt 1990).

Critical of the overemphasis on economic development, recent work explores alternative ways of empowering women. From the late 1970s into the 1980s, reports from several groups and international meetings proposed the empowerment of women in the political process as one of the paramount goals of development to remove both ideological and structural forms of oppression (APCWD 1979; IWTC 1980; CEPAL 1983; Sen and Grown 1987). The essential point these reports make is that the oppression of women is rooted in political and economic systems based on gender, race, and class. If development programs are to affect women's lives, they must take into account not only women's practical but also their strategic interests, including their emancipation and empowerment (Molyneux 1985). Moser (1987) demonstrates how housing programs for poor women could either satisfy a practical need for shelter or fulfill a strategic need for change if women were permitted to house themselves. Departing from the welfarist approach to women's basic needs, new policies need to include consciousness raising, mobilization for political participation, and other legal and structural changes (CEPAL 1983). Multifaceted strategies in areas of political, economic, educational, and cultural empowerment are used to link research with collective action (Everett 1989).

Furthermore, as Bunch and Carrillo (1990, p. 77) succinctly explain, "Power for women was seen as essential, not in its traditional patriarchal definition as domination over others but as a sense of internal strength, as the right to determine one's choices in life, and the right to influence the direction of social change." Therefore, feminism is defined as global, providing a political basis for this new consciousness for diverse kinds of women, for cultural resistance to all forms of domination, and for collective solidarity of women in different parts of the world.

A Third World women's group called DAWN (Development Alternatives with Women for a New Era) formed to define the issues of development from the vantage point of women and to advocate alternative development processes. DAWN emphasizes that a movement for change needs to draw its ethical basis from women's daily lives by rejecting the competitive and aggressive nature of the male-dominated system and by advocating a system that derives "a sense of responsibility, nurturance, openness, and rejection of hierarchy" out of feminist vision. Sen and Grown (1987, p. 79) point out the importance of a unified "commitment to breaking down the structures of gender subordination and a vision of women as full and equal participants with men at all levels of societal life."

In sociology, a recent upsurge of interest in bringing "the state back in" has occurred in comparative-historical studies over the past decade (Evans, Rueschemeyer, and Skocpol 1985). This trend has brought about a paradigmatic shift moving from the "society-centered" or "grand theory" approach advocated by structural-functionalists and Marxists to the "state-centered" or "middle range" approach suggested by the comparative social scientists. Reconceptualizing the state as an autonomous actor, Evans and others (1985) examine how states affect social processes through their policies and their relationships with groups in the world-economic, geopolitical, and transnational settings. However, studies about the formation of state policies need to take gender into account. Skocpol (Evans et al. 1985, p. 30) specifically cited Charrad's work (related to the chapter in this book) as a prime example illustrating how state formation in Tunisia resulted in policies that expanded women's legal rights while perpetuating gender inequality.

Moving beyond the focus on the economic transformation of

gender relations, recent in-depth analyses by feminist scholars have reconceptualized the state and studied the effects of the state's role in capital accumulation and industrialization on gender relations (Afshar 1987; Charlton et al. 1989; MacKinnon 1989; Peterson 1992; Staudt 1990). Defining the state as a set of institutions, Charlton and others (1989) see state-gender relations as one dimension of state-society relations interconnected with other dimensions (including class, race, and religion), all of which are tied closely to various forms of structural inequality. For the most part, these analyses contend, the state has helped to reproduce gendered power relationships and to maintain women's subordination in society through the influence of state elites, the nature of state policies, and the political discourse shaped by state institutions.

Throughout the world, women have employed various types of household strategies, used collective forms of resistance, and shown a considerable degree of empowerment as women's community groups have become politicized at the grass-roots level to ensure family survival. These responses from women, their families, and their communities, though traditionally perceived as relatively insignificant, may in fact affect state policies and eventually lead to policy changes (Bookman and Morgen 1988; Charlton et al. 1989; Mohanty et al. 1991). Recent feminist analyses suggest that this bottom-up approach in which women and their grass-roots organizations exert control in the development process, provide input to policy-makers at different levels, and influence national politics has enhanced women's interests. The connection between state policy at the macro-level of politics and of the economy and women's lives at the micro-level of the individual and of the household needs further analysis.

Family, Development, and the State: An Emergent Analytical Framework

Over the past two decades, feminist thought in family sociology, women and development, and the state has contributed to the theoretical convergence of these three fields. The commonalities of these fields have advanced global analysis of macro- and micro-linkages between the individual and society and between the family and other social institutions. They have transformed our understanding of how gender, the family, the economy, and the state interact.

The unifying theme of this book is how the interlocking of families, economies, and states perpetuate gender inequality within and outside of the family, shaping women's life experiences globally. Representing a range of scholarly interests and theoretical perspectives, the contributors offer original empirical research, especially from various Third World settings, that reveal how women and their families respond to state policy as they struggle to meet basic needs and to deal with the interface of work and family life. This book represents only a beginning point for addressing the complementarity of the three fields and for systematic discussion of their theoretical convergence.

The Global Approach to Studying Women and the Family

Global feminism, as embodied in theory, research, and practice, has legitimized gender as a general principle of social organization and has increased our understanding of the diversity of family patterns. Increasing sensitivity to gender, race, class, cultural, and national differences characterizes the fields of family sociology and of women and development (Baca Zinn 1990; Beneria and Roldan 1987; Fernandez Kelly 1989; Mohanty et al. 1991). A comparative approach provides a means for testing generalizations developed in a single society in other cultural settings. Cross-cultural comparisons help illuminate the causes and consequences of family patterns in particular countries.

For example, women's status and family patterns vary according to the structural conditions that prevail in a society at different points in time. The form, extent, and significance of household work vary according to a society's stage of economic transformation. In subsistence economies, household and nonhousehold production are so closely linked that it is hard to distinguish them. In agricultural societies, the proportion of production for the household's own consumption is higher than in societies where a large proportion of home production has become commoditized. As Berheide and Segal show in their chapter, domestic and agricultural work contribute most to subsistence needs in farming areas. By contrast, in industrialized urban societies, the burden of subsistence falls upon the wage; domestic work transforms the wage into use values consumed in the household (Beneria and Sen 1981, pp. 292–293). Thus incorporating women and development research into the study of the family broadens the perspective of family sociology to encompass macro-forces affecting households globally.

However, scholars from both fields have different concepts of what the family is. Critical of family as a Western concept, women in development scholars point out that worldwide variations in household and kinship relations exist (e.g., extended or fictive kin, female-headed households). Even in the United States, female-headed households outnumber the traditional nuclear family composed of a bread-winning father, homemaking mother, and children, as the former constitute 17.6 percent of all households while the latter constitute only 13.6 percent (U.S. Bureau of Labor Statistics 1992). Women and development researchers prefer to use the term "household" rather than "family." "Household" generally refers to a residential unit in which members live in close proximity and which forms the locus of a set of activities that maintain these members' daily lives.

Critiquing the global economy approach, however, Bourque and Warren (1987) note that using the household as a unit of analysis downplays competing interests within the family. Challenging the view of the household as a harmonious unit with a single decisionmaker, women and development scholars analyze the household as an arena of conflict over resource allocation that tends to serve patriarchal or kinship interests, to reinforce women's subjugation within the family, and to shape different household arrangements (Chow 1993; Dwyer and Bruce 1988; Papanek 1990). When Third World women are able to control their own income and to set allocation priorities, they negotiate, bargain, and trade to improve their families' positions. Blumberg (1991 and also in this volume) suggests that gender-differentiated control of economic resources within the household matters for the family's well-being, for the relative status of women, and for the success of development projects. She explains how development planning in Africa ignores the "internal economy" of households, thus reducing women's opportunities in food production and contributing to the food crises in that region.

In this book, we use family and household interchangeably. We prefer to use the term "family" partly because it embodies a richer and broader meaning than "household" and partly because some users limit "household" to a merely economic term. We define family as a socioeconomic unit that includes household and as a system of interacting personalities which offers a cultural context in which the material relations of the household take place and are normatively regulated. Family is also linked to kinship, which describes the structured network in which the boundaries of several households intersect.

The Role of Patriarchy and the Family

Patriarchy is generally defined as the principle of male dominance that forms both a structural and ideological system of domination in which men control women. It consists of "a set of social relations between men that have a material base and which, though hierarchical, establish interdependence and solidarity among men that enable them to dominate women" (Hartmann 1976, p. 138). However, patriarchy is not a monolithic conception of male domination; men and women of various backgrounds have different places in the patriarchy. In different historical periods and in different countries, the specific forms of women's subjugation to male dominance vary by class, race, and age. For example, Kandiyoti (1988) identifies two distinct systems of patriarchy which exert a powerful influence on women's gendered subjectivity, determine the nature of gender ideology, and affect women's forms of resistance in the face of oppression under different cultural contexts. Women in sub-Saharan Africa gain autonomy through protest against patriarchal practices that reduce their status, whereas women from North Africa, the Muslim Middle East, and South and East Asia show subservience while using manipulation to maintain their status within classic patriarchy.

Patriarchy's chief institution is the family, within which men hold the power to determine the privileges, statuses, and roles of women and children. Such a structure is buttressed by traditional gender-role ideology and is further institutionalized and reproduced in gendered power relationships throughout society, contributing to the perpetuation of gender inequality. In particular, Hartmann (1976) points out that patriarchy, as an independent system of domination preceding capitalism, influences the particular forms the sexual division of labor takes in the family as well as in the waged labor economy. Household work, childcare, emotional labor, and home-based production are examples of how the family serves as locus of control and how men benefit from women's labor, paid or unpaid, at home.

Feminist debates about whether patriarchy is an inherently ahistorical concept and whether control over children should be placed under the same rubric as control over women led to a distinction between "private" and "public" patriarchy and between different historical stages of patriarchy to clarify the changing relationship between gender- and age-based inequality (Boris and Bardaglio 1987; Brown 1981; Walby 1990). At different stages of capitalist development, Ferguson (1984) explains how "father patriarchy" (men's economic benefits from and power over their children and wives) was changed to "husband patriarchy" (men's control over women) due to child labor laws and public education requirements that directly limit paternal control over children and replace the economic benefits of having children with economic costs, which women pay.

"Private" patriarchy becomes a "public" one when the power of fathers is replaced by the power of men who use the state to dictate laws, to control scarce resources, and to shape gender ideology (Folbre

1987). With the development of capitalism, patriarchal control of unpaid domestic labor in household production extends to the labor market, as the gender-segregated occupational structure clearly indicates (Hartmann 1981; Reskin and Roos 1990; Sokoloff 1980). Furthermore, patriarchal control of unpaid work extends to the labor market extracting surplus values from women volunteers, such as those in Australia (see Baldock's chapter in this volume). The following sections will discuss further how the interlocking of patriarchy, modes of production (e.g., capitalist or socialist), and the state form a system of domination that shapes the lived experience of women.

The Interplay of Patriarchy and the Economy on Family and Work

As "private" patriarchy becomes "public," its interaction with the economy creates another dimension of domination that affects the relationship between work and family. Socialist feminists clearly link capitalism and patriarchy to the productive and reproductive roles of women in society (Beneria and Roldan 1987, p. 9; Hartmann 1981). The literature on the international division of labor has also documented how capitalist accumulation on a world scale interacts with patriarchal family structures in shaping women's place in the division of labor in the global economy and in the household (Beneria and Stimpson 1987; Leacock and Safa 1986; Mies 1986; Nash and Fernandez Kelly 1983).

One theme that integrates many chapters in this book is the interconnectedness between family and work in the lives of the world's women. The three theoretical models—separate spheres, spillover effects, and system interdependence respectively—represent conflicting world views concerning the roles of men and women. In various modes of economic production, whether capitalist or socialist, the separate spheres model is an ideological support for existing patriarchal arrangements. Bourque and Warren (1979) argue specifically that men use separate sphere arguments to justify continued male dominance and female subordination because men have a stake in asserting that women are incapable of doing men's work and thus of sharing men's power even when women do "men's work." This underlying ideology often contradicts public policy related specifically to women and helps perpetuate gender inequality. The patriarchal ideology implicit in the one-child family-planning policy in the People's Republic of China is a case in point, as the chapter by Chow and Chen in this book shows.

Family and work or private and public spheres are analytically distinct only at a theoretical level, and they are, in fact, empirically interrelated in women's lives. Beneria and Sen (1981, p. 293) assert that a clear separation between domestic and commodity production exists only in modern industrialized societies. Tiano (1984) is critical of the split Marxist feminist theories posit between the public sphere of commodity production and the private sphere of reproduction and consumption, especially when applied to Third World women's work. Some Marxist scholars even contend that production vs. reproduction is a false dichotomy and suggest reconceptualizing the two as alternative modes of production (Beechey 1979; Kusterer 1990).[4]

In this book, we argue that even in industrialized societies such as the United States, family and work are intertwined, with each system highly permeable as a result of individuals' simultaneous memberships in both (Chow and Berheide 1988). Using the interdependence model, we treat the work and family systems as analytically distinct at a conceptual level while examining their interconnectedness. As Beneria and Roldan (1987, p. 10) note, "The specificity of real life does not present itself in a dualistic manner but as an integrated whole, where multiple relations of domination/subordination—based on race, age, ethnicity, nationality, sexual preference—interact dialectically with class and gender relations."

The differential effects of the interaction between patriarchy and modes of production on family and work are gendered. Gender inequality is socially constituted through the differences in men's and women's work and family activities. On the one hand, the interplay of these social institutions has provided economic independence, means to meet basic family needs, and well-being for women. On the other hand, these institutions have promoted exploitation of women both as low-paid workers in the labor market and as unpaid workers in the home. Field research from Guatemala and Tanzania demonstrates that development, whether in capitalist or socialist economies, continues to marginalize women and to take their domestic contributions in the household for granted (Blumberg 1991; Ehler 1983). The fact that women perform household labor while men do not reflects the "essential nature" of each sex, adding a double shift to women's paid work in the economy (Hochschild 1989) and making a "triple day" for Third World women workers (Blumberg 1991; Parpart 1990; Sen and Grown 1987; Ward 1990).

The gendered nature of both work and family systems and its transformation is dialectical, producing contradictions at different historical times. As U.S. families increasingly depend on two incomes, "Reliance on wives' services at home [has] produced husbands who both resisted and encouraged their wives' employment and women who were ambivalent—not simply resentful—about their double burden" (Gerstel and Gross 1987, p. 8). Some women and development scholars question whether the pursuit of paid work in the labor market (that is, in the public sphere with men) is the basis for building an egalitarian society. Whether such employment offers job opportunities which enable women to ensure family survival or whether it creates super-exploitation of Third World women epitomizes the dialectical nature of work-family connections. In this book, Yi's chapter shows the dilemmas that Chinese women face when combining work and family roles in Taiwan. The chapter by Tiano demonstrates that having children tends to create problems for women employed in the maquila factories at the southern U.S. border. Issues associated with the dialectic between work and family become complicated, yet theoretically interesting, when the role of the state is added to the framework of analysis.

Patriarchy, the Family, the Economy, and State Policy

This book seeks to understand the critical linkage between feminist theory and action by addressing how state policy relates to women and their families specifically and to structurally based inequality generally. It studies the relationships among a set of patriarchal social institutions in both private (the family) and public (the economy and the state) domains, forming a system of domination which affects women's lives and family well-being globally.

Kamerman and Kahn (1978) note that the United States, unlike many European countries, does not have either explicit family policies or a comprehensive national policy.[5] Gerstel and Gross (1987) explain that the absence of a coherent national family policy in the U.S. is due to the lack of agreement on the meaning of being pro-family, the government's reluctance to legislate family relations, pluralism in family life, persistent variations from state to state, and the ideology of the family as a bastion of privacy. Reviewing maternity-leave, child-support, childcare, AFDC (Aid to Families with Dependent Children), and tax policies, Folbre (1987) shows how they have served the interests of men while disadvantaging women by failing to recognize mothering as work, by assigning disproportionate amounts of the cost of child-rearing to mothers, and by contributing significantly to the pauperization and dependency of mothers.

This book's framework of analysis shows how male dominance as manifested in the state has both ideological and material bases, collaborating with the economy and the family to shape policies that reinforce gender inequality. Afshar (1987, p. 2) points out that studies of many countries reveal that state policy (with some of its underlying ideological contradictions) influences private and personal lives, especially women's. She shows specifically how fear of women's sexuality and perception of women as "seditious" agents led to Iranian legislation supporting women's seclusion at home as the most important symbol of their honor and dignity, thereby justifying the benefits men receive by excluding women in the public domain and by controlling them within the household. The chapter by Chow and Chen reveals how Chinese state patriarchy reflected in the only-child policy tends to place a greater emphasis on child-centeredness ideology than on gender egalitarianism to increase women's responsibilities for childbearing and rearing, and potentially to limit their full participation in society, thus increasing rather than diminishing gender inequality.

Recent feminist analyses have begun to examine the role of the state and its relationship to public policies and state apparatuses which have significant effects on women's strategic and practical interests as well as on their families' well-being. Identifying three main approaches—liberal-pluralist, Marxist, and statist—to the state, Charlton et al. (1989) indicate that liberal-pluralist approaches typically view the state as a government or decision-making apparatus which serves as an arbitrator between competing interest groups. The state, which is presumed to be gender-blind, is largely responsible for resource allocation in meeting citizen demands. Marxist theory views the state as the apparatus through which the dominant capitalist class seeks to preserve its interests. Although Charlton et al. (1989, p. 4) recognize the utility of Marxist analysis in demonstrating how the patriarchal family and state are sustained through control of female labor, they argue that this approach does not take into account "the vitality of gender ideologies, conflict between men and women of the same class, the distinctiveness of women's organizations, or gender conflicts in socialist countries."

The statist approach views the state simultaneously as "a bureaucratic, coercive, legal, and normative order" (Charlton et al. 1989, p. 4). This approach does not treat gender as merely another interest group or as of secondary importance to class relations. More specifically, Charlton et al. (1989, p. 5) assert that "Institutionalized male privilege exists independently of the dominant class, and it means that women occupy a different, and subordinate, role in intergroup competition (when it exists). The challenge is to locate the boundaries that define state autonomy and to explain those forces that both enhance and limit autonomy, whether international or domestic."

Following a similar approach, Staudt and others (1990) discuss the contexts under which paternalism is manifested in statist apparatus, in bureaucratic structures and staff (such as those of the Commission on the Status of Women, the World Bank, the Inter-American Foundation, and the Swedish International Development Authority), and in constituencies outside the official apparatus. State paternalism affects the women's groups that these apparatuses are supposed to serve. These scholars question whether more women inside bureaucracy will actually empower women outside of it and whether women will infuse a new sort of politics into male-oriented bureaucracy. Therefore, this book's emphasis on the connections among the family, the economy, and the state challenges the deterministic view of the economy as the only public domain by bringing the state and other organizations under scrutiny.

Studies included in this volume examine the conditions, structural and ideological, that produce policies that promote or limit women's interests and that enhance or impede their socioeconomic status. We identify three kinds of state policies—women-centered, women-sensitive, and women-peripheral—that vary in the degree to which they are inclusive of women's concerns and in the extent to which they intend to benefit women. Women-centered policies are those which are designed with concern for or the intention of benefitting women, such as Swedish welfare policies adopted to promote gender equality. Second, women-sensitive policies are ones which are formulated with other primary concerns (e.g., family planning or economic goals), but are also sensitive to women's interests, such as China's one-child policy. Lastly, women-peripheral policies are ones made for purposes ostensibly unrelated to women and pay little or no attention to women's interests. We argue for more women-centered or at least gender-sensitive policies to promote the wealth of nations, the well-being of women and their families, and equality for all people.

Conventionally, the term "politics" refers to the activities of public officials and the workings of the state, taking place exclusively in the public domain. The feminist principle that "the personal is political" embodies the understanding that a deep, direct relationship exists between politics and everyday life and between social change and women's practical and strategic interests. This reconceptualization of political terrains as existing in both personal and social life bridges the Marxist dichotomies of production vs. reproduction, interweaves the private and public spheres, and captures the dialectical connection as well as the tension between macro-structures of domination and the micro-level interaction of maintenance and resistance. For a full understanding of international politics, Enloe (1989) expands this feminist insight from "The Personal is Political" to "The Personal is International" to show how public life is constructed out of daily struggles in the private domain which define masculinity, femininity, and gender relationships in ways that bolster male-dominated political control globally.

Women around the world adopt multiple strategies, including building coalitions among women's groups, labor movements, political movements, and the like, to force social change. Many women's groups with varying goals share a common strategy of political empowerment. To Bookman and Morgen (1988, p. 4), empowerment connotes "a spectrum of political activity ranging from acts of individual resistance to mass political mobilizations that challenge the basic power relations in our society." The goal of transforming women's position through empowerment fundamentally challenges the very logic, the very primacy of the profit motive as well as of the traditionally patriarchal role of the state. Globally, by not only responding to changing political-economic and family conditions, but also actively resisting adverse conditions and seeking creative strategies for ensuring family survival, women are politicized and empower themselves in both the private and public domains (Jaquette 1991). Their struggle forms an important pre-condition for their becoming politically active in challenging and even transforming state policy.

Overview of the Book

In short, this book introduces an analytical framework by integrating feminist thought and Third World perspectives in three specialized fields—the sociology of the family, women in development, and gender and the state. Family sociology in the United States tends to place greater emphasis on the micro-level; its macro-level analysis is mostly limited to a single country. As this book demonstrates, incorporating the literature on women and development into family studies broadens the perspective of the latter. The applied, policy-oriented focus of the women and development literature allows us to assess the validity of existing sociological theories on the family cross-culturally while enlarging our understanding of the diversity of women's experiences globally. Both family and development studies achieve new insight from a feminist perspective about the politics of gender which specifically examines how macro-social forces are linked to micro-interaction in women's everyday lives, and how the state apparatus and political ideology serve as control mechanisms which perpetuate various forms of inequalities globally.

The chapters in this book place women at the center of the analysis, regard the family as interdependent with other social institutions, provide cross-cultural insight into family issues, and examine the effects of policy on the status of women and their families. They focus on family issues ranging from mundane everyday ones, such as housing and childcare, to specific family patterns, such as divorce and female-headed households. These issues are major concerns not only in modern Western societies such as Australia and Sweden but also in such diverse societies as the People's Republic of China, Taiwan, Malawi, Tunisia, Guatemala, and Costa Rica. These countries, many of which are in the Third World, vary in sociocultural, political, and economic settings, providing a more contextualized understanding of cross-cultural patterns. The chapters included also demonstrate the value of both qualitative and quantitative studies for understanding the objective conditions and subjectivity in women's lives.

The book is organized into two sections. Part I focuses on the effects of various policy changes on the status of women and families. The chapters by Acker, Charrad, Chow and Chen, Baldock, and Blumberg illustrate how the state operates differently in various types of political economies (i.e., socialist or capitalist), in the varying stages of development (i.e., industrializing, newly industrialized, and advanced industrialized). Although women-centered policy changes are primarily designed to benefit women, they may have unintended negative consequences for women's status. In Chapter 1, Acker suggests that in Sweden progressive policies, including some of the very ones created to eliminate gender inequality, actually help maintain it. Similarly, Charrad in Chapter 2 shows both the positive and negative effects of changes in divorce laws on the status of women in Tunisia. The one-child policy China promulgated to reduce population growth to help realize its modernization goals has some sensitivity toward women's interests initially. In Chapter 3, Chow and Chen find that this policy has generated some unintended adverse effects on women.

Finally, women-peripheral policies, though they may have positive consequences for the system and/or for the individual, largely produce intended or unintended effects that marginalize women. In Chapter 4, Baldock delineates a set of specific circumstances and particular government policies which, taken together, limit women's access to paid work and exploit their unpaid labor not only at home, but also in the not-for-profit sector. In Chapter 5, Blumberg's analysis reveals how lack of attention to women's roles resulted in a change in agricultural practices that actually harmed the well-being of women and their families.

Part II of this book addresses how women struggle to meet their own and their families' practical needs while advancing their strategic interests in the global political economy. As Chapter 6 by Berheide and Segal as well as Chapter 7 by Tinker indicate, women's participation in income-generating activities, whether in the formal or informal sector, and their ability to control the fruits of these activities are highly related to their degree of economic and political power within the household and in the public domain. Chapter 8 by Sagot illuminates how political activism by grass-roots women within a feminist organization helped meet family housing needs while empowering women by involving them in the political process surrounding state housing policy.

Gender inequality deeply embedded in patriarchal family structures affects women's status both inside and outside of the family. While women participate in production, they still assume the primary responsibility for reproduction. Therefore, social policies affecting childbearing and childrearing have far-reaching influence on women's status. While Tiano (Chapter 9) focuses more on the effects of corporate recruitment practices on women's fertility and their position in society, Yi (Chapter 10) studies the effects of women's employment on their childcare arrangements.

This book contains studies illustrating how women in different parts of the world struggle for their family's survival in the process of development. These studies, in each of their unique ways, epitomize the essential meaning of the feminist slogans "The Personal is Political" and "The Personal is International," as they reveal the blurring of the dichotomy between private and public spheres and the direct linkages between macro- and micro-level social forces impinging upon women and their families. The micro- and macro-level analyses reveal that conflict and contradiction as well as consensus and stability characterize relationships within the family as well as among the family, the economy, and the state.

Notes

1. Feminist frameworks include liberal feminism, cultural feminism, radical feminism, traditional Marxism, and socialist feminism (see Donovan 1985; Jaggar and Rothenberg 1984; Tong 1989). In the women and development field, also see the discussion by Bandarage (1984).

2. Mohanty et al. (1991, p. ix) define Third World as "the colonized, neo-colonized or decolonized countries (of Asia, Africa, and Latin America) whose economic and political structures have been deformed within the colonial process, and to black, Asian, Latino, and indigenous people in North America, Europe, and Australia." In this case, Third World is a sociopolitical designation rather than a racial or biological identification.

3. To avoid economic and political evaluation attached to countries at various stages of development, practitioners and researchers in women and development have begun to use the North and the South to refer to industrialized and developing countries (Tinker 1990; The North-South Institute 1990).

4. Kusterer (1990) describes the economy as a system of multiple modes of production, dominated usually by the capitalist mode but fundamentally rooted in a patriarchal domestic mode. Interaction of these modes leads to both poverty and gender inequality in developing societies.

5. The United States has policies and government initiatives, such as tax and social security plans, welfare and work-incentive programs, and a child-support system, that often have enormous effects on families despite their focus on individuals as the relevant social units.

References

Acosta-Belen, Edna, and Christine E. Bose. 1990. "From Structural Subordination to Empowerment: Women and Development in Third World Contexts." *Gender & Society* 4:299–320.

Adams, Bert. 1986. *The Family: A Sociological Interpretation*. 4th edition. New York: Harcourt Brace Jovanovich.

Afshar, Haleh, ed. 1987. *Women, State, and Ideology: Studies from Africa and Asia*. Albany, NY: State University of New York.

Andersen, Margaret A. 1993. *Thinking About Women: Sociological Perspectives on Sex and Gender*. Third edition. New York: Macmillan Publishing Company.

APCWD (Asian and Pacific Centre for Women and Development). 1979. "Feminist Ideology and Structures in the First Half of the Decade for Women." Report of a workshop held in Bangkok, June 23–30. Republished in IWTC, 1980, *Developing Strategies for the Future*.

Baca Zinn, Maxine. 1990. "Family, Feminism, and Race in America." *Gender & Society* 4:68–82.

Baca Zinn, Maxine, and D. Stanley Eitzen. 1988. "Transforming the Sociology of the Family: New Directions for Teaching and Texts." *Teaching Sociology* 16:180–184.

Bandarage, Asoka. 1984. "Women in Development: Liberalism, Marxism, and Marxist-Feminism." *Development and Change* 15:495–515.

Beechey, V. 1979. "On Patriarchy." *Feminist Review* 3:66–82.

Beneria, Lourdes, ed. 1982. *Women and Development: The Sexual Division of Labor in Rural Societies*. New York: Praeger.

Beneria, Lourdes, and Martha Roldan. 1987. *The Crossroads of Class and Gender*. Chicago, IL: University of Chicago Press.

Beneria, Lourdes, and Gita Sen. 1981. "Accumulation, Reproduction and Women's Role in Economic Development: Boserup Revisited." *Signs: Journal of Women in Culture and Society* 7:279–98.

Beneria, Lourdes, and Catharine R. Stimpson, eds. 1987. *Women, Households, and the Economy*. New Brunswick, NJ: Rutgers University Press.

Bernard, Jessie. 1987. *The Female World from a Global Perspective*. Bloomington, IN: Indiana University Press.

Blumberg, Rae Lesser. 1991. "The 'Triple Overlap' of Gender Stratification, Economy, and the Family." Pp. 7–32 in *Gender, Family, and Economy: The Triple Overlap*. Newbury Park, CA: Sage.

Bookman, Ann, and Sandra Morgen, eds. 1988. *Women and the Politics of Empowerment*. Philadelphia, PA: Temple University Press.

Boris, Eileen, and Peter Bardaglio. 1987. "Gender, Race, and Class: The Impact of the State on the Family and the Economy, 1790–1945." Pp. 132–151 in *Families and Work*, edited by Naomi Gerstel and Harriet Engel Gross. Philadelphia, PA: Temple University Press.

Bose, Christine, Roselyn Feldberg, and Natalie J. Sokoloff, eds. 1987. *Hidden Aspects of Women's Work*. New York: Praeger.

Boserup, Ester. 1970. *Woman's Role in Economic Development*. London: George Allen and Unwin.

Bourque, Susan, and Kay Warren. 1979. "Female Participation, Perception and Power: An Examination of Two Andean Communities." In *Political Participation and the Poor*, edited by John Booth and Mitchell Seligson. New York: Holmes and Meier.

———. 1987. "Technology, Gender, and Development." *Daedalus* 116:173–97.

Brown, Carol. 1981. "Mothers, Fathers and Children: From Private to Public Patriarchy." Pp. 239–267 in *Women and Revolution*, edited by Lydia Sargent. Boston: South End Press.

Bunch, Charlotte, and Roxanna Carrillo. 1990. "Feminist Perspectives on Women in Development." Pp. 70–82 in *Persistent Inequalities: Women and World Development*, edited by Irene Tinker. New York: Oxford University Press.

CEPAL (Economic Commission for Latin America). 1983. *Five Studies on Situation of Women in Latin America*. Santiago: UN/ECLA.

Chafetz, Janet Saltzman. 1990. *Gender Equity: An Integrated Theory of Stability and Change*. Newbury Park, CA: Sage.

Charlton, Sue Ellen M., Jana Everett, and Kathleen Staudt, eds. 1989. *Women, the State, and Development*. Albany, NY: State University of New York.

Chow, Esther Ngan-ling. 1993. "The Impact of the Interplay Between the Economy and Patriarchy on Intrahousehold Dynamics: The Case of High-Tech Workers in Taiwan (ROC)," paper presented at the Conference on Engendering Wealth and Well-Being at the University of California, San Diego.

Chow, Esther Ngan-ling, and Catherine White Berheide. 1988. "The Interdependence of Family and Work: A Framework for Family Life Education, Policy, and Practice." *Family Relations* 37:23–28.

Christensen, Harold T., 1964. "Development of the Family Field of Study." Pp. 3–32 in *Handbook of Marriage and Family*, edited by Harold T. Christensen. Chicago, IL: Nelson-Hall.

Christensen, Kathleen E. 1987. *The Unspoken Contract: Women and Home-Based Work*. New York: Henry Holt and Company.

Collins, Patricia Hill. 1991. *Black Feminist Thought: Knowledge, Consciousness, and the Politics of Empowerment*. New York: Routledge.

Crouter, A. C. 1984. "Spillover from Family to Work: The Neglected Side of the Work-Family Interface." *Human Relations* 37:425–442.

Daniels, Arlene Kaplan. 1987. "Invisible Work." *Social Problems* 34:403–415.

Diamond, Irene, ed. 1983. *Families, Politics, Public Policy: A Feminist Dialogue and the State*. New York: Longman.

Dill, Bonnie Thornton. 1988. "Our Mother's Grief: Racial Ethnic Women and the Maintenance of Families." *Journal of Family History* 13:415–31.

Donovan, Josephine. 1985. *Feminist Theory*. New York: Frederick Ungar Publishing Company.

Dwyer, Daisy, and Judith Bruce, eds. 1988. *A Home Divided: Women and Income in the Third World*. Stanford, CA: Stanford University Press.

Ehler, Tracy B. 1983. "The Decline of Female Family Business: A Guatemalan Case Study." Pp.7–21 in *Women and Developing Countries: A Policy Focus*, edited by Kathleen Staudt and Jane S. Jaquette. New York: Haworth Press.

Enloe, Cynthia. 1989. *Bananas, Beaches, and Bases: Making Feminist Sense of International Politics*. Berkeley, CA: University of California.

Evans, Peter, Dietrich Rueschemeyer, and Theda Skocpol, eds. 1985. *Bringing the State Back In*. New York: Cambridge University Press.

Everett, Jana. 1989. *The Global Empowerment of Women*. Washington, DC: Association for Women in Development.

Ferguson, Ann. 1984. "On Conceiving Motherhood and Sexuality: A Feminist Materialist Approach." In *Mothering: Essays in Feminist Theory*, edited by Joyce Trebilcot. Totowa, NJ: Rowman Allenheld.

Fernandez Kelly, M. Patricia. 1989. "Broadening the Scope: Gender and International Economic Development." *Sociological Forum* 4:611–635.

Ferree, Myra. 1990. "Beyond Separate Spheres: Feminism and Family Research." *Journal of Marriage and the Family* 52:866–884.

Folbre, Nancy. 1987. "The Pauperization of Motherhood: Patriarchy and Public Policy in the United States." In *Families and Work*, edited by Naomi Gerstel and Harriet Engel Gross. Philadelphia, PA: Temple University Press.

Gerstel, Naomi, and Harriet Engel Gross, eds. 1987. *Families and Work*. Philadelphia, PA: Temple University Press.

Hartmann, Heidi. 1976. "Capitalism, Patriarchy, and Job Segregation by Sex." *Signs: Journal of Women in Culture and Society* 1:137–169.

———. 1981. "The Family as the Locus of Gender, Class and Political Struggle: The Example of Housework." *Signs: Journal of Women in Culture and Society* 6:366–394.

Hartsock, Nancy C. M. 1987. "The Feminist Standpoint: Developing the Ground for a Specifically Feminist Historical Materialism." Pp. 157–180 in *Feminism and Methodology*, edited by Sandra Harding. Bloomington, IN: Indiana University Press.

Hass, Linda. 1992. *Equal Parenthood and Social Policy: A Study of Parental Leave in Sweden*. Albany, NY: State University of New York Press.

Hochschild, Arlie. 1983. *The Managed Heart: Commercialization of Human Feeling*. Berkeley, CA: University of California Press.

———. 1989. *The Second Shift: Working Parents and the Revolution at Home*. New York: Viking.

Hyde, Janet Shibley, and Marilyn J. Essex. 1991. *Parental Leave and Child Care: Setting a Research and Policy Agenda*. Philadelphia, PA: Temple University Press.

IWTC (International Women's Tribune Centre). 1980. *Developing Strategies for the Future: Feminist Perspectives*. New York: IWTC.

Jagger, Alison M., and Paula S. Rothenberg. 1984. *Feminist Frameworks: Alternative Theoretical Accounts of the Relations Between Women and Men*. Second edition. New York: McGraw-Hill.

Jaquette, Jane S. 1991. *The Women's Movement in Latin America—Feminism and the Transition to Democracy*. Boulder, CO: Westview Press.

Jones, Jacqueline. 1985. *Labor of Love, Labor of Sorrow: Black Women, Work, and the Family from Slavery to the Present*. New York: Basic Books.

Kamerman, Sheila B., and Alfred J. Kahn, eds. 1978. *Family Policy: Government and Families in Fourteen Countries*. New York: Columbia University Press.

Kandiyoti, Deniz. 1985. *Women in Rural Production Systems: Problems and Policies*. Paris: UNESCO.

———. 1988. "Bargaining with Patriarchy." *Gender & Society* 2:274–89.

Kanter, Rosabeth Moss. 1977. *Work and Family in the United States: A Critical Review and Agenda for Research and Policy*. New York: Russell Sage Foundation.

Kusterer, Ken. 1990. "The Imminent Demise of Patriarchy." Pp. 239–255 in *Persistent Inequalities: Women and World Development*, edited by Irene Tinker. New York: Oxford University Press.

Leacock, Eleanor, and Helen I. Safa, eds. 1986. *Women's Work*. South Hadley, MA: Bergin and Garvey.

Lengermann, Patricia Madoo, and Jill Niebrugge-Brantley. 1988. "Contemporary Feminist Theory." Pp. 400–443 in *Contemporary Sociological Theories*, edited by George Ritzer. New York: Alfred A. Knopf.

Lim, Linda Y. C. 1983. "Capitalism, Imperialism, and Patriarchy: The Dilemma of Third-World Women Workers in Multinational Factories." Pp. 70–91 in *Women, Men and the International Division of Labor*, edited by June Nash and M. Patricia Fernandez Kelly. Albany, NY: State University of New York Press.

MacKinnon, Catharine A. 1989. *Toward a Feminist Theory of the State*. Cambridge, MA: Harvard University Press.

Mies, Maria. 1986. *Patriarchy and Accumulation on a World Scale*. London: Zed Books.

Mohanty, Chandra Talpade, Ann Russo, and Lourdes Torres, eds. 1991. *Third World Women and the Politics of Feminism*. Bloomington, IN: Indiana University Press.

Molyneux, Maxine D. 1985. "Mobilization Without Emancipation? Women's Interests, State, and Revolution in Nicaragua." *Feminist Studies* 11:227–54.

Moser, Caroline O. N. 1987. "Women, Human Settlements, and Housing: A Conceptual Framework for Analysis and Policy-Making." In *Women, Human Settlements, and Housing*, edited by Caroline Moser and L. Peake. London: Tavistock.

Nash, June, and M. Patricia Fernandez Kelly. 1983. *Women, Men and the International Division of Labor*. Albany, NY: State University of New York.

Ollenburger, Jane C., and Helen A. Moore. 1992. *A Sociology of Women: The Intersection of Patriarchy, Capitalism, and Colonization*. Englewood Cliffs, NJ: Prentice Hall.

Papanek, Hanna. 1990. "To Each Less Than She Needs, From Each More Than She Can Do: Allocations, Entitlements, and Value." Pp. 162–181 in *Persistent Inequalities: Women and World Development*, edited by Irene Tinker. New York: Oxford University Press.

Parpart, Jane L. 1990. "Wage Earning Women and the Double Day: The Nigerian Case." Pp.161–182 in *Women, Employment and the Family in the International Division of Labour*, edited by Sharon Stichter and Jane L. Parpart. Philadelphia, PA: Temple University Press.

Parsons, Talcott, and Robert E. Bales. 1955. *Family, Socialization and Interaction Process*. New York: Free Press.

Peterson, V. Spike, ed. 1992. *Gendered States: Feminist (Re)Visions of International Relations Theory*. Boulder, CO: Lynne Rienner Publishers.

Piven, Frances Fox. 1984. "Women and the State: Ideology, Power, and the Welfare State." *Socialist Review* 74:18–25.

Pleck, Joseph H. 1977. "The Work-Family Role System." *Social Problems* 24:417–427.

Reskin, Barbara F., and Patricia A. Roos. 1990. *Job Queues, Gender Queues: Explaining Women's Inroads into Male Occupations*. Philadelphia, PA: Temple University Press.

Rogers, Susan. 1983. "Efforts Towards Women's Development in Tanzania: Gender Rhetoric vs. Gender Realities." Pp. 23–41 in *Women in Developing Countries: A Policy Focus*, edited by Kathleen Staudt and Jane Jaquette. New York: Haworth Press.

Sen, Gita, and Caren Grown. 1987. *Development, Crises, and Alternative Visions*. New York: Monthly Review Press.

Smith, Dorothy E. 1979. "A Sociology of Women." Pp. 135–187 in *The Prism of Sex: Essays in the Sociology of Knowledge*, edited by J. Sherman and E. Beck. Madison, WI: University of Wisconsin Press.

———. 1987. *The Everyday World as Problematic: A Feminist Sociology*. Boston, MA: Northeastern University Press.

Sokoloff, Natalie J. 1980. *Between Money and Love: The Dialectics of Women's Home and Market Work*. New York: Praeger.

Staudt, Kathleen, ed. 1990. *Women, International Development, and Politics: The Bureaucratic Mire*. Philadelphia, PA: Temple University Press.

The North-South Institute. 1991. *The Future for Women in Development*. Ottawa, Canada: The North-South Institute.

Thorne, Barrie, and Marilyn Yalom. 1992. *Rethinking the Family: Some Feminist Questions*. Revised edition. Boston: Northeastern University Press.

Tiano, Susan. 1984. "The Public-Private Dichotomy: Theoretical Perspectives on 'Women in Development'." *The Social Science Journal* 21:11–28.

Tilly, Louise A., and Joan W. Scott. 1978. *Women, Work and Family*. New York: Holt, Rinehart and Winston.

Tinker, Irene. 1987. "Street Foods: Testing Assumptions about Informal Sector Activity by Women and Men." *Current Sociology* 35 (3), whole issue.

———. 1990. *Persistent Inequalities*. New York: Oxford University Press.

Tong, Rosemarie. 1989. *Feminist Thought: A Comprehensive Introduction*. Boulder, CO: Westview.

United Nations, Division for Economic and Social Information. 1980. *Women: 1980*. Conference booklet for the World Conference of the United Nations Decade for Women, Copenhagen, July 1980.

———. 1991. *The World's Women 1970–1990: Trends and Statistics*. New York: United Nations Publication.

U.S. Bureau of Labor Statistics. 1992. "Work and Family: Child-Care Arrangements of Young Working Mothers." Report# 820. Washington, DC: Department of Labor.

Walby, Sylvia. 1990. *Theorizing Patriarchy*. Cambridge, MA: Basil Blackwell.

Ward, Kathryn, ed. 1990. *Women Workers and Global Restructuring*. Ithaca, NY: School of Industrial and Labor Relations, Cornell University Press.

Part I

Changing State Policies,
Women, Families, and
Economic Development

Chapter 1

Women, Families, and Public Policy in Sweden

Joan Acker

State policies in Sweden, having eliminated legal ties and limits that in many other countries reinforce women's secondary place, now provide ample money and services to support family life and the employment of women. The Swedish state, under the leadership of the Social Democratic Party and the confederation of blue collar unions (LO), has created many policies to help both parents to participate fully in paid work and family life. In the post-World War II period, the Swedish compromise between capital and labor that included commitments to full employment and rapid economic growth also created new prosperity and the material resources for the welfare state. As a result, Swedish women enjoy public programs and economic guarantees that have made Sweden a model for women in other countries as they attempt to solve the problems of gender inequality.

Yet the relative subordination of Swedish women persists, with a highly sex-segregated labor market; a paucity of women in higher-level positions in education, the trade unions, and private business; and a still traditional sex division of work in the home and family. Swedes often dismiss this state of affairs as unimportant, or simply don't recognize it.

Why has gender equality been elusive in Sweden, a country with a strong commitment to equality? In the following I offer an interpretation of this reality which has puzzled me since I first went to Sweden 12 years ago. First, I will summarize Swedish welfare state family policy and how it has affected the family, as well as women's and men's places within it. Next, I will briefly examine the evidence about continuing inequality, particularly in working life. Then I look at historical and structural explanations for the relative lack of impact family policy has had on gender equality in employment compared with public goals and the hopes of many Swedish women. I conclude with some hesitant predictions about Swedish women and families in the 1990s.

Public Policy and the Family

Families in Sweden are affected by a broad range of public policies such as labor market and tax policies, as well as policies more directly concerned with families such as day-care, parental leave, and child allowance measures. Many changes in the family are the result of conscious policy decisions (Baude 1979). Increasing the labor market participation of women has been public policy in Sweden since the 1960s, when labor shortages began to be met by recruiting women (Kyle 1979). Labor demand coincided with feminist analysis that women could not be equal to men unless they were financially independent from individual men. Financial independence was furthered by the 1971 income tax reforms which facilitated, or forced, the entry of women into employment.

Central to these reforms was the principle, based on the assumption that every adult should be self-supporting, that each individual should be taxed separately. As a result, tax deductions for dependents were severely reduced, pushing married women into paid work; and wives' relatively low incomes were no longer added to husbands' incomes to produce a high marginal tax, a positive incentive toward wives' employment (Gustafsson 1988). This tax policy, added to the early and rapid expansion of welfare state services which created many new jobs, resulted in very high employment rates for Swedish women well before comparable expansion in the United States.

The expansion of welfare state services has also resulted in a concept infrequently found in discussions of women and work in the United States. That concept is "caring work." Caring work refers to all the activities that have to do with caring for children, the ill and handicapped, and the fragile elderly. A substantial proportion of that work is now done in the paid public sector in Sweden. Nurses, assistant nurses, nurses aides, children's nurses, pre-school teachers, and home helpers are among the largest female occupations.

By 1986, 89.8 percent of Swedish women between the ages of 25 and 54 were in the labor market, including 85.6 percent of women with children under the age of seven (Persson-Tanimura 1988). The combination of work and parenting is eased for Swedish parents by tax-supported day-care. In 1986, 31 percent of children under two years old and 57 percent of three- to six-year-olds were in public childcare. Public childcare includes day-care centers and licensed family care homes. It is organized by the local community, and subsidized by both the community and the state. Parents pay about ten percent of the cost (Persson-Tanimura 1988).

Day-care is more available in large cities than in small towns or the countryside. Thus, whether the ordinary family has such services depends to a degree on where they live. Children of single parents have priority for often scarce day-care places, as do multiple children in a family. These priorities reflect the public purpose of day-care policy in Sweden, to facilitate the paid employment of parents. That policy would not be served if one child in a family received childcare, but the mother still had to stay at home to care for the second child (or children) for whom no room existed. When public day-care is not available, children are cared for by relatives, by unlicensed care providers, or by parents who arrange their work so that one of them is always home. Recently, some parents have organized cooperatives, which receive municipal subsidies. Day-care is still an important political issue, but the government's goal of a place for every child by 1992 has been delayed indefinitely.

Parental leave insurance is probably the most spectacular of the Swedish policies encouraging women's labor force participation. Parental leaves are available to both women and men, with the distribution of time to be decided by the couple based on their own wishes and needs. Parents taking leave are guaranteed by law that they may return to the same job. The parents of a newborn or a newly adopted baby are entitled to 360 days of leave at normal sick pay, which in 1988 was 90 percent of normal income, with a limit of about $2300 per month, plus an additional 90 days at a flat sum of around $10 per day (Nasman and Falkenberg 1989).

In addition, new fathers are entitled to 10 days of "paternal leave" at normal sick pay rate. Until the child is 12 years old the parents are entitled to stay at home with sick pay if the child or the person caring for her is ill. Parents may take up to 60 days per year per child for these caring responsibilities. In addition to all this, parents are entitled to two "contact days" per year per child to visit the child's day-care center or school.

Swedish policy also recognizes that a long working day for both parents may leave little time at home with the children. Therefore, the law establishes the right of parents to reduce their hours on the job to 3/4 of normal working time, at 3/4 of normal pay, until the child is eight years old or has finished the first year of school.

All families, regardless of class or income, receive a basic child allowance for all children up to the age of 16; in 1989 it amounted to approximately $900 per year per child. Families with three or more children receive an additional child allowance. Single parents may receive a maintenance advance if the absent parent fails or is unable to pay an agreed upon maintenance allowance. This advance, to be reimbursed by the absent parent if possible, was around $150 per month in 1989 (Nasman and Falkenberg 1989).

A housing allowance, based on income, number of children, and housing costs within certain limits, also eases economic problems. In 1987, housing allowances went to 25 percent of all families with children, including 60 percent of families with three or more children (Svenska Institutet 1987). Even with all these financial supports for families with children, most families must have two wage earners to get by. One reason for this is that taxes are very high—the Swedish people pay for the welfare state, usually willingly.

Taken together, these services, employment guarantees, and money transfers create positive support for a secure family life as well as paid employment for women, producing a new family model in which, as many have noted (for example, Hernes 1987; Holter 1984; Siim 1987), much caring work has been moved out of the home to hospitals and day-care centers, and most families have two income providers.

The typical Swedish family today consists of two working parents and children who are (or have been) in state-supported day-care. In the typical family, the woman is likely to work part-time and the man full-time. Among women aged 25–54 in the labor force in 1986, 10.9 percent worked "short" part-time: 1–19 hours per week, and 37.9 percent worked "long" part-time: 20–34 hours per week (Persson-Tanimura 1988, p. 7). Over 67 percent of employed women with children under the age of 7 worked part-time. Among men, only 10.5 percent worked part-time, and most of these were either students or older workers with partial retirement rather than fathers of young children (Sundstrom 1987). These differences in work hours contribute to differences in earned incomes; in 1987 women earned 69 percent of the earnings of men (SCB 1989, Table 22), although those who worked full-time attained 80 percent.

Many Swedish couples are not married. The special word for unmarried partners in marriage-like relationships is "sambo", or living together. In 1985, 19 percent of couples living together were "sambo," or unmarried partners. Of these, 57 percent had children (Nordic Council of Ministers 1988). About one-third of Swedish babies are born to unmarried parents, but many of these parents later marry. Marriage has declined in importance as its legal advantages have been removed, illegitimacy has been abolished as a civil status, and the force of religious commandments has declined. On the whole, marriage or its absence seem to make little difference in family daily life. Single-parent families have increased. In 1985 approximately 16.5 percent of all mothers were living alone with their children. Single fathers totalled around 3 percent of all fathers (Nordic Council of Ministers 1988). Families are small: In 1985, married couples with children under age 18 had an average of 1.8 children (SCB 1986, p. 30). From 1988 to 1992 a mini-baby boom occurred in Sweden, but it is too soon to know if an increase in average family size will result.

Swedish women and men divide their unpaid work in the home along conventional lines in spite of public exhortations, starting in the early 1960s, that men share childcare and other home tasks with women. Different types of data give somewhat different pictures. According to one set of time-use studies, in 1983 "women aged 25–44 who had families worked an average of 24 hours per week in the market and 38 hours at home. Their husbands were gainfully employed for 41 hours and spent 19 hours per week on home chores" (Persson-Tanimura 1988, p. 10). Full-time employed mothers had a 73 hour workweek, 34 of those hours at home. Men did the maintenance chores and women the household work and childcare. Of course there are variations. Some fathers do a lot of childcare; in Stockholm, it is not surprising to see a man pushing a baby carriage down the street in the middle of a working day. This is confirmed by several studies showing that fathers of young children are spending more time at childcare (Moen 1989, p. 20).

Public childcare and parental leave together constitute a package of rights that can be used to design individual solutions to the parenting/paid work problem (Nasman 1986; Nasman and Falkenberg 1989). In practice, some solutions, such as the following example, are more common than others.

A young woman I know recently had a baby. During her pregnancy she had considerable physical trouble, but she continued to work between periods of pregnancy leave paid for by the state sickness insurance fund. When the baby was born, her husband took the 10 days of paternal leave, also with normal sick pay, to which he is entitled as a new father. The new mother is now on parental leave from her job, with the guarantee that she can return to her former work. She plans to take the total 360 days of fully paid leave that the law allows and may possibly stay home for the additional 90 days at lower compensation to which she is also entitled.

The father in this typical family takes some days of parental leave to care for the baby and give the mother a rest. According to the law, as discussed above, either parent may take parental leave, but in practice that parent is most often the mother. In 1985 fathers took 1.9 percent of the total days of fully-paid parental leave to care for infants (Persson-Tanimura 1988) and around 9 percent of the additional lower paid days. Fathers participate more in the transitory care of older children, taking 44 percent of the total number of paid days in 1985. A more recent study suggests that by 1990 fathers were increasing their share of parental leave (Dagens Nyheter 1992).

When my friend returns to work, she will be on the job half-time at first, a work-time reduction above that guaranteed by law that was negotiated by her union, while her son is cared for in a nearby family care home. If she is lucky, her son will get a place in a day-care center by the time he is three years old. The local center has a waiting list and children of two-parent families have low priority. After one or two years, my friend plans to work six hours a day, or 3/4 time. After-school care may be available for my friend's son once he is in school. However, this kind of care is less plentiful than day-care for younger children, and the family may have to make other arrangements. By the time that her son is eight years old, my friend will be back in full-time paid work.

This example comes from the life of a professional woman, but represents a typical pattern of using services and guarantees to their fullest. High-income women are more likely to have husbands who share parental leave with them than are low-income women. Working-class women often have a somewhat different experience. Men working in the public sector are more apt to stay home with the baby than are men in the private sector, particularly those doing blue-collar work. Working-class families use public day-care less frequently than professional families (LO 1987), and working-class women more often continue part-time work over long periods of time.

In summary, in Sweden the feminization of the paid labor force has been almost complete, resulting in the transformation of family daily life and the lives of women. This transformation has been powerfully shaped by state policy. The archetypal figures of industrial capitalist society have changed. No longer is there a worker and a housewife with their separate but interdependent roles. Instead there are two workers—the classical, male-defined worker and a new worker in whose life the tasks of reproduction and production are intertwined. Welfare state measures make possible, as I have described above, many different lifetime patterns of combining paid work and family, but it is primarily women who take up these options. It is still women who do most of the caring work. Thus reproduction and the family are still women's responsibilities.

The Swedish solution to the problem of combining family life and labor market work for women is the most advanced in the world, although other Nordic countries have similar but less extensive provisions. Yet this new and woman-friendly family work life coexists with sex segregation, a gendered wage gap, the concentration of women in low wage, low status jobs, and the same exclusions and invisibilities that women suffer in work organizations in the United States (Baude and Gonas 1989).

These inequalities in working life are reflected in various sorts of data. For example, sex segregation data show that in 1985, of the 30 largest occupations in Sweden, 26 were occupations composed of over 70 percent of either women or men workers, while only four occupations had more equal distributions of women and men. About 52 percent of all Swedish women employees were in just 12 occupations (SCB 1989). An Organization for Economic and Cultural Development (OECD) study (Bakker 1988) comparing sex segregation in industrial countries found that in 1977 Sweden, with the United States and Canada, had the highest index of occupational sex segregation. When sex segregation by industrial sector was measured, Sweden was the most segregated. This is probably still true because well over half of all employed women work in the public care sector. Swedish sex segregation declined by two percentage points at the end of the 1970s (Jonung 1984), and unpublished data indicate that this trend is continuing, although very slowly.

Segregation by race and ethnicity also exists in Sweden. The most common occupation for immigrant women is charworker, or cleaner. Immigrant women are also over-represented in routine manufacturing, as kitchen maids, and as nursing aids (Leinio 1988). Thus, for all groups sex segregation remains the predominant pattern in the labor force.

Sex segregation is also reflected in hierarchies within organizations. As in other countries, the higher the level, the fewer the women. For example, among white-collar employees in Swedish industry in 1988, women occupied 5 percent of upper management positions (excluding top management), 16 percent of middle management and skilled technical jobs, 43 percent of lower management and technical jobs, and 80 percent of routine clerical positions (SCB 1989). Similar distributions are found in trade unions and educational institutions. For example, a woman was elected to the top position in a blue-collar trade union for the first time in 1989, although several of these unions have had a high predominance of women members for many years. Universities, where only about 5 percent of professorial positions are filled by women, are another example.

The wage gap between women and men is lower in Sweden than in most other countries. Women fare better in some parts of the economy than in others. Industrial women workers earn about 90 percent of the earnings of their men co-workers, primarily because blue-collar unions have been committed to wage equality. However, white-collar women earn only about 75 percent of their male equivalent. In all sectors, some of the wage differences are due to sex segregation, but a difference remains within occupations and within hierarchical levels of responsibility and expertise (SCB 1989).

Unfinished Revolution or the Limits of Reform?

We might interpret the situation described above as a stage in ongoing societal development which in time will result in gender equality, even a revolution in gender relations. However, I believe that it represents the limits to feasible reform in contemporary welfare capitalism and reveals an underlying contradiction in our societies. The limits come into view as the logic of reform policies are developed to the full, as in Sweden. Sweden, of course, has its own history, and it is this history that makes visible the contradictions embedded in the successes of a well-developed welfare state policy.

The Swedish welfare state, like every other welfare state, developed historically from efforts to alleviate the most destructive effects of industrial capitalism on the working class (Polanyi 1944). This development assumed and used the unpaid or poorly paid labor of women. The destructive effects included poverty-level wages, long working hours, periodic unemployment caused by depressions and other economic events, work injuries, illnesses and deaths, and generally poor working and living conditions. This dismal past is still very close to many Swedes, who can remember how hard their parents labored and how difficult winters were without adequate housing, indoor plumbing, or a hot water supply. If they can't remember, they are reminded by an exhibit at the Nordisk Museum in Stockholm about the difficulties of working class family life through the 1930s.

These destructive effects indicate a contradiction between the dynamic of the capitalist economy, or production, and the human needs of at least substantial parts of the population, or reproduction. The capitalist economy is fundamentally indifferent to human needs because its aim is profit, not human welfare. In all late capitalist countries, this contradiction was met in the 19th Century by the organization of labor movements that fought for higher wages so that men could support their families, by middle-class social reform, and in the

20th Century by the development of the welfare state. The family wage for men, to the extent that it was actually achieved, allowed women to stay at home and do the hard and necessary labor of creating family life. The worker, ideally, was a man and the organization of production assumed that his daily maintenance was taken care of outside work, probably by a wife. Women did the caring, nurturing work, the raising of children, the nursing of the sick, and the tending to the infirm elderly, as well as the daily cooking, cleaning, and washing. This hidden but essential work alleviated the contradictions between production and reproduction. When the welfare state began to be built, it was for this gender-divided world peopled by workers and housewives.

As the welfare state began to develop in the 1930s and 1940s, Sweden was a society in which most married women were, or aspired to be, at home. The solution to the serious deprivations of the working class was to be sought in the development of a secure and comfortable family life that was available to all. A major part of social democratic ideology was the concept of the "People's Home," the good society that would develop the good life within Swedish homes (Hirdman 1987). Creating these homes, and the families within them, were women as housewives. Workers were men whose trade union solidarity built a strong movement that could negotiate effectively with management and could support a winning political party, the Social Democrats. Together, the unions and the party could work with private industry and business to achieve an expanding economy that could then support the welfare state, a major part of the People's Home concept. This model has been remarkably successful, but underlying the success is a deep but often unrecognized gender division.

The new family model seems almost as firmly grounded in gender divisions as was the old family model (in the People's Home), but now the divisions are as much within the arena of paid work as they are between the family and the public sphere, or within the family. The world of paid work is still primarily organized around the assumption of a male worker. Research on the consequences of this assumption is still underway, but some patterns seem clear (Caleman et al. 1984; Nasman and Falkenberg 1988). Work is organized in most places as an eight hour day; part-time work and parental leave is often difficult to accommodate. Employers expect full commitment from employees, and it is easy for them to assume that a mother of small children cannot make such a commitment. Frequently, career tracks are cut short or changed with parental leave. Many jobs predominantly held by women, such as aides in the public care sector, are structured as part-time employment, so that part-time work may be the only employment available. Such jobs, requiring relatively low education, are apt to be low-waged work.

There is space for the new worker, the woman, but the very rights she uses, those granted by the welfare state, set her apart from the standard, full-time, life-long worker. The measures designed, in part, to make women economically independent also solidify their status as different workers and confirm their obligations as the primary organizers of family life and providers of care, thus limiting their economic independence (Widerberg 1991). The unintended consequences of welfare state measures to promote equality actually recreate the underlying gender structure. In this way, the incipient contradiction between production and reproduction has been alleviated in Sweden, but, at the same time, the gendered sub-structure of the society has been reorganized but not eliminated.

This gender division is difficult to attack because of particular features of the Swedish model. The goals of the People's Home, a just and humane society with employment and security for all, were dependent upon the development of a strong economy; but this economy was conceptualized as gender-neutral, as it is by all economists everywhere.

Women's particular problems became politically visible only when they were relevant for this apparently gender-neutral economy. As a result, most reforms that have helped women have come to fruition only when they could be interpreted as necessary for the economy. Thus, women were recruited into paid labor in the post-war period of high labor demand because this was seen as a better alternative than recruiting more foreign labor. Income tax reform that made each individual separately taxed, symbolizing the ideal of equality, was a mechanism for drawing more women into the labor force. Daycare and parental leave have been ways to tie women to the paid labor force while at the same time encouraging childbearing. Other issues, such as the sex segregation of the labor force and the economy, that were not clearly seen as of "general" interest were given little attention.

In addition, the welfare state was achieved through the solidarity of the trade unions and the Social Democratic Party, which was in power for most of the period between 1938 and 1991 (Esping-Andersen 1985; Korpi 1978). Feminist challenges to the male dominance of these institutions were interpreted as undermining solidarity, and thus undermining the very institutions that have been responsible for the vast improvements in women's lot. The trade unions have been seen as the avenues through which the working lives of Swedes will be improved and, indeed, the unions have had great success in doing so. However, the other side of this reality is that unions have often opposed any measures that would weaken their exclusive power.

For example, the blue-collar unions and the Social Democratic Party opposed a law on equality between women and men in working life, only finally supporting it when, with conservatives in power, its passage was assured in 1979. The law provides for protection against sex discrimination and mandates positive measures to promote equality. The "Equality Ombudsman" carries out both functions.

This law has not been particularly effective partly because it assumes that unions and management are able to deal with all workplace issues. This means that if an agreement is reached on gender equality measures between a union and an employer and both parties are satisfied with the agreement, the state cannot intervene through the use of the equality law. Consequently, in practice, women workers have little recourse if male union leaders and employers see no problem.

Individual discrimination cases are handled first by unions. If no resolution is found, the office of the ombudsman may intervene, but successful interventions have been few. Although provisions through which individuals can take their own discrimination cases to court are available, this rarely happens because it is expensive and difficult to do without organized support which, for workers, must come from the union.

The law on equality was revised in 1991, with strengthened anti-discrimination provisions as well as the prohibition of sexual harassment. At this writing, it is too soon to know if these new measures will improve women's situations in the labor market.

In sum, social provisions to ease women's labor force participation and support family life have increased women's security and independence, creating a new life pattern for women as paid and unpaid workers. The very programs that were intended to increase gender equality through financial independence lock women into sex-segregated and often low-level, dead-end positions in an economy still organized around the male worker who has few home responsibilities. The powerful voices of reform were those of men in male-dominated institutions who supported reforms that contributed to economic growth, but ignored, on the whole, the gender structure of the economy and employment. This helps to explain the Swedish paradox— high levels of employment for women and exceptional social supports for that employment existing alongside male dominance and advantage. Swedish women have benefitted greatly from social democracy, through its ability to pass and implement the most advanced welfare measures in the world. This success, in itself, may increase the difficulty in confronting the failures. People who work with equality problems in employment seem to be faced with an often unspoken resistance that could be articulated as "What more do women want? They have gotten everything they asked for. It's boring to talk about this anymore."

Strains in Paradise—Into the 1990s

The picture I have drawn of the ways that Swedish women can combine family and employment is a wonderful one in comparison with the situation in most countries, in spite of the unintended negatives. However, strains in paradise reveal the unresolved, underlying contradiction. These strains have their roots in Sweden's place within the restructuring of the global economy.

During the 1970s, in Sweden, as in all other wealthy industrial countries, old manufacturing industries declined and new service jobs were created, a majority in the public sector. However, Swedish export-oriented industries remained strong and, except for periods of downturn that affected the world economy, were very profitable in the 1980s. They moved much of their manufacturing abroad and invested heavily in mergers and acquisitions of foreign firms. These large firms are now no longer as dependent upon the Swedish economy and its politics.

This has led to changes in the power relations between capital and labor. As a result, the Social Democrats and the labor unions have been unable to resist cutbacks in the welfare state and tax reforms that favor the wealthy over the poor. At the same time, high profits have produced a booming economy with labor shortages and very low unemployment. This causes the spokesmen of capital to demand higher unemployment to avoid inflation and to increase the available labor supply. Supporting all these developments is a new conservative economic ideology, not unlike that of Reagan and Thatcher, that places a higher value on market rationality than on a rationality of care.

These changes have practical consequences for women: A crisis in the care sector and a growing wage gap between women and men. The crisis in the care sector has developed as most women have moved into the labor market. Employed women are dependent on other employed women to relieve them of some of the care-giving work that women previously did in the home. As more and more care work is done for pay in the public sector, the magnitude of this kind of work becomes more visible. As mothers working in care jobs take parental leave and as new work opportunities for better pay in the private sector open up, personnel shortages increase in the public care sector, affecting the ability of other women to fulfill their paid work responsibilities and increasing the pressures of daily life. The stress in caring work increases with personnel shortages, while the undervaluation of care work in relation to other work is increased by budget tightening spurred by the present emphasis on market rationality. At the same time, the labor reserve for the care sector, middle-aged housewives with little previous employment who are willing to work at relatively low wages, is gone.

Thus, when unemployment rates are low, the welfare state seems to reach a saturation point. The "crisis of the welfare state" in Sweden, at least, is a crisis of the conflict between production and reproduction—who will care for the children and the aged when women are no longer in the home full-time or available as a low-wage labor reserve? And how will care be paid for, now that leaders of business and industry are succeeding in their campaign to reduce welfare spending? What will happen to the values of family life, welfare, and care in an economy increasingly turning to a capitalist technical rationality focused on production and profit?

As the question of care becomes more visible, so does the related problem of women's continuing relative disadvantage. The wage gap between women and men is growing larger (Gustafsson 1988). The increase in the gap is small but significant because it reverses a twenty-year trend toward more equality. The reasons for the reversal are related to the restructuring of the economy. For example, the majority of women are employed in the public sector where wages are stagnating, while a large majority of men are in the private sector where wages and salaries are relatively high and rising, particularly in professional and managerial jobs, where demand is high for new technical and organizational skills. Management strategies to reduce centralized bargaining weaken the labor unions' wage solidarity policy and contribute to the increasing gap. New individual wage-setting practices are probably also involved. In addition, part-time and temporary jobs that facilitate the combination of family and paid work tasks contribute to disadvantages for women in terms of pay and work opportunities.

Women in the care sector are reacting strongly to pay inequities and to the implications of low pay on status and respect. For example, recently several groups of specialized nurses (such as midwives and anesthesiology nurses) have quit their jobs when the pay raises they demanded were denied. Others, such as day-care workers, vote with their feet, going to new jobs.

These actions create almost unsolvable problems for public authorities. Welfare state budgets were built upon the assumption of certain low wage levels. Even these budgets are under attack by conservative attempts to reduce welfare spending and direct more money to the private sector. To raise the wages of hundreds of thousands of workers, as might be required with a comparable-worth wage strategy, is budgetarily extremely difficult under these conditions. Nevertheless, women need to support themselves and contribute to their families. That need becomes stronger all the time. Thus, the undervaluation of women's caring work, hidden when it was unpaid work in the home, becomes an urgent public issue, exposing the dependence of the society on the relative disadvantage of women and, possibly, also exposing the limits of the Swedish family model.

The more conservative Swedish critics of the Swedish model are pushing for the privatization of parts of the healthcare, eldercare, and childcare systems and for payments to mothers of children past infancy who leave the labor market to care for their children. If such changes occur, wives of affluent men would find it easier to leave the labor market than wives of ordinary workers. On the other hand, high-income women can also afford to hire domestic help. Au pairs from the United States and Canada are already not uncommon.

Privatization would lead to a two-tier system of family services and increasing class differences in the quality of care available. Working-class women, single women, and (especially) single mothers would have increasing difficulty. As users, they would face declining quality of publicly provided care as resources are reduced. As providers of care, they would have to deal with increasing pressures working in an underfunded public system. Some professional workers might benefit from private employment, but lower-level workers in the private sector would find lower wages and worse working conditions if privatization in Sweden follows the patterns in, for example, the United States.

Another possibility is to reorganize work to encompass family or social needs in new ways and to give increased value, both monetary and in terms of respect, to caring work. That the present organization and assumptions of paid work are contradictory to many social needs (Sassoon 1987) and that it is not enough to modify those assumptions for women if they are not modified for men would have to be recognized before reorganization is called for. This will take something more than public statements (now commonplace) that both men and women have the same responsibilities to support and care for their children. Real social relations and practices are otherwise. Social Democratic women have made a start with a demand for a six-hour working day at eight hours' pay. This might be a step toward eliminating the disadvantage of being a part-time worker. But, some have warned, the result might well be that men simply have more time for relaxation and union work, while women's lives remain unchanged. In any case, with broad opposition from men the six-hour-day proposal has made no progress.

Whether the Swedish family-work model will continue to function is unclear. Family life is highly valued. A recent study showed that 80 percent of young Swedes between 17 and 27 years old want to have a family and to live in a house that they own, many in the town in which they grew up. They expect to achieve this goal within the next few years (Svenska Dagbladet 1989). However, for all the reasons discussed above, the model is apt to function with increasing difficulty. Local innovations in childcare, such as parent cooperatives and employer-sponsored centers, are beginning to appear. These are likely to provide solutions for relatively highly paid, professional and managerial families. The booming economy in 1989 and 1990 created good employment opportunities and higher wages for some women, but increased the wage disadvantages for many others. Should the economy go into a recession, with increased unemployment, the shortages of workers for the public sector could disappear, removing one strain on the welfare state but exacerbating problems with funding. With internationalization of the economy and a strong private business sector, the values of capitalism—rationality, efficiency, productivity—overshadow the values of welfare—care, nurturing, community. These are the values not only of women's work in the family, but also of the People's Home and of social democracy. The challenge is to keep pursuing these values in the face of new economic conditions.

The trade unions are responding to this challenge with new efforts to bring women into union leadership, to raise the wages of poorly paid women workers, and to improve the working conditions of women who do the most physically demanding labor, as assembly line workers and as care workers for children and the chronically ill. The government has committed 60 million kronor to promote gender equality in the first part of the 1990s. In addition, the government is beginning a new campaign to encourage fathers to take more responsibility for children and more time off for parental leave. All these efforts may be the beginning of a new assault on gender inequality at work and at home.

However, my analysis implies that much more is needed to reach a more fundamental equality between women and men. The Swedish experience shows, I think, what a large proportion of a society's total work must be expended on the care and nurturing of human beings if everyone is to have equality of access to what we might call "a decent life." If production has the highest priority, and reproduction—including caring work—is only secondary, then secondary workers who attend to people are likely to be women, or, alternatively, many people will go untended and uncared for. A reorganization of social and economic life that puts production at the service of the reproduction of life is what is needed.

The Swedish model is not a failure. On the contrary, it shows that a capitalist economy can support an adequate standard of living and a humane life for all women and men if a people's movement committed to those goals retains political power and the economy is functioning well. However, gender equality will not necessarily be a result unless work is reorganized to meet the demands of daily life, caring work becomes as valued as producing profits, and the issue of male power is directly confronted. Still, if women in all countries could organize to achieve the standards Swedish women enjoy, that would be a huge step on the way to equality.

Postscript

More recently, two things have happened that make the future insecure for Swedish women. First, Sweden has been affected by the world recession, and unemployment has escalated. Second, the Social Democrats lost the election of September 1991, and women's parliamentary representation dropped from 38 percent to 33 percent. The new conservative coalition government moved rapidly to push through its agenda that will change and cut back the welfare state. By the summer of 1992, measures such as the privatization of day-care and other services, the introduction of market principles into health-care systems, and the general reduction of public employment were in the planning or early implementation stages. A proposal of a new benefit for mothers who stay at home after the parental leave period was controversial because it would encourage women to leave the labor force and would be financed by reductions in programs that encourage such participation, such as day-care and parental leave.

In response, some Swedish women were organizing within the political parties and unions, as well as outside traditional organizations, to save welfare state programs and to reverse the decline in their political power. Openly defining themselves as feminists, these new activists challenge male power and, at the same time, argue that Sweden may have to develop a new economic policy in order to recommit itself to the values of care and community. These women warn that they will form a new women's party if the old parties do not actively work for women's interests. While the outcome is still unclear, the centrality of gender conflicts in welfare state politics is escalating in Sweden.

Notes

1. The ideas expressed in this paper owe much to many discussions with colleagues in Sweden and Norway. I wish to particularly thank Annika Baude, Eivor Englund, Joke Esseveld, Eva Falkenberg, Lena Gonas, Harriet Holter, Wuokko Knocke, and Arnlaug Leira.

References

Bakker, Isabella. 1988. "Women's Employment in Comparative Perspective." Pp. 17–44 in *Feminization of the Labor Force*, edited by Jane Jenson, Elisabeth Hagen, and Ceallaigh Reddy. New York: Oxford University Press.

Baude, Annika. 1979. "Public Policy and Changing Family Patterns in Sweden 1930–1977," in *Sex Roles and Social Policy: A Complex Social Science Equation*, edited by Jean Lipman-Bluman and Jessie Bernard. London and Beverly Hills: Sage Studies in International Sociology 14.

Baude, Annika, and Lena Gonas. 1989. "Den Nodvandiga Kvinnoperspektivet." *Tiden*, 20–28.

Calleman, Catharina, Lena Lagercrantz, Ann Petersson, and Karin Widerberg. 1984. *Kvinnoreformer pa Mannens Villkor*. Lund: Studenlitteratur.

Dagens Nyheter. February 12, 1992, 10.

Esping-Andersen, Gosta. 1985. *Politics Against Markets*. Princeton, NJ: Princeton University Press.

Gustafsson, Siv. 1988. "Loneskillnade Mellan Kvinnor och Man-Gapet Okar Igen." *Ekonomisk Debatt*, April.

Hernes, Helga Maria. 1987. *Welfare State and Woman Power: Essays in State Feminism*. Oslo: Norwegian University Press.

Hirdman, Yvonne. 1987. *The Swedish Welfare State and the Gender System: A Theoretical and Empirical Sketch*. Uppsala, Sweden: The Study of Power and Democracy in Sweden. English Series. Report No. 7.

Holter, Harriet, ed. 1984. *Patriarchy in a Welfare Society*. Oslo: Universitetsforlaget.

Jonung, Christina. 1984. "Patterns of Occupational Segregation by Sex in the Labor Market," in *Sex Discrimination and Equal Opportunity: The Labor Market and Employment Policy*, edited by Gunter Schmid and Renate Weitzel. Berlin: Wissenschaftszentrum, WZB-Publications.

Korpi, Walter. 1978. *The Working Class in Welfare Capitalism*. London: Routledge and Kegan Paul.

Kyle, Gunhild. 1979. *Gastarbeterska i Manssamhallet*. Stockholm: LiberForlag.

Leinio, Tarja-Liisa. 1988. "Sex and Ethnic Segregation in the 1980 Swedish Labor Market." *Economic and Industrial Democracy* 9:99–120.

LO. 1987. *LO-medlemmar i Valfarden*. Rapport 8. Stockholm: LO.

Moen, Phyllis. 1989. *Working Parents: Transformations in Gender Roles and Public Policies in Sweden*. Madison, WI: The University of Wisconsin Press.

Nasman, Elisabet. 1986. "Work and Family—A Combination Made Possible by Part-time Work and Parental Leaves?" Stockholm: Arbetslivscentrum.

Nasman, Elisabet, and Eva Falkenberg. 1989. "Parental Rights in the Work and Family Interface." Stockholm: Arbetslivscentrum.

Nordic Council of Ministers. 1988. *Kvinnor och Man i Norden*. Stockholm: Nord.

Persson-Tanimura, Inga. 1988. "Economic Equality for Swedish Women—Current Situation and Trends," in paper prepared for New Sweden seminars.

Polanyi, Karl. 1944. *The Great Transformation*. Boston: Beacon Press.

Ruggie, Mary. 1984. *The State and Working Women: A Comparative Study of Britain and Sweden.* Princeton, NJ: Princeton University Press.

Sassoon, Anne Showstack. 1987. "Women's New Social Role: Contradictions of the Welfare State." Pp. 158–88 in *Women and the State,* edited by Anne Showstack Sassoon. London: Hutchinson.

SCB (Statistiska Centralbyran). 1986. *Kvinno och Mans Varlden.* Stockholm: Statistics Sweden.

———. 1989. *Income Distribution Survey in 1987.* Stockholm: Statistics Sweden.

Siim, Birte. 1987. "The Scandinavian Welfare States—Towards Sexual Equality or a New Kind of Male Domination?" *Acta Sociologica* 30, 3/4:255–270.

Sundstrom, Marianne. 1987. *A Study in the Growth of Part-time Work in Sweden.* Stockholm: Arbetslivscentrum.

Svenska Dagbladet. 1989. "Villa och Familj Drom For Unga." June 9.

Svenska Institutet. 1987. Fact Sheets on Sweden: Housing and Housing Policy in Sweden. Stockholm: The Swedish Institute.

Widerberg, Karin. 1991. "Reforms for Women—On Male Terms—The Example of the Swedish Legislation on Parental Leave." *International Journal of the Sociology of Law* 19:27–44.

Chapter 2

Repudiation versus Divorce: Responses to State Policy in Tunisia

Mounira Charrad

Law is inescapably two-faced. It reproduces existing inequalities; yet it also embodies ideals and provides channels through which the ideals can be pursued. In that it protects the existing social order while sometimes offering possibilities for change, law has at the same time a "reproductive" and "transformative" vocation. The particular balance between reproduction of inequality versus transformation of existing social relations varies depending on the specific context.

Reform of family law in Tunisia constitutes an interesting case of intended and dramatic innovation in the legal norms governing gender relations and family life. It is an example of a government enacting a law as an instrument of social change in an Islamic country where family matters had been regulated by traditional Islamic legal doctrine. Gaining significance outside of Tunisia, the reforms became a model for advocates of women's rights elsewhere in the Islamic world.

In 1956, immediately after achieving national independence from French colonial rule, Tunisia adopted its Code of Personal Status (CPS). By consensus among scholars, the Code and its amendments

The University of California, San Diego, and the American Institute of Maghrebi Studies, Los Angeles, provided partial support for this research. I wish to thank the Center for Research and Publications, Law School, University of Tunis and the Center for Maghrebi Studies, Tunis, for their generous hospitality during several research trips.

brought about far-reaching reforms in family law, reforms so fundamental that many have characterized them as revolutionary in the context of an Arab and Islamic country.

Tunisia has been at the forefront of the Arab Islamic world with
respect to family law.[1] The thrust of the new legislation is to redefine
the rights and obligations of men and women within the family. As
originally enacted and in its subsequent amendments, the Code out-
laws polygamy, transforms the procedure for marriage and divorce,
and makes changes in the law of succession, adoption, custody and filiation (Tunisia 1991). In particular, the CPS abolishes "repudiation," or
the husband's unilateral prerogative to terminate the marriage at will
without judicial intervention.

This chapter takes divorce as a pivotal issue to examine the
implementation of the Tunisian reforms embodied in the Code and
their impact on women. Legally, divorce has become more equal for
men and women. The Code also intends to decrease the harm, both
financial and social, that divorce causes in the cultural context of
Tunisia. In light of such ambitious objectives, it is important to know
whether the legislators' philosophy about family and gender roles
found its way into jurisprudence, what problems have been encountered in the application of the new laws, and how judicial decisions
have affected women. These are some of the key issues to be investi-
gated as we assess how the state legal policy has influenced women's
family experiences and what factors have been at work in the process.

In theoretical terms, the analysis presented here builds on the
system interdependence model discussed by Chow and Berheide in
this volume. Underlining the complexity of the interface between family and social structure, the interdependence model examines a full
range of reciprocal effects between macro-sociological processes and
the family (Acker 1988; Blumberg 1991; Boserup 1970; Tilly and Scott
1978; Tinker 1990). Most studies that develop the model concentrate on
the economy. In a somewhat different vein, and while recognizing the
importance of economic considerations with respect to divorce, I propose to venture into the less covered territory of the interplay between
family and state.[2] Conceptualizing the legal/judicial system as part of
the state, I will examine linkages between state action, law, and cultural images of gender roles in the family.

The analysis centers on the tensions involved in the application
of secularly minded legal norms in an Islamic country. By considering
an Islamic country—such as Tunisia—the study aims to enrich our
understanding of the diversity of women's experiences globally. A tradition of excellent scholarship on divorce law in the United States
(Weitzman 1985) contrasts with the dearth of research on the same

topic in the Middle East.[3] In order to develop a more global and less ethnocentric perspective, we need to incorporate culture into the study of family and gender. Sensitivity to culture provides an opportunity to develop a more internationally informed social theory on the linkages between gender and other institutions.

Contemporary Tunisia offers an unusually appropriate locus for the exploration of such issues. Since the reforms started in the mid-1950s, they have been in effect for over thirty years; we thus have enough of a time perspective to study their implementation. The divorce laws contained in the Code of Personal Status and its amendments constitute a clearly defined state-initiated innovation. Such a configuration of events provides a vista on the relationships between a country's legal/judicial system and its social/cultural system. While several studies of women's roles in the Middle East (Gadant and Kasriel 1990; Hijab 1988; Mernissi 1987; Fernea 1985) have been done, none has focused sufficiently on the interplay between legal change, culture, and gender; a very important issue at the intersection of family experiences and state institutions.

The chapter begins by considering the legal innovations of the CPS and the critical role of the judicial system. Drawing evidence from in-depth interviews with lawyers, the analysis proceeds with a focus on the issues surrounding the application of the new divorce laws in judicial practice, their impact on women, and their symbolic meaning. The study shows that, even though the divorce legislation has been unevenly applied, the Tunisian reforms were no mere paper pronouncement.

Islamic Culture and Legal Reform

In promulgating the Code of Personal Status in 1956, the Tunisian government took the precaution of reasserting its allegiance to Islam. An integral part of the original religious texts and appearing in the Quran itself, family law is the kernel of the Islamic tradition. A reform can easily be construed as an attack on religion, a position which the Tunisian government never took. When Turkey, another Islamic but non-Arab country, made equally significant reforms under the leadership of Ataturk in the 1920s and 30s, the Turkish legislators opted for the unambiguous adoption of the Swiss civil code, thus enacting legislation clearly defined as secular in political discourse. In marked contrast, the Tunisian lawmakers emphasized the continuing faithfulness of Tunisian law to the Islamic heritage. They presented the reforms as a reinterpretation of the Islamic tradition in a newly independent country faced with the unavoidable dilemmas of development. While some of these changes may appear to conflict with doctrines of Islamic family law, members of the government described them in political discourse as a legitimate innovation, similar to earlier phases of legal interpretation that have occurred intermittently throughout Islamic history.[4]

Even though it made reforms that were among the most radical in the Arab-Islamic world, the Tunisian government of the mid-1950s went only as far as it felt necessary for its objectives. Its primary project at the time was an overall modernization of the country, and changes in family life were part of that project. The newly formed national state was able to make reforms because it faced no effective opposition in 1956. The likely supporters of Islamic law, regions where kinship was organized along the lines of Islamic law and the Islamic establishment, had lost all political leverage at the time—which left the Tunisian government with free rein (Charrad forthcoming and 1990). While promulgating the CPS, the government also unified the judicial system by creating a nationwide network of courts. Here, then, we have an instance of fundamental legal reform in an area of deeply held values, together with a reorganization of the country's judiciary.

How the Law Changed

Before we consider the issues involved in implementation, we must first see the difference between the old legal principles and those embedded in the new laws. The reforms of divorce law started with the CPS in 1956, which changed several aspects of family law, and continued with the promulgation of a law specifically on divorce in 1981.

Islamic law, called the Shari'a, was in effect in Tunisia prior to the reforms. The Shari'a is a comprehensive legal system embedded in the original texts of Islam, including the Quran. It gives a man the right to divorce his wife at will, even though it depicts divorce (called repudiation or "tallaq") as abhorred and only tolerated by God. The husband has the right to repudiate his wife by making a solemn declaration, usually the pronouncement of the sentence "I divorce thee." The verses most pertinent to divorce in the Quran are the following (*Holy Quran* 1946):

> For those who take
> An oath for abstention
> From their wives,
> A waiting for four months
> Is ordained

> (Surah II, Verse 226)

> But if their intention
> Is firm for divorce,
> God heareth
> And knoweth all things
>
> (Surah II, Verse 227)

The presence of two witnesses is sufficient to make the repudiation valid and no judicial intervention is required. Repudiated women have the right to retain their dowry. They may receive a lump sum of money from the husband but no provision is made for continuous alimony. One of the reasons for the waiting period advised in the verse above is to detect a possible pregnancy and settle ensuing issues of filiation.

In contrast to the ease of divorce for a man, the Shari'a seriously restricts a woman's possibility of obtaining a divorce. If a woman wants a divorce, she must appeal to a religious judge ("qadi") and provide evidence that her husband has harmed her. The Shari'a limits the grounds on which a woman may be granted a divorce to extreme cases, identifying each one specifically, such as the husband's failure to provide food and shelter to his wife and children, or his prolonged and unexplained absence for several years. If he considers that the woman has a case, the religious judge may pronounce the termination of the marriage.

The lawmakers enacting the CPS found four principal problems with traditional Islamic divorce law. First, Islamic law did not require a court procedure for all cases of divorce. Second, it gave only men the right to get a divorce. Third, it did not impose any financial responsibilities on the men who wanted a divorce by repudiation. Fourth, it was too easy for men to get a divorce.

The CPS also responds to these problems first and foremost by abolishing the man's unilateral right of repudiation. It introduces the necessity of judicial intervention in all cases: "No divorce shall take place save before the court," reads Article 30. The CPS also makes it possible for women to get a divorce and gives them the same rights and obligations as men in this respect. It states that the party not desiring the divorce, man or woman, should get compensation. Presenting a new conception of divorce, the CPS requires the party wanting the divorce to go to court, go through a session of reconciliation, reflect on the situation, and consider the possibility of having to make a payment to the other spouse. The Tunisian Code thus establishes the principle of equal divorce rights and obligations for men and women.

The CPS makes three forms of divorce possible: divorce by mutual consent, divorce based on fault, and divorce at the request of one of the spouses. The third form is similar to a no-fault divorce, since the party requesting the divorce does not need to prove fault on the part of the other, but it requires the spouse initiating the divorce to pay a compensation to the non-consenting spouse. The courts determine the nature and amount of compensation, which can be either in a lump sum or as ongoing alimony. An amendment to the Code, the 1981 law on divorce, introduces the possibility of "life-long alimony" for a divorced woman. (Prior to 1981, compensation was paid in a lump sum.) A divorced woman can now select to receive a regular monthly or yearly payment until death or until she remarries. The judge may adjust the amount as the circumstances of the husband and wife change. The legal principle involved is to allow a divorced woman to maintain the standard of living she had in marriage.

The CPS and the 1981 law also make changes in custody and, to some extent, in guardianship. Under Islamic law before the reforms, children of divorced parents were in the custody of their mother until the age of puberty, at which time custody passed automatically to the father or one of his relatives.[5] The CPS states that both parents are equally eligible for custody and that the judge is to consider the best interest of the child as the only criterion in attributing custody, thus increasing a woman's chance to keep her children even after they reach puberty.

While increasing women's custody rights, the CPS nevertheless maintains male power in making a distinction between custody and guardianship. Whereas custody involves day to day care, guardianship refers to legal responsibilities for the child such as authorizing a passport, signing official papers for school enrollment, and the like. When the father is alive, the CPS systematically makes him the child's guardian after divorce, even when the mother has custody and thus takes daily care of the child. In case of the father's death, the original CPS required the judge to select a guardian for the child among a wide range of potential candidates including paternal and maternal relatives. The mother was considered among other possible guardians, depending on the judge's assessment of the child's best interest. The 1981 law introduces a modification. It automatically makes the mother the guardian in case of the father's death, and in that case only. In the event of divorce, guardianship continues to rest with the father as it did before 1981.

In summary, the CPS abolishes repudiation. It makes divorce a matter to be administered by the courts. It gives women and men the same rights and obligations both with respect to initiating a divorce and paying its cost to the other party. It also establishes the principle of alimony and increases women's rights to child custody, while maintaining men's advantage through guardianship.

Delicate Mission Assigned to the Judicial System

To understand the problems involved in implementation, it is important to underscore the distance between the new laws and social practice at the time of their promulgation. Formulated on the initiative of the government, the Code of Personal Status did not adjust the law to conform to social practices of the mid-1950s. Even though no systematic information is available on divorce cases before the reforms of 1956, anthropological studies and memories of older people confirm the gap between the reforms and previous practices. The new legal norms, especially those on divorce, were overall at variance with prevailing legal practice and dominant patterns of social conduct.[6] In such a context, the judiciary must play a critical role in the application of the new laws. Since a law is only as strong as the court system in charge of its implementation, the operation of the judicial system is one of the most important factors shaping the fate of reforms. Successful reform depends on the understanding of the new laws by the courts and on their willingness to apply them.

Judges were, in effect, given a difficult mission. In the years following the reforms, Tunisian judges were mainly teachers in religious schools or Islamic scholars hastily trained to fulfill their new role. They were asked to apply new legal norms which departed not only from their own training, but also from the dominant cultural patterns of the country. Even though the government gave them what appeared as a simple mandate, namely to apply the CPS directly, members of the judicial system repeatedly had to choose between continuity of Islamic legal tradition versus conformity to values embodied in the new laws. Judges had to translate abstract legal norms into actual decisions intended to produce observable behaviors. For example, judges had a significant amount of discretion to determine levels of alimony and how one identifies the child's best interest.

On issues on which the CPS is not explicit, the courts in practice had a series of choices ranging from referring back to Islamic doctrine to formulating creative solutions based on the legal principles embodied in the CPS and legislative policies. In actuality, however, because of their general cultural values, members of the courts shifted back and forth between the legal philosophy of Islamic doctrine and the principles of the new legislation.

Impact of the New Legislation

Given the context just described, the impact of the reforms on women has been complex and double-sided. And so have been women's responses to the new laws. The new laws have made little difference on some divorce issues, such as alimony. Contrary to the intent of the reforms, women usually receive low levels of financial support after divorce. On other issues, such as child custody, the new laws have made a major difference. For example, a woman's actual chances of obtaining custody have increased considerably.

In order to assess the impact and meaning of the reforms, I conducted in-depth interviews with fourteen lawyers and four legal scholars, both male and female. The lawyers specialize in family law and have extensive experience with divorce cases. They all practice in the city of Tunis and their clientele covers a wide range of socioeconomic groups. The legal scholars do research on family law and personal status at the University of Tunis. The advantage of interviewing both lawyers and legal scholars is that they have knowledge of many cases, and are thus in a position to give an overall assessment of the situation. Each two to three hours long, the interviews focused on the impact of the reforms and the problems encountered in their application.

Repudiation Replaced by Divorce

The interviewees agree that the abolition of repudiation and the right of women to initiate a divorce constitute major changes in Tunisian family law. These are, by consensus, significant steps towards women's and men's equality before the law. All lawyers comment that a consequence of the Code has been to render divorce more difficult for men, if only because it now requires a court procedure when it was previously a private action. Furthermore, the prospect of having to pay alimony, possibly for the rest of their former wife's life, makes men think twice about divorce. All lawyers report cases of women initiating divorce.[7]

A legal scholar explains:

> In the past, all marriages were affected by the possibility that the husband might repudiate his wife and leave her without support. The Code introduces a new conception of marriage.

A lawyer states:

> Divorce is more difficult because you have to go to court. It is more trouble, there is publicity, so that by comparison with the situation where the husband was able to repudiate his wife without cause, he is likely to give more thought to it now, especially

since he may have to pay support. In addition, the Code certainly gives women access to the courts and the right to file for divorce themselves. In my view, this is critical.

Another says:

The great advantage of the Code for women is that women now have the right to divorce their husbands.

Calling repudiation a "Sword of Damocles," still another declares:

In my opinion, among the changes brought about by the Code, the abolition of repudiation is the most important. When a woman marries now, she can have a greater sense of permanence. She is not at risk to be repudiated any day, whenever the husband feels like it. She no longer has this Sword of Damocles hanging over her head.

Some judges still find it difficult to accept the idea that a woman can initiate a divorce simply because she is unhappy in her marriage, a notion that conflicts with traditional Islamic doctrine. Consequently, this is something which, in practice, remains more difficult for a woman. Nevertheless, many women do initiate divorce and succeed in obtaining it—which, in most cases, would have been unlikely before the Code. Furthermore, if a woman is able to fight her way through the judicial system and willing to face appeals, she can usually reach her goal. The lawyers I interviewed agree that a woman who is determined to get a divorce will most likely get it in the end.[8]

If women continue to suffer in marriage rather than file for divorce, it is no longer because of restrictions imposed by the law as it was in the past. Instead, it is because of the lack of financial support, often combined with fear of the social ramifications. As in the United States (Weitzman 1985), social and economic inequalities restrict the potential advantages of legal equality for women. According to national statistics, Tunisian women represent only 21.2 percent of the population classified as "economically active" (Moghadam 1990). The women who initiate a divorce are those who either have their own source of income or can be supported by their family of origin. While urbanization makes this increasingly difficult, some extended families will take care of divorced women relatives and their children, thus providing a measure of security for women who choose divorce despite limited economic resources.

Custody and Guardianship

Laws on child custody have been among the most effective in improving women's position and family experiences, and judges overwhelmingly have interpreted the new laws in favor of women. Lawyers report that this has been the case even in rural areas. Prior to the new laws, members of the extended paternal family—and not judges— made decisions on matters of custody after divorce. They usually gave the responsibility of caring for the child to a female relative of the child's father. Now that the courts decide and the CPS makes the child's best interest the paramount concern, the judge may choose custody arrangements quite different from those that the extended paternal family would have made. Several of the lawyers whom I interviewed estimate that, in nine cases out of ten, the mother now gets custody of children after divorce.

The legal distinction between custody and guardianship has caused difficulties, however. The law gives guardianship (or legal responsibility for the child) to the father, while the mother has custody—and therefore the day to day care. In everyday life, the lines between guardianship and custody become blurred, giving rise to conflicts between the two parents. For example, a lawyer reported a case in which the mother wanted to take her son on a trip abroad, but the father refused to sign the necessary papers for the son to obtain a passport. In another case, the father, who had the legal responsibility to sign the forms for his child's enrollment in school, insisted on choosing a school with a curriculum to his taste, even though the school was located far from the area where the mother and child lived, thus causing serious transportation problems. Clearly, the change that has taken place in custody patterns is important, but many women feel that it is not enough. They want further changes, which will give them guardianship at the same time as custody.

Financial Support for Women After Divorce

The law of 1981 establishing alimony has failed to provide divorced women with appropriate resources. All the lawyers and legal scholars interviewed agree that women receive low levels of financial support after divorce. As mentioned earlier, in principle, the judge is supposed to consider the standard of living which the woman enjoyed during marriage, and then calculate the level of compensation she should receive after divorce. This seldom happens in reality, however. Many judges continue to be influenced by the Islamic principle that allowed a man to terminate the marriage at will without incurring much financial responsibility for his former wife.

A legal scholar says: "Many judges, influenced by the Shari'a, accept the idea behind repudiation and give little in the way of compensation or alimony."

"In my experience," a lawyer notes, "alimony is ridiculously low, reflecting the views of judges who refuse to give large support payments to women when they think that the husband has a right to a divorce without having to make such payments."

Confirming this, another lawyer calls the levels of support for divorced women "unrealistically low," and says that on this point "a majority of judges interpret the Code in a way which is as ungenerous to women as possible." In her estimation, about 90 percent of the women who divorce experience a drop in their standard of living as a result. This is similar to what happens to U.S. women after divorce, where many also face a decrease in income, sometimes of considerable proportions.[9]

One of the reasons for the low levels of alimony resides in the relative faithfulness of the judicial system to Islamic doctrine; another is economic: The low income of most Tunisian men. Tunisia has a per-capita annual income of 1,315 dollars (Lacoste 1991, p. 453). A man is often unable to give much alimony to his former wife, especially if he remarries and has children with a second wife.

The law, however, is more frequently a deterrent to divorce in higher income groups, because men are aware that, under the new law, the financial stakes may be high and that they may be required to make large payments to their former wives. Several highly publicized divorces have resulted in substantial life-long alimony for the women. These cases involved educated women, who are in the best position to avail themselves of their legal rights. But the cases have taken on meaning even outside of educated circles. During my research in Tunis, I heard illiterate women in lawyers' waiting rooms mention these cases and say that they, too, would try to fight in court for a satisfactory level of support.

Under the CPS, the party initiating the divorce is more likely to be required to pay compensation to the other spouse. A consequence of the new divorce laws is that women have the same obligations as men; therefore, if they are the ones initiating the divorce, they may be required to pay compensation. This has led to a manipulation of the law. Men who want a divorce will try to force their wives into seeking the divorce, instead of initiating the divorce procedure themselves, in the hope of avoiding alimony and perhaps even of receiving a compensation payment.

Several of the lawyers indicate that, even though the law of 1981, which created the life-long alimony, has not been as positive an enactment as hoped, it has had a significant psychological effect. It induces the judge to consider the welfare of the woman after divorce. This represents a new conception of divorce and its financial consequences, a conception which was absent from the previous legislation.

Meaning of the Reforms

The new legislation matters a great deal in terms of cultural meaning. The CPS has become a national symbol of women's rights, a symbol that feminists, liberals, and democratic forces want to preserve. Lawyers, legal scholars, and women themselves all feel that women are better off under the new legislation. Yet, the aftermath of divorce is still difficult for women, who tend to become culturally marginalized and pay a high personal cost for divorce.

Women's Awareness of Their Rights

The extent to which Tunisian women of all walks of life know about the existence of the Code is striking. Especially in the 1960s and 1970s, the government sponsored radio programs and other campaigns to explain the content of the CPS. Of course, those who are best informed are the highly educated, professional women. They often know specific provisions on marriage, divorce, inheritance, etc. The Code is published as a small booklet readily available in bookstores, is easy to obtain, and is relatively understandable to non-lawyers.

But awareness of the Code does not stop with the educated. Since 60 percent of the female population is illiterate (A.F.T.U.R.D. 1992, p. 154), many women can only have learned about the new legislation through hearsay and government campaigns. The lawyers interviewed report that illiterate women know that the CPS exists and vaguely understand that parts of it protect women's interests without knowing specific provisons. That in itself is important. Many of them also know that the new legislation gives them the right to divorce their husbands and keep their children.

While sitting in lawyers' waiting rooms, I overheard underprivileged women saying a couple of popular phrases: "Thanks to Bourguiba," and "It's only because Bourguiba helped us." They were referring to the President who headed the government responsible for the promulgation of the Code. Bourguiba is seen as the author of the Code and an advocate of women's rights in Tunisia. The women were expressing their awareness that Bourguiba (or his government) had enacted a set of laws that could now make a difference in their lives. While Bourguiba was President, another expression was common in everyday parlance. A woman unhappy with her husband's behavior would say to him: "I will go and complain about you to Bourguiba," which then became a common scolding joke between husband and wife.

A Tunisian magazine conducted a series of informal interviews with women, the majority illiterate, in the countryside in the mid-1970s, twenty years after the adoption of the CPS. The findings confirm my observations in lawyers' offices. The women expressed their gratitude to Bourguiba for having done something good on their behalf. While not knowing most of the CPS content, they did know through hearsay that the man's right to unilateral repudiation had been abolished (Chaouchi 1976).

Even though the application of divorce laws has met with obstacles, the new legislation means much to Tunisians because of its symbolic value. The Code symbolizes emancipation for women. Since its enactment in 1956, the Code has been gradually making its way into Tunisian culture. Some people, men *and* women, are starting to take it for granted, as they do with other aspects of their culture.

Asked to summarize the effects of the Code since its inception, one of the best known family lawyers comments:

> The most important effects might be psychological. Man is no longer sovereign. He can no longer beat his wife freely, without fear of punishment. Women who know the exact provisions of the Code feel in a stronger position than before. Even those who don't know the details know somehow that power has shifted in their direction at least to some degree.

Another echoes this statement when she says: "Although there have undoubtedly been problems of implementation, the Code constitutes a major step in the modernization of Tunisian society. It has become a national symbol of greater equality for women. As such, it is immensely important."

High Personal Cost of Divorce

A theme that emerged strongly from the interviews concerns the social cost attached to divorce. Women pay a high price for it. In the Islamic cultural context of Tunisia, where marriage is seen as a woman's proper place, divorce has harsh consequences. Despite the highly significant symbolic meaning of the CPS, deeply seated cultural images of women's roles continue to shape people's perceptions of divorcees. Cultural values hamper the changes that the law could potentially bring to social conduct.

Traditionally, a woman is defined as belonging to an extended family, a lineage, often referred to as a "house," first her father's and then her husband's. A divorced woman lacks such identification. Her social status is ambiguous and culturally marginal. A lawyer describes the situation of a divorced woman as follows:

> If a divorced woman has children, it is extremely difficult for her to remarry. She is in a tough situation with regard to her own family and society generally. She will rarely be free of her family. They don't want her to live alone because the fact of her living alone would make people question her morality. Often she will not have the means to live alone in any case. She will have no choice but live with relatives. If she has a flock of children, she will often have difficulty finding a place to stay. In many cases, a woman's sexual life is over because she will be unable to remarry and it will be extremely difficult for her to have love affairs. In any case, a love affair would subject her to moral criticism.

Likening divorced women to the subterranean, informal economic sector in the cultural context of Tunisia, a woman lawyer says: "What counts is youth and beauty. Men give little consideration to a woman who is not young, beautiful and a virgin. Divorced women play the same role in society as the informal sector does in the economy." What she means by this metaphor is that divorcees are seen as available to receive the sexual energy which is not channeled into marriage, in the same way as the informal, subterranean sector of the economy absorbs the surplus labor which cannot be integrated into the more formally organized economic structures.

Without a doctrine of original sin, the Islamic tradition views sexuality as basically good, especially for men, and encourages it. But cultural rules prohibit sexual activity outside of marriage, particularly for women. The image of a divorcee has traditionally been that of a libertine and the conception persists today. In having sexual relations, divorced women break cultural rules. They are stigmatized for it and placed in a difficult social position.

"The relationships enjoyed by divorced women are very superficial," a lawyer comments. "Men expect to have sexual relations with them [divorcees], but not to marry them."

Another agrees: "Society views divorced women as available and dangerous." And yet another gives this overall assessment: "Divorced women have a hard time. Life punishes them."

As these quotes illustrate, the personal cost of divorce remains high for most women. Even when they have the resources necessary to choose divorce over a bad marriage, women face the risk of becoming socially marginal. The Tunisian example shows how cultural ideals and images shape women's experiences in ways that legal innovations cannot change directly. In presenting a new conception of divorce, however, the current laws have changed the terms in which men and women think about divorce. They also have made women aware of new possibilities and new challenges.

Conclusion

The application of divorce laws shows a tension between continuity of Islamic tradition and conformity to new values embodied in new legislation. The new laws have clashed with prevailing gender roles. Not surprisingly, therefore, the implementation has met with difficulties. On some critical points affecting women's lives, such as alimony, judges have been reluctant to depart from Islamic legal philosophy. As a result, they have failed to protect women's welfare.

Yet—and this may be the less expected outcome for Western audiences—the laws have clearly *not* been in vain. The judicial system has shifted away from traditional legal doctrine and followed the legislative intent to bring about change. Women have gained custody rights. They can no longer be repudiated at the whim of their husbands. They have also obtained—and used—the right to initiate a divorce.

A very great majority of Tunisian women, including those who are illiterate, know that something has changed in the last generation, even though most may not know specific points. They know that there is a difference between the family law which applies to them and that which applied to their mothers, and they feel that they are better off than their mothers. Finally, the Code of Personal Status has an important cultural meaning in Tunisian society and in the Islamic Middle East generally: It constitutes a powerful symbol of women's liberation in an Islamic context.

If we return to the metaphor of the law as having two faces—reproduction of existing inequalities and transformative vocation—it is fair to say that the application of divorce laws in Tunisia has combined reproduction of gender inequality with a measure of transfor-

mation in gender relations and family experience. In Tunisia, as in
other countries, economic considerations continue to limit women's
options and to prevent many women from using the law to its full
potential.

Nevertheless, the new laws and their application by the judiciary
have redefined divorce for the majority of Tunisians. A return to repudiation would be a significant loss of rights for women. Because the
relationship between state and family is a dynamic one which changes
with shifts in political power, the application of divorce laws could
take a different turn in the years to come. Whether and how current
struggles for state power affect family law in the future is a question
for further research. In the last thirty years, however, the new divorce
laws have been no mere paper pronouncement.

At present, the feminist agenda in Tunisia includes issues pertaining to divorce. In an attempt to influence policy formation, feminists are making several demands. First, they ask that the law be
applied in conformity with the spirit of the legal texts and, in particular, that the courts give more than token alimony to women. Second,
they request further changes in the text of the law to improve women's
family experiences. They want an end to the power over children that
the law still grants to the father, even when the mother has custody.
Third, they strive to protect the legal rights that women have gained so
far. With the wave of Islamic fundamentalism sweeping the Middle
East and the concomitant call for a return to Islamic law, Tunisian feminists feel a threat to their rights and the need to be especially vigilant.

The analysis of the Tunisian case has broader implications for an
internationally informed understanding of the interplay between
state-enacted social policy, law, and gender. In Tunisia, as in the United
States, feminists fight for changes in the law (Equal Rights Amendment and abortion rights in the United States, divorce and other
aspects of family law in Tunisia). Feminists in vastly different cultural
contexts engage in such fights because of the transformative potential
of legal innovations, despite the limitations or difficulties encountered
in implementation. It is often assumed that the judicial system functions, albeit imperfectly, yet well enough to make fighting for legal
change worth the effort in liberal democracies.

This study has shown that legal rights are equally critical and
meaningful in other countries. No law can be expected to transform
social reality by itself. Yet, legal rights matter a great deal for at least
two reasons. Once the law is in place, proponents of democracy and
freedom have a chance to work toward their enforcement. And, even if
unevenly applied, legal rights create an opening that can then be used
to bring about further change.

Notes

1. The relevant context here is the world in which Arab and Islamic identities overlap. Another Arab and Islamic country, the People's Democratic Republic of Yemen, also made significant reforms in promulgating its Family Law in 1974. The Republic of Yemen did not go as far as Tunisia, however, in that it only restricted polygamy, whereas Tunisia banned it. Turkey, an Islamic but non-Arab country, made reforms similar to those made in Tunisia, but did so by rejecting the Islamic legal tradition altogether and adopting an entirely secular law. The fact that Turkey stands outside of the Arab world has created a different set of conditions for the promulgation of reforms and their implementation.

2. For another example of an analysis of state, gender, and law, see Charrad forthcoming; and 1990. On the social construction of sexuality and systems of domination, see MacKinnon (1989). Afshar (1987), Charlton et al. (1989), Stacey (1983), and Staudt (1990) emphasize the role of the state in shaping policies of economic development and reproducing gender inequality. Afshar (1987) and Stacey (1983) examine gender ideologies in social revolutions.

3. Jansen (1987) shows how widows, orphans, divorcees, and other women without men cope with their social status in an Algerian town. Hermassi and Hmed (1983) present a social psychological study of divorce in Tunis. Neither, however, focuses on the application of divorce law.

4. On legal innovation and interpretation in the Islamic tradition, see Esposito (1982).

5. This was especially true in the case of sons. There was more flexibility for daughters who might remain in the custody of their mother.

6. In an effort to find out about law and divorce before the 1956 reforms, I interviewed the chief statistician at the National Institute of Statistics. He reported that very little was known pre-1956 because notaries recorded important events (such as marriages and divorces) in handwriting in their notebooks. The events were recorded chronologically as they occurred. The only way to obtain systematic information on divorce prior to 1956 would be to study the notaries' notebooks, a monumental task that no one has yet attempted. There are studies, however, that give a sense of family life in the past in Tunisia (Cuisenier 1975 and Camilleri 1973, for example).

7. Figures available for 1985–1986 show that women did initiate divorces, although men did so in greater numbers. In that period, the total number of divorces came to 6,640, out of which men initiated 5,079 divorces and women 1,561 (Republique Tunisienne 1986). During the 1980s, one marriage out of seven ended in divorce (*Realites* 1988). Hermassi and Hmed (1983) indicate that the overall divorce rate exhibits only minor fluctuations from the 1960s to the early 80s.

8. Divorce and legal proceedings are not nearly as expensive a process in Tunisia as they are in the United States, and they are thus available to a wide range of women. For the majority of women, the lack of financial support after divorce constitutes a greater obstacle than does the expense of the legal proceeding.

9. Weitzman indicates that the standard of living of divorced women and their children drops by as much as 73 percent in the year following divorce (Weitzman 1985, p. xii). See also Arendall (1991).

References

Acker, Joan. 1988. "Class, Gender and the Relations of Distribution." *Signs* 13:473-479.

Afshar, Haleh, ed. 1987. *Women, State and Ideology: Studies from Africa and Asia.* Albany, NY: State University of New York.

A.F.T.U.R.D. (Association des Femmes Tunisiennes pour la Recherche et le Developpement). 1992. *Tunisiennes en Devenir*, Vol.2, *La Moitie Entiere.* Tunis: Ceres Productions.

Arendall, Terry. 1991. "Downward Mobility." *The Family Experience: A Reader in Cultural Diversity*, edited by Mark Hutter. New York: Macmillan.

Beck, Lois, and Nikki Keddie, eds. 1978. *Women in the Muslim World.* Cambridge, MA: Harvard University Press.

Blumberg, Rae, ed. 1991. *Gender, Family and Economy: The Triple Overlap.* Newbury Park, CA: Sage.

Boserup, Ester. 1970. *Woman's Role in Economic Development.* London: George Allen and Unwin.

Camilleri, Carmel. 1973. *Jeunesse, Famille et Developpement.* Paris: Editions du Centre National de la Recherche Scientifique.

Chaouchi, Aly. 1976. "Vingt Ans Apres le 30 Aout 1956: L'Emancipation de la Tunisienne se Poursuit-elle avec Bonheur?" *Dialogue* 19.

Charfi, Mohamed. 1983. *Introduction a l'Etude du Droit.* Tunis: Centre d'Etudes, de Recherches et de Publications.

Charlton, Sue Ellen, Jana Everett, and Kathleen Staudt, eds. 1989. *Women, the State and Development.* Albany, NY: State University of New York.

Charrad, Mounira. 1990. "State and Gender in the Maghrib." *Middle East Report* 20(2):19-24.

———. Forthcoming. *States and Women's Rights: A Comparison of Tunisia, Algeria and Morocco.* Berkeley, CA: University of California Press.

Cherif Chamari, Alya. 1991. *La Femme et la Loi en Tunisie.* Casablanca: United Nations University and le Fennec.

Cuisenier, Jean. 1975. *Economie et Parente.* Paris: Mouton.

Esposito, John L. 1982. *Women in Muslim Family Law.* Syracuse, NY: Syracuse University Press.

Fernea, Elizabeth W., ed. 1985. *Women and the Family in the Middle East.* Austin: University of Texas Press.

Gadant, Monique, and Michele Kasriel, eds. 1990. *Femmes du Maghreb au Present*. Paris: Editions du Centre National de la Recherche Scientifique.

Glendon, Mary Ann. 1989. *The Transformation of Family Law: State, Law and Family in the United States and Western Europe*. Chicago, IL: University of Chicago Press.

Hermassi, Abdelbaki, and A. Marie Hmed. 1983. *Le Divorce dans la Region de Tunis: Evolution et Aspects Psycho-Sociologiques*. Tunis: Union Nationale des Femmes de Tunisie et Institut El Amouri de Psychologie Appliquee.

Hijab, Nadia. 1988. *Womanpower: The Arab Debate on Women at Work*. New York: Cambridge University Press.

Holy Quran. 1946. New York: Hafner.

Jansen, Willy. 1987. *Women Without Men*. Leiden: Brill.

Lacoste, Camille and Yves, eds. 1991. *L'Etat du Maghreb*. Tunis: Ceres Productions.

Ladjili, Jeanne. 1980. "Recherche d'une Responsabilite Egale des Pere et Mere dans la Garde de l'Enfant Mineur en Droit Tunisien." *Revue Tunisienne de Droit*.

MacKinnon, Catharine. 1989. *Toward a Feminist Theory of the State*. Cambridge, MA: Harvard University Press.

Mernissi, Fatima. 1987. *Beyond the Veil*. Bloomington, IN: Indiana University Press.

Moghadam, V. M. May 1990. "Determinants of Female Labor Force Participation in the Middle East and North Africa." *World Institute for Development Economics Research* (Helsinki).

Realites (Tunis). 1988. December, No. 175:16–22.

Republique Tunisienne. 1986. *Les Statistiques Juridiques*. Tunis: Ministere de la Justice, Inspection Generale.

Stacey, Judith. 1983. *Patriarchy and Socialist Revolution in China*. Berkeley, CA: University of California Press.

Staudt, Kathleen, ed. 1990. *Women, International Development, and Politics: The Bureaucratic Mire*. Philadelphia, PA: Temple University Press.

Tilly, Louise A., and Joan W. Scott. 1978. *Women, Work and the Family*. New York: Holt, Rinehart and Winston.

Tinker, Irene. 1990. *Persistent Inequalities: Women and World Development*. New York: Oxford University Press.

Tunisia. 1991. *Code du Statut Personnel*. Edition 1991. Imprimerie Officielle de la Republique Tunisienne.

Weitzman, Lenore J. 1985. *The Divorce Revolution*. New York: Free Press.

Weitzman, Lenore J., and Ruth B. Dixon. 1986. "The Transformation of Legal Marriage Through No-Fault Divorce." Pp. 338–350 in *Family in Transition*, edited by Arlene S. Skolnick and Jerome H. Skolnick. 5th ed. Boston: Little Brown.

Chapter 3

The Impact of the One-Child Policy on Women and the Patriarchal Family in the People's Republic of China

Esther Ngan-ling Chow and Kevin Chen

The one-child family policy implemented by the People's Republic of China (PRC) since 1979 is one of the most significant, yet controversial, programs of planned fertility that China has ever attempted.[1] The Chinese government designed this policy to launch planned social changes through altering household composition for the purposes of restricting population growth and advancing economic prosperity in China. The policy also represents one of the Chinese government's several efforts since liberation in 1949 to eliminate the centuries-old feudalist system and to address the issue of women's oppression through legislation, policy, and program intervention. Hence, the implementation of such a policy has had profound effects on the lives of the Chinese people and their families, directly impacting on women's roles in production and reproduction.

Central questions of concern are: Does the one-child policy tend to strengthen or weaken the patriarchal family in China? Does this policy

Paper presented at the Annual Meetings of the American Sociological Association held in San Francisco in August 1989. Special thanks go to Anna Sullivan and Myle Loung for their help in data processing and to Elaine Stahl Leo, Xu Wu, Xiaolan Bao, Mei Yue, and Lin Nan for reading early versions of this paper.

promote gender equality, as Chinese officials claim? In the early years of its implementation, gender issues related to the one-child policy were basically ignored by policy-makers as well as researchers, but these issues have recently begun to attract scholarly attention (Dalsimer and Nisonoff 1987; Davin 1987; Hong 1987; Johnson 1986; Robinson 1985). The one-child policy affects women, in particular, not only because they assume primary responsibilities in childbearing and childrearing, but because the policy intends to change the family, an institution which is still vitally important in shaping and limiting the lives of Chinese women. Recent debates over the impact of the one-child policy reveal its dialectic nature, showing that, despite some positive effects, it tends to reinforce women's traditional roles as household laborers and reproducers and to perpetuate the patriarchal family system, especially in rural China.

Based on a survey of 1,130 households in Beijing, the purposes of this study are to examine empirically the extent to which the one-child policy has influenced the Chinese family system and shaped gender relationships within it. First, we describe briefly the background of the one-child policy to elucidate the historical and social contexts of its implementation. Then we analyze the impact of the policy on patriarchal family and gender relationships by comparing the structural and ideological conditions of the family and the gendered household division of labor and of childcare between only-child and multiple-child families. Finally, we discuss linkage between macro-change in state population policy and micro-change in family and gender relationships.

Family Planning Policy: Background and Implementation

In traditional China, population fluctuation through history usually resulted from epidemics, natural disasters, or political upheavals which led to wars, dynastic changes, and other social turbulence. Because feudal ideology values fecundity and favors male offspring to maintain paternal lineages, birth control was, by and large, alien to Chinese culture. No clear policy on planned fertility was attempted by the Chinese government prior to 1949; such would have conflicted with the cultural values and gender-role ideology that supported the Chinese patriarchal system for centuries.

The recent demographic explosion in China is attributed to high birth rates (primarily in the 1960s), a falling mortality rate, and inconsistent policies on family planning issued from the 1950s to the early 1970s. The country's population size has almost doubled in the past thirty years and could double again in the next 45 years if families average three children each (Banister 1984; Chen and Tyler 1982). With a population then approaching one billion, the PRC was the first country in the world to institute a one-child per married couple policy, in 1979. The goal of this policy is to achieve zero population growth by limiting China's population to 1.2 billion by the year 2000. Based on the fourth census of July 1990, China's population was estimated to be 1.133 billion (*People's Daily*, October 31, 1990) and reached 1.17 billion by early 1993 (Sun 1993). In view of the pressing demographic situation, greater acceptance of birth control in the urban than in the rural areas, housing problems in urban areas, limited childcare for preschool children, increasing living costs due to inflation, hidden unemployment, and the need to provide basic food and services for all, China must solve its overpopulation problem if it is to realize its "four modernization" programs for economic growth in agriculture, industry, national defense, and science and technology. The birth-control campaign from 1971–79, which advised Chinese people to marry late, not to have a first child until the age of 25, to have children spaced at longer intervals, and to have fewer offspring, laid the groundwork for the one-child policy in the 1980s.

After successful experimental implementation of the one-child policy in Sichuan province in 1979, the Chinese government officially presented the policy to the National People's Congress, which subsequently approved it in 1980 for the whole nation. The Chinese government offered four major rationales for planned fertility: It would contribute to better health care for both children and mothers, establish better social conditions for raising future generations, increase work efficiency and political awareness, and promote equality of the sexes (Huang 1982). To achieve the one-child family objective, the government has undertaken a number of implementation measures, including economic rewards, media promotion, fertility education publications, planning of social security for the aged, special training for medical and family planning personnel, free birth control and abortion, and even courses teaching parents and grandparents how to raise only children properly. Couples who comply receive an honorary certificate entitling their family to such special privileges as extra maternity leave, a monthly allowance, housing or a private plot of land, food, bonuses or gifts, and special access to health services, education, and job opportunities. Parents who defy the policy by giving birth to a second child are severely penalized, losing work points and wages, paying fines, experiencing job demotion, and forfeiting other social benefits.

Policy implementation varies greatly in its effectiveness and is sometimes met with resistance. Because enforcement regulations for the one-child policy are issued by provinces, municipalities, counties, and communes, these regulations and exemptions often differ geo-graphically. In general, the policy has greater acceptance in urban areas but is far less rigidly enforced by local officials in rural areas and for certain national minorities, which can have a second child under special circumstances.[2] Assessment of the policy's implementation and impact generally shows rather mixed outcomes (Chen 1985; Cheung 1988; Ching 1982; Croll et al. 1985; Dalsimer and Nisonoff 1987; Davin 1987; Davis-Friedmann 1985; Falbo 1987; Huang 1982; Poston and Yu 1985; Shanghai Preschool Education Study Group 1980; Sun and Wei 1987; Tien 1983; Wong 1984). More negative than positive and some unintended consequences are reported by officials and researchers in different locations. Their critical concerns are potential lack of old-age security, breakdown of kinship structure, forced abortion and steriliza-tion, female infanticide, wife battering, and only children's personality development. At this juncture, it is too soon to evaluate long-term pol-icy impact. Ideally, such an assessment will use longitudinal data to scrutinize systematically the policy's effectiveness over time in various regions of China. In this paper, we offer some preliminary evidence from a cross-sectional study of only-child families in Beijing, the capi-tal city and one which supposedly exemplifies successful implementa-tion of the policy.

The Demise or the Perpetuation of the Patriarchal Family?

For centuries, the traditional Chinese family has been basically patri-lineal, patriarchal, and patrilocal in nature and has played a decisive role in perpetuating male dominance, gender inequality, and the exploitation of women. The key question is: Will the one-child policy lead to the disintegration of the traditional Chinese family and to the promotion of gender equality in China? The one-child policy may have three possible outcomes: weakening of the patriarchal family with primarily positive effects for gender equality, strengthening of it with largely negative results, or its modification with mixed results. If the one-child policy achieves what Chinese officials claim it ideally will, it will eventually undermine the patriarchal family and effect some degree of gender parity.

Posing an argument in support of the first outcome, Hong (1987, p. 319) suggests that "The one-child policy, if widely accepted, could transform Chinese society into one in which the patrilineal kinship system may finally cease to be a significant factor in everyday life, where uxorilocal marriages [couples residing in the wife's household] may vie with virilocal marriages in popularity, where greater gender equality may become a reality." With the patrilineal network reduced to direct lineal kin (i.e., parents, grandparents, and surviving great-grandparents), Hong reasons that the power of the patriarchy and its influence on the individual, the village, and work would dwindle. The favoring of male offspring and frequently reported female infanticide would result in an unbalanced sex ratio and in women using their scarcity as a leverage to negotiate for uxorilocal marriage. Uxorilocal marriage is not unprecedented in traditional China and is also one of the exemptions under the current policy, which allows couples to have a second child when the mother is the only child in the family.

Furthermore, Hong predicts that the one-child policy, together with marked increases in life expectancy, would reduce women's time spent on childbearing and thus free them to devote longer spans of their lives and more energy to activities traditionally dominated by men. Therefore, the new demographic realities, together with the possible disintegration of patrilineal kinship, would create a favorable climate that could bring Chinese women social equality heretofore unattainable.

In contrast, Stacey (1983) offers an interesting argument that China's family reform policies have actually strengthened patriarchy rather than undermined it. This argument also applies to the impact of one-child policy on women and the family. Chinese women historically have never had much control over their bodies and fertility; these were matters determined by the elders or male members of the family. Now, the state has assumed that role. Chinese women are caught in a tug-of-war between the state and the patriarchal family, a war in which both sides seek control over the reproductive process, including contraception, menstrual cycle, pregnancy, abortion, childbirth, and even childrearing (e.g., classes for parents on how to bring up an only child). When familial and state control are in direct conflict, women are victimized, particularly in the rural areas (e.g., see Dalsimer and Nisonoff 1987).

Criticizing Hong's assumption that the one-child policy will radically alter gender inequality, Mandle (1987) thinks that Hong underestimates the extraordinary power of patriarchy and the economic, cultural, and social supports for gender inequality in China. Hong's model of social change is too simplistic, Mandle says, to deal fully with the complexity and depth of the major social and political changes necessary to achieve gender equality. Other researchers (Davin 1987; Dalsimer and Nisonoff 1987; Johnson 1986; Robinson 1985) concur, pointing out a broad range of gender issues associated with the adverse effects of the one-child policy, such as female infanticide; the burden of pregnancy on women; forced abortion and sterilization; hazards to women's health; wife beating and abandonment; losses in status, wages, and job; and, in some cases, more severe penalties for mothers than for fathers if they defy the policy. As patriarchy is still deeply rooted in Chinese society, implementation of the one-child policy in certain parts of China has actually accentuated the ill-treatment of women.

Unlike in the rural areas, where great resistance to the policy persists and many adverse effects as mentioned above are found, families in major urban areas show greater compliance with the one-child policy with mixed positive and negative effects. We reason that the one-child policy may have partially laid some ideological and structural conditions for family change and for a more egalitarian relationship between men and women in urban areas. If that is the case in Beijing, we would specifically expect several major changes in the family and in the gendered division of labor to be more evident in only-child families than in multiple-child families there. Any significant differences found between these two family types may be indicative of the on-going process of transforming traditional family structure and redefining gender relationships in which one-child policy plays an important part.

Changing Family Size and Structure

One of the most obvious one-child policy effects is change in family size and structure due simply to the reduced number of children in the household. Contrary to the widespread notion that the Chinese extended family is large, with several generations living under one roof, the average size of the Chinese household has been relatively small because of the limited availability of land and other resources (Chen 1985; Goode 1963; Hsu 1959; Levy 1949). The 1982 Chinese National Census reported that the average size of the domestic household was 4.4 persons, a figure which does not significantly depart from the five persons per household reported in 1949 (Aird 1983; Chen 1985). With the exception of a fluctuation in birth rates from 1955 to 1965 due to famine and an economic recovery that followed, the average number of children born per family has decreased (from 6.08 in 1965 to 2.63 in 1981), becoming rather stable in recent years (Qian and Xiao 1983). With the introduction of the one-child policy, Chinese officials expect that the average birth rate per family will be kept far below 2.0.[3]

Some social scientists have predicted that the Chinese family, like those in the West, will change into a nuclear type as China becomes modernized and industrialized (Freedman 1970; Goode 1963; Levy 1949). Using Freedman's formulation, Croll (1985) empirically demonstrates four models of family size and their relationships to changing fertility norms in China from 1949 until the 1980s. For economic and other sociopolitical reasons, as family patterns have changed—from the joint family (prevailing around 1949), to the complex peasant family (1950-70), then to the small family (1970-1979), and most recently to the single-child family (1979 to present)—the number of children in Chinese families has decreased over time.

Since the one-child policy will necessarily lead to a trimming of the family tree (i.e., fewer cousins, aunts, uncles, and in-laws), the consanguinity of Chinese extended families will be limited. The present study groups Chinese families into three major categories: extended or joint, stem, and nuclear. "Extended or joint family" refers to a social unit that is composed of a couple with married or unmarried children and grandchildren and/or relatives living together in the same household. The "stem family" is a social unit that includes a couple with one married child and the child's spouse and, sometimes, offspring. The "nuclear family" is a much smaller unit, consisting simply of a couple and their unmarried children. Due to the short history of the one-child policy and its implementation, its impact on family structure may not yet be substantial. However, it is reasonable to predict that types of family structure will vary and that the small nuclear family type is more likely to be a dominant one (Hypothesis 1).

Family Ideology

In traditional China, family relationships as prototypes of other major social relationships were deeply rooted in the ethical principle of filial piety, in which paternal authority reigned over children and women, demanding their obedience. Maintenance of the patrilineage instilled a feudal ideology that valued fertility, favored sons to carry on the family name, and emphasized primogeniture (the inheritance right of the eldest son), thus devaluing the worth of women. While the traditional belief was that fate determined fecundity, women were held responsible for the sex of infants. To some extent, these beliefs still prevail in China today.

Introduction of the one-child policy appears to have revitalized feudal ideology concerning the value of children. This feudal ideology has accentuated the importance of seeing the only child as the "only lifeblood" of family procreation, as the "only fulcrum" in the family triangle of father-mother-child relationships, and as the "only hope" for old-age security. Numerous reports indicate significant concerns among parents, educators, researchers, and policy-makers regarding preference for males, personality development of the only child, and extravagant economic consumption for the only child (Baker 1987; Bian 1986; Falbo 1987; Wu 1986). These concerns suggest that the one-child Chinese family has tended to shift from adult-centered to child-centered. We therefore hypothesize that parents in one-child families will emphasize a child-centered ideology more than those in multiple-child families do (Hypothesis 2).

Furthermore, if the ideology of gender equality is as widely accepted by the Chinese people as the central government advocates, family egalitarianism should be clearly evident. By the same token, if the one-child policy is a vehicle to promote gender equity as officially claimed, it is logical to predict that parents in one-child families will subscribe to gender egalitarianism to a greater extent than those in multiple-child families do (Hypothesis 3).

Household Division of Labor by Gender

Adherence to gender egalitarianism may be manifested not only in ideology but also in behavior, especially in the division of household labor. In this study, we specifically examine gender equity in six major aspects of the division of labor between husbands and wives. Spouses of Chinese women are expected to participate in domestic and child-care responsibilities. Therefore, we hypothesize that various aspects of division of household labor will be shared more equally between husbands and wives rather than mostly performed by wives as tradition-ally expected (Hypothesis 4).

In addition, reduction in fertility may mean that the younger generation of mothers will spend less time on pregnancy, childbirth, lactation, and childcare. Lowered fertility may also mean that young urban women especially will have more opportunities to pursue alter-natives to the roles of mother and homemaker, will suffer less from the double demand of work and family responsibilities, will have fewer interruptions in their careers, and will have more leisure time (Davin 1987). Some women may also engage in sideline occupations and thereby raise their economic status and power in the family (Dalsimer and Nisonoff 1987, p. 591). If one-child policy really makes a positive difference from the traditional roles expected of Chinese women, then mothers may do less and fathers may do more domestic chores and childcare in one-child than in multiple-child families. Thus we hypoth-esize that gender equity in household division of labor will be greater in one-child than in multiple-child families (Hypothesis 5).

The Study

This is a cross-sectional survey of 1,130 Chinese, only and non-only children, aged three to fifteen, and their families residing in Beijing in 1985. A combination of multistage area sampling and matching techniques was used to select two subsamples which had similar social characteristics for systematic comparison, the "only" and the "non-only."[4] First, multistage cluster sampling was employed to divide sampling selection into four major stages—by district, school, grade level, and individual student.[5] Twenty kindergartens, six elementary schools, and four junior high schools in urban areas as well as five kindergartens in suburban areas were included in the final sample.[6] After class lists for each grade were obtained from the schools, individual students were carefully selected to meet matching criteria in terms of "only" versus "non-only," sex, and age. Among the 1,130 children, 605 (53.54 percent) only children and 525 (46.46 percent) non-only children were included, forming the basis for dividing the sample into two family types: one-child and multiple-child families.[7]

Data were collected by questionnaire with special assistance from a six-person research team from Beijing University. Each school child was given a questionnaire to be filled out by her/his parents at home and to be returned to the school one week after distribution. 1,400 questionnaires were distributed to the children and 1,244 were returned, resulting in a response rate of 89 percent. Due to missing information, 114 questionnaires were discarded, leaving 1,130 cases for data analysis.

Major relevant variables included in this analysis can be classified into five categories: (1) family and child characteristics; (2) socioeconomic attributes of the couple; (3) family ideology concerning child-centeredness and gender egalitarianism; and (4) division of labor in housework and childcare by gender.[8] All these variables are compared and contrasted by family type (only-child or multiple-child). Respondents were also asked to report their household size and explain its composition and were grouped according to "nuclear," "stem," or "extended" family structure.[9]

Family ideology refers to beliefs concerning the value of children and gender relationships within the household. This ideology consists of four major components: each of the parents' attitudes respectively toward child-centeredness and gender egalitarianism. Composed of five major items, the index of child-centeredness measures attitudes toward the child as the focal point of the family, the child as embodying the parents' highest hope in life, the meaning of having children, the importance of having children, and children compared with other meaningful life pursuits (e.g., work/career or family). High score values mean a high degree of child-centeredness, low values a low degree. Gender egalitarianism is measured by two separate measures of the couple's belief in an egalitarian marital relationship. Both mothers and fathers were asked to respond to the statement, "An unequal hierarchical relationship between husband and wife is the best way to avoid family conflict" in terms of three response categories—"agree," "no opinion," and "disagree." Those who agreed with this statement were assumed to favor male dominance in marital relationships; those who disagreed were considered to favor egalitarian marital relationships. The scores were later reversed, with high scores indicating agreement and low scores disagreement with gender egalitarianism.

Household division of labor by gender, the major dependent variable in this study, is indicated by four measures—housework division of labor by couples, childcare by couples, and time spent in childcare by each spouse respectively—to capture both qualitative and quantitative aspects of household organization. Respondents were asked by whom and how household chores and childcare were shared.[10]

Research Findings and Discussion

General Sample Characteristics

Table 3.1 shows frequency distributions for the child and family variables. Female children constituted 51 percent and male children 49 percent of the total number of respondents' children.[11] The mean age of the children was about seven years old; only children were slightly younger than non-only children. The average number of children per family was 1.51, a figure which the Chinese government is attempting to maintain or even reduce. The average educational level completed by both husbands and wives was about junior high school, with the fathers' level of education generally higher than the mothers'. Although fathers' level of education did not differ much by family type, mothers with one child had a slightly higher level of education than those with more than one. Approximately one-third of the parents were both reported to be factory workers. Another one-fourth of the fathers and 15 percent of the mothers worked as government officials/cadres, while an additional one-fourth of both the fathers and the mothers worked in educational and technical fields. About 12 percent of the fathers and 16.8 percent of the mothers were peasants. Except for the age of children, family and child characteristics did not differ significantly.

Table 3.1 Characteristics of the Beijing Sample by Family Type
(N = 1, 130)

	Total Sample		Only-Child Families		Multiple-Child Families	
	#	%	#	%	#	%
Sample total:	1130	100.0	605	53.5	525	46.5
Gender of children:						
Male	553	48.9	298	49.3	255	48.6
Female	577	51.1	307	50.7	270	51.4
Median age:	7 yrs.		6.88 yrs.		7.28 yrs.	
F's education:						
Elementary school	89	7.9	46	7.6	43	8.2
Junior high school	435	38.5	252	41.7	183	34.9
High school or vocational school	288	25.5	144	23.8	144	27.4
College/university	318	28.0	163	26.9	155	29.5
M's education:						
Elementary school	146	13.0	59	9.8	87	16.6
Junior high school	491	43.6	293	48.6	198	37.8
High school or vocational school	325	28.8	158	26.2	167	31.9
College/university	165	14.6	93	15.2	72	13.7
F's occupation:						
Peasant	144	12.7	74	12.2	70	13.3
Sales/service worker	28	2.5	18	3.0	10	1.9
Factory worker	384	34.0	226	37.4	158	30.1
Cultural worker	13	1.2	10	1.7	3	.6
Cadre/official	267	23.6	127	21.0	140	26.7
Educational/ technical worker	246	21.8	125	20.7	121	23.0
Others	48	4.2	25	4.1	23	4.4
M's occupation:						
Peasant	188	16.8	96	16.0	92	17.7
Sales/service worker	105	9.4	56	9.3	49	9.4
Factory worker	356	31.8	200	33.3	156	30.0
Cultural worker	7	.6	5	.8	2	.4

Table 3.1   *Continued*

	Total Sample		Only-Child Families		Multiple-Child Families	
	#	%	#	%	#	%
Cadre/official	164	14.6	88	14.7	76	14.6
Educational/ technical worker	260	23.2	131	21.8	129	24.8
Others	40	3.6	24	4.0	16	3.1
Mean family income (monthly):	123.6 Yuan		120.7 Yuan		127.5 Yuan	
Mean number of children:	1.51		1.00		2.10	

Toward Small and Nuclear Family Structure

Table 3.2 presents the major findings resulting from empirical testing of hypotheses. Adherence to the Chinese government's rigorous family planning program is expected to result in changes in family size and structure. It is expected that more one-child than multiple-child families will exhibit small nuclear rather than stem and extended types of family structure. Data partially support Hypothesis 1 with regard to family size but not family structure.

Findings showed that one-child families were substantially smaller than multiple-child families (3.66 vs. 4.65 household members respectively, t-test = 13.42, p<.001). Although over 70 percent of the families were of the nuclear type, no marked difference in family structure was found between one- and multiple-child families. Simply because the number of children is smaller, it was expected that one-child families would be significantly smaller than multiple-child families. The finding is consistent with a downward trend in Chinese family size which began even before the Communist government took power in 1949. After 1949, as Chen (1985, p. 195) points out, average family size declined moderately and then remained stable over most of the next thirty years (5.3 in 1949; 4.4 in 1957; 5.3 in 1964; 4.5 in 1978; 4.4 in 1982). A series of land reforms, promulgation of two New Marriage Laws in 1950 and 1980, and agricultural collectivization can account for these decreases in family size over time.

As the Chinese government proceeds with its modernization programs and implements the one-child policy, a further decrement in

Table 3.2 Distribution and Correlation of Major Variables by Family Type (N = 1, 130)

	Total Sample		Only-Child Families		Multiple-Child Families	
	#	%	#	%	#	%
Family size:						
Mean	4.12		3.66		4.65	
s.d.	1.18		1.28		1.10	
Type of family structure:						
Nuclear	755	71.2	395	70.9	360	71.6
Stem	206	19.4	107	19.2	99	19.7
Extended	99	9.3	55	9.9	44	8.7
Mothers' child-centeredness ideology:						
Low	548	53.8	265	47.7	283	61.1
High	471	46.2	291	52.3	180	38.9
Mean	12.10		12.45		9.41	
s.d.	2.31		2.25		2.32	
Fathers' child-centeredness ideology:						
Low	455	45.7	231	42.2	224	50.0
High	541	54.3	317	57.8	224	50.0
Mean	11.63		11.89		11.32	
s.d.	2.30		2.25		2.33	
Mothers' gender egalitarianism:						
Agree	473	32.1	255	32.1	218	32.1
No opinion	291	25.9	155	25.7	136	26.1
Disagree	361	42.0	194	42.4	167	41.8
Fathers' gender egalitarianism:						
Agree	472	28.6	255	27.1	217	30.3
No opinion	318	28.8	179	30.1	139	27.2
Disagree	316	42.7	161	42.9	155	42.5
Household work:						
Mostly wife	318	29.4	178	30.8	140	27.7
Equally shared	720	66.5	372	64.4	348	68.9
Mostly husband	45	4.1	28	4.8	17	3.4

Table 3.2 *Continued*

	Total Sample		Only-Child Families		Multiple-Child Families	
	#	%	#	%	#	%
Childcare:						
Mostly wife	207	18.3	115	19.0	92	17.5
Equally shared	829	73.4	438	72.4	391	74.6
Mostly husband	93	8.3	52	8.6	41	7.8
Mothers' time spent in childcare:						
Mean (in minutes)		96.30		103.86		87.98
s.d.		65.58		67.48		62.80
Fathers' time spent in childcare:						
Mean (in minutes)		70.52		78.66		60.93
s.d.		58.46		66.61		45.04

family size is anticipated. This study confirms that such has already been the case for Beijing, as the household size for only-child families was lower than for multiple-child families (see comparable figures in Croll et al. 1985). This finding is consistent with recent reports showing a slight decline in average household size for Beijing in 1987, to 3.59 as compared to 4.23 for the whole nation (State Statistical Bureau 1988).

While the nuclear family type is clearly the most dominant one in this study (over 70 percent of all families), no marked difference in family structure was found between one-child and multiple-child families. Such findings lend support to a general prediction that, as China becomes modernized and industrialized, the nuclear family type will gradually replace the traditional extended Chinese family (Croll et al. 1985; Freedman 1970; Goode 1963; Levy 1949). Thus, the data indicate that observed change in family structure is not a function of the one-child policy, but rather of other macro-forces that have gradually transformed the traditional family over time. These findings suggest that the impact of the one-child policy on family structure has not been as great as other scholars have expected it to be.

The sample for this study was primarily drawn from a metropolitan area where urbanization tends to separate family from their kin, where a housing shortage makes it difficult for the traditionally large extended family to reside together, and where geographical mobility has been strictly monitored by the state. Small nuclear family structures flourish under these social conditions. Yet the Changsha study found that one-child families with special housing privileges had the highest average amount of living space per person (Poston and Yu 1985). If this is generally true, one-child families may find it easier to fit more than two generations into a single household.

Taking such complex social forces into consideration, we suggest that, instead of a linear change toward nucleation, more diverse family structures may coexist in China at least for a while, as the small nuclear family emerges as dominant. Our study found very little difference in family structure between families located in the urban areas and those situated in the suburban areas of Beijing. Had the sample included Chinese families from the rural areas, where a second child might be allowed, particularly if the first child was a girl, family structure would doubtless be more diverse and the nuclear family less dominant than in the present study.

Ideologies of Child-Centeredness and Gender Egalitarianism

Patriarchal structure cannot persist without an ideological base supporting the male status quo. Family ideology is measured in four aspects relevant to the one-child policy, namely child-centeredness ideology and gender egalitarianism of each spouse respectively in each sample household. As predicted by Hypothesis 2, data (in Table 3.2) clearly show that both mothers and fathers from one-child families tended to subscribe to the child-centeredness ideology to a greater degree than did those from multiple-child families (t-test = 5.21, p<.001 for the mothers and t-test = 3.88, p<.001 for the fathers). Regardless of family type, mean scores for child-centeredness ideology generally tended to be higher for mothers than for fathers (12.10 as compared to 11.63).[12] Mothers of one-child families scored the highest in this regard, followed in turn by fathers of one-child families, fathers of multiple-child families, and mothers of multiple-child families. Parents of one child had a greater tendency than other parents to underscore the importance of having children, to rank having a child as the most meaningful aspect of life, to consider having a child a major life aspiration or fulfillment, to see children as embodying the only hope in life, and to invest in children rather than in other aspects of life as their central life interest. Ideological consensus within couples was exceptionally high (r =.45, p<.001, see Table 3.3) for the total sample and also for both types of family.

Given several legislative attempts by the Chinese central government over the last three decades to eradicate gender inequality, it

Table 3.3 Correlation Coefficient Matrix of Major Variables

	Family Size	Family Structure	Mothers' Child-Centeredness	Fathers' Child-Centeredness	Mothers' Gender Egalitarianism	Fathers' Gender Egalitarianism	Household Division of Labor	Childcare	Mothers' Time Spent in Childcare	Fathers' Time Spent in Childcare
Family size	—	.83***	.00	.04	.01	.01	-.04	.06***	-.01	-.04
Family structure		—	.06*	.06*	.02	-.06*	.06*	.02	.04	-.01
Child-centeredness:										
Mothers			—	.45***	-.18***	-.06*	-.03	.01	.08**	.07**
Fathers				—	.06*	-.07*	-.01	.00	.08**	.13***
Gender egalitarianism:										
Mothers					—	.42***	.15***	.04	.00	.02
Fathers						—	.13***	.09***	-.04	.00
Household division of labor							—	.19***	-.03	.07
Childcare								—	-.05*	.09**
Time spent in childcare:										
Mothers									—	.24***
Fathers										—

* $p < 0.05$
** $p < 0.01$
*** $p < 0.001$

would be reasonable to expect an ideological transformation in the minds of the Chinese people disposing them to favor the norm of gender egalitarianism. However, the findings presented in Table 3.2 indicate that 42 percent of the couples tended not to support egalitarian ideology regarding marital power relationships. About one-third of them showed support for an egalitarian relationship between husbands and wives, and another one-fourth had no opinion on this matter. Couples showed a high degree of ideological consensus concerning gender egalitarianism (r =.42, p<.001, see Table 3.3). No difference by family type was found in this regard. Therefore, the data do not support Hypothesis 3.

More importantly, gender egalitarianism was negatively associated with child-centeredness ideology for both only-child and multiple-child couples. Couples who supported an egalitarian gender relationship in the family were less likely to consider children as the focal point of the family. In particular, mothers who endorsed an equal power relationship within couples tended to score lower in child-centeredness ideology (r = -.18, p<.001, see Table 3.3). Fathers showed a similar inclination, but to a lesser degree (r = -.07, p<.05, see Table 3.3). The inverse relationship between gender egalitarianism and child-centeredness was much stronger for the mothers than for the fathers and was much stronger in only-child than in multiple-child families.

The absence of pronounced structural variations in the family and ideological differences in gender egalitarianism between the one-child and multiple-child families seems to indicate both socially and culturally a limited impact of one-child policy on the family system. As a matter of fact, we argue that the policy may have revived feudal ideas of the value of fecundity, preference for male offspring, and importance of parenting for old-age security. Couples' belief in the significance of children is largely shaped by the limited number of children that the policy allows them to have. According a greater importance to having children inevitably burdens women in terms of childbirth, childrearing responsibilities, health risk, and social pressures associated with motherhood. Unless such cultural ideology changes in the minds of the Chinese people, they will continue to desire male or more children, discouraging women's liberation from traditional roles and statuses.

The data seem to reveal a conservative ideological outlook among the Chinese couples as indicated by their low degree of acceptance of gender egalitarianism and their tendency to adhere to child-centeredness ideology. These findings lend support to Margery Wolf's (1972) conceptualization of the "uterine family," one based on mother-son bonds, and a central aspiration of Chinese women to create their own sense of family through their children in traditional families. A woman idealizes the family because having a son provides her with a primary means for overcoming the powerlessness, loneliness, and low status which the patrilineal, patriarchal family structure and norms seek to impose on her (see also Chodorow 1978; Kandiyoti 1988). Having a daughter would be a fateful blow to a Chinese woman, precipitating her further decline in family status. The one-child policy aiming to dismantle some remnants of the traditional family came as a threat to many women of childbearing age who were hoping to produce sons but had not yet done so. As a consequence, particularly in one-child families, many mothers may tend to cling to their only child, regardless of its gender, as a "sole lifeblood" who embodies singular hope for life fulfillment. Such a strong propensity toward child-centeredness will no doubt shape future parent-child relationships in China.

When couples in the present study were asked about their vital concerns regarding the only-child issue, over 60 percent of the respondents singled out old-age security as the most serious drawback. The policy clearly jeopardizes the traditional old-age security system in which elderly rely on children, especially sons, for support after retirement. In 1980, only 19 percent of the total work force in China was eligible for retirement benefits (Davis-Friedmann 1985, pp. 151–152). Unless the Chinese government provides adequate old-age security, Chinese elderly will remain dependent on their children for support, and the stem or extended family structure will coexist with the dominant nuclear family pattern. Assuming smaller cohorts with strict population control over time, longer life expectancy, and lower death rates, China's National Committee on Aging recently predicted that one child will eventually shoulder the burden of care for two parents and four grandparents. Local governments in certain provinces have even stipulated a new policy that requires a formal support agreement to be signed between children and their elderly parents in certain provinces (Sun 1990b).

Household Division of Labor, Childcare, and Gender Relationships

Assuming that the implementation of the one-child policy may have laid partial ideological and structural conditions for a more egalitarian relationship between men and women within the family, we would expect that some degree of gender equity would be manifest in the ways that Chinese couples organize their families. In this study, we specifically examined gender equity in four major aspects of couples' division of labor within the family—household work, childcare, and time spent in childcare by mother and by father respectively.

First, data in Table 3.2 provide some support for Hypothesis 4, which states that household division of labor will be shared more equally between husbands and wives in only-child families. Two-thirds (66.5 percent) of the respondents in the total sample claimed that the couples shared household chores equally, and nearly three-fourths (73.4 percent) of them reported that they equally shared child-care responsibilities as well. When work was not shared, however, 29.4 percent of the respondents reported that domestic chores were done mostly by the wives; 4.1 percent said that such chores were performed mostly by the husbands. Similarly, 18.3 percent of respondents reported that childcare was done mostly by the wives; 8.3 percent said that it was assumed mostly by the husbands. Although childcare was reported to be equally shared, there were marked quantitative differences in the amount of time each parent estimated spending per child. What "sharing" may mean is that fathers participated substantially even though mothers still did more. Mothers' average estimate was 96.30 minutes per day; fathers' was 70.52 minutes. The average difference, 25.78 minutes, was statistically significant (t-test = 11.34, p<.001). Thus, mothers devoted significantly greater time to caring for children than fathers did, resulting in an inequity in this regard.

If the one-child policy has had any effects on gender roles in the family at all, we would expect (as posited in Hypothesis 5) that division of labor would depart from the traditional mode, with greater equity between husbands and wives in one-child than in multiple-child families. However, data in Table 3.2 show little support for this hypothesis. Indeed, they reveal a slight tendency toward greater gender equity in sharing household work and childcare between husbands and wives in multiple-child families. First, both parents in one-child families spent substantially more time in childcare per day than did those in multiple-child families (t-test = 4.23, p<.001 for the mother; t-test = 5.28, p<.001 for the father). Mothers continued to spend more time than their spouses in caring for children in both types of family, and the gender differences in this regard were statistically significant (t-test = 7.35, p<.001 for one-child families; t-test = 9.24, p<.001 for multiple-child families).

The above findings clearly indicate behavioral changes that may have resulted from the institutionalizing of certain forms of gender equality over the last three decades rather than from implementation of only-child policies. The apparent greater sharing of household work and childcare by couples in the sample is probably due to labor force conditions that require couples to juggle their time (e.g., staggering work hours and work days) and to manage many aspects of family responsibilities. Yet, the behavioral changes toward greater gender equity may be more qualitative than quantitative. Regardless of family type, mothers spent notably more time than their male counterparts did in caring for the children.

Contrary to a common notion that more children in the family will require parents to spend more time with them, in the present study, both fathers and mothers in one-child families spent significantly more time on childcare than those did in multiple-child families. These findings seem to support concerns in China about only children becoming "Spoiled Brats," "Little Emperors," and "China's Pampered Darlings" (Chen and Kols 1982; Poston and Yu 1985; Shanghai Preschool Education Study Group 1980; Yang et al. 1980; *The Washington Post* 1987). Parents of only children have more time to devote to caring for them, while parents of more may have the advantage of help from older children. Fear that improper care may cause loss of an only child may also motivate both fathers and mothers to invest extra time and effort in rearing these children.

Finally, we examine the extent to which family structural and ideological characteristics shape the family's division of labor. Table 3.3 summarizes the correlation coefficients of all the major variables analyzed. The findings indicate that larger household size and stem or extended family structure tended to require that the couples share childcare responsibilities and that husbands have become more involved in childcare even though kin assistance might be available. The two measures of family ideology differentially affected the four aspects of family division of labor. Mothers' and fathers' gender egalitarianism tended to influence couples' sharing of housework and father's assuming of childcare responsibilities, whereas mothers' and fathers' child-centeredness tended to motivate the couple to spend more of their time on childcare.

In view of these results, we argue that one-child policy has an unanticipated consequence, quite contrary to official expectations, in that it tends to encourage the privatization of women in domestic labor and reproduction in the home. Robinson (1985, p. 55) once predicted that, ". . . in five year's time, we will find that Chinese mothers are spending as much or more time on household and childcare in one-child families as is now spent in families with two or more children. The preciousness of the single child may prompt more housework and motherhood, not less." Our findings clearly support this prediction, leaving less time for mothers to devote to work, leisure, and other activities outside of the home.

Robinson (1985) also points out another paradox: As the standard of living increases, so too does time spent on domestic labor, as new levels of nutrition and comfort and more consumer durables require greater expenditures of time. And it is still women who are responsible for most household labor, despite increases in the amount of time men devote. For example, a Chinese study of urban workers found that the difference in hours per day expended in housework between a woman with one child and a woman with two children is less than one half hour (Wang and Li 1982). The one-child policy exerts new demands: ensuring the physical well-being, security, safety, personality development, education, and happiness of their only progeny. Shouldered with increasing pressure to bear male offspring, and to devote more time in domestic labor and childcare, women will remain or become more privatized, reinforcing the traditional roles of women as homemakers, reproducers, and nurturers. The recent popularity of hiring domestic help in major urban centers such as Beijing and Shanghai may alleviate burdens faced by employed parents, especially mothers. Except for a few professional couples and well-to-do families who can afford to do so, however, the majority of Chinese women must face the pressures of working the double day and the second shift (Hochschild 1989).

Policy Implications and Conclusion

With the planned changes launched in China for population control and economic development, the implications of the one-child policy for women and their families are complex. Whether the present one-child policy strengthens or weakens the patriarchal family will require longitudinal data based on a national sample that examines the long-term impact on the family and changing gender-role relationships. The present study offers some preliminary evidence to illustrate the interlocking of the state, economy, and family, each separately and jointly shaping policy formulations that tend to strengthen the patriarchal system that subordinates women structurally and controls their lives ideologically.

Here, we discuss several major policy implications related to transformations of family structure, gender relations, and gender equality. First, this study demonstrates the important role of the state in shaping the experience and lives of the Chinese people. Understanding the macro- and micro-linkages between changes in society and the individual, between the public and private spheres, requires careful scrutiny of the role of the state as an autonomous entity which controls resources and implements social interventions to attain its official goals (Charlton et al. 1989). This study illustrates how state initiatives such as the one-child policy have profound, sometimes dialectical effects on people's lives.

Second, policy formation is often made under a particular set of political and economic realities. China's one-child policy originated as a population policy to limit fertility, thereby cutting state expenditures, and later on became a family policy facilitating modernization. Hence, the one-child policy emerged as a panacea for the country's many pressing problems, including population growth, poverty, inflation, overcrowding, agricultural stagnation, inadequate school facilities, and unemployment. These social and economic concerns often override concerns for benefits to women and their families.

We argue that the one-child policy may be seen as one vehicle whose ultimate goal is economic development rather than gender equality. A great discrepancy is evident between the policy's official goals and its practical implementation, resulting in many unintended, negative consequences. Without necessarily solving old problems as planned, the one-child policy creates new ones. Hence, China needs a comprehensive family policy which thoroughly assesses political and economic situations and takes into consideration the human side of the one-child policy.

Third, the relationship between the state and the macro-economy is compounded by patriarchal rule. The state acts as a socialist patriarchy, determining women's reproductive behaviors. Women are caught in the politics of reproduction, and the status of being a mother has far-reaching political consequences. To a large extent, the one-child policy is a prime example illustrating the role of politics in reproduction where mothering is socially constructed by the state and the family (Chodorow 1978; O'Brien 1981). The findings of this study provide some evidence that the one-child policy, in fact, revives the feudal ideology valuing fecundity and encourages the traditional role definitions of women as household laborers and reproducers of men, despite the government's intention to promote women as productive workers. Faced with competing ideological beliefs concerning child-centeredness and gender egalitarianism, the majority of women with only-child families in this study unequivocally chose concern for their only progeny over struggle for gender equality. Therefore, neither the formation nor implementation of the one-child policy has comprehensively taken into account the long-term strategic and practical interests of women and men. The state has not adequately compensated Chinese couples for their losses in having an only child.

Fourth, the one-child policy has no doubt threatened the male-dominated family system but has by no means weakened it. With its short history and limited enforceability, the policy's impact on family structure (other than its impact on family size) apparently remains minimal at this time. Finding that in Beijing the most dominant family pattern in this study was the small nuclear type did not appear to result from the only-child policy because the structural characteristics of only-child versus multiple-child families did not differ much. Small nuclear families may reflect the effects of urbanization, modernization, and industrialization in breaking down the extended family structure, affecting only-child and multiple-child families equally.

Fifth, one dimension of demographic change such as planned fertility may be a necessary but not a sufficient condition for overturning the centuries-old tradition of gender inequality in China. Regardless of family type, a majority of couples in the present study reported that they equally shared housework chores and childcare duties, yet women still assume greater household responsibilities and childcare than men do. We observe a new tendency toward the reprivatization of women, particularly those in only-child families. If such a tendency becomes widely prevalent, it will reinforce traditional gender-role relationships in families and strengthen the patriarchal family, contradicting Hong's prediction and confirming what Andors (1983) calls "the unfinished liberation of women" in China.

Sixth, with little change in family structure and in gender relationships, and with the revival of traditional family ideology, it is doubtful whether the one-child policy will automatically lead to the disintegration of China's patrilineal, patriarchal, and patrilocal family. Hong seems to underestimate how deeply patriarchy is embedded in the family as well as in the state. The key point is that massive sociopolitical changes are needed to uproot patriarchal rule and to eliminate the structural and ideological sources of women's oppression. The one-child policy may set a stage for family change in China, but unless Chinese state officials seriously consider gender concerns as high priorities, the policy's impact on family structure and gender relationships may remain minimal.

Finally, given the drawbacks of the one-child policy, the Chinese government should explore alternative policies for population control. Recent analyses point out that allowing a second child will not seriously jeopardize China's long-term population goal if other measures such as mandatory spacing between the two births, late marriage, late childbearing, and avoidance of unplanned births are simultaneously adopted (Bongaarts and Greenhalgh 1985; Dalsimer and Nisonoff 1987; Wang 1988). A two-child policy would be accepted better, particularly in rural areas; would be easier to implement; would ease the burden of the only child in caring for the elderly; would alleviate the pressures and risks women take on as the childbearers and parents or grandparents take on as childcaregivers; and would lessen other detrimental consequences. Careful policy analyses should also be conducted to see how family planning links with other public policies (e.g., housing, old-age security, marriage and family laws). With comprehensive policies explicitly formulated to take gender interests into account, the impact of family planning policy on family life and gender equality will be greatly enhanced.

Notes

1. With funding from the Chinese government, the second author and his research team at the Beijing University collected the data. The first author did the data processing, data analysis, and writing. The feminist critique here reflects the viewpoint of the first author rather than the official Chinese position on the one-child policy.

2. For example, special circumstances allowing couples in either urban or rural areas an exemption to have a second child include when: (1) the first child suffers from a non-hereditary handicap; (2) both parents belong to national minorities; (3) both parents are returned overseas Chinese; (4) the husband is the son of a revolutionary martyr; (5) one spouse has a major handicap; (6) the bride is an only child; (7) only one son has been born to the family for three consecutive generations; and (8) the spouses are themselves both only children. How these exemptions are granted varies greatly by region.

3. According to one expert's calculation (Ching 1982), if the birth rate remains at an average of 2.3 children per family, China's population will climb to approximately 1.3 billion by the year 2000 and to 2.1 billion by 2080. If, from 1985, China averages 2.0 births per family, its population by the end of the century will be 1.25 billion and by 2050, more than 1.5 billion. If China, by 1985, achieves 1.5 children per family, it will have a population of 1.15 billion by the year 2000. In recent years, however, Coale et al. (1991) reported the overall fertility rate rose in 1985 and 1986 to well above that of 1980, suggesting China's failure to limit births (Sun 1990a). However, since then China's fertility rate declined slightly, dropping to 2.0 births per woman in 1992 (Sun 1993).

4. Several factors were considered in designing the sampling procedure: (1) heterogeneity of the sample to ensure representativeness; (2) availability of sampling or sub-sampling frames; (3) prior knowledge for the identification of only and non-only children; (4) comparability of individual characteristics and family background; and (5) adequate numbers of only and non-only children at different levels for subgroup comparison.

5. The multistage cluster sampling entailed four major stages. The first stage involved random selection of districts in Beijing that were characterized by residents with heterogeneous backgrounds. Four out of nine districts in an urban area and two out of six counties in a suburban area were randomly selected. Within each of the districts or counties, schools were randomly cho-

sen in accordance with the availability of sampling information, accessible location, and willingness to participate. Thirty-one schools in both urban and suburban areas were then selected. Schools were further divided into three grade levels—kindergartens, elementary schools (first and third grades), and junior high schools (ninth grade). Within each grade, equal numbers of only and non-only children with matching characteristics were finally chosen.

6. Due to greater success of the one-child policy in urban than in rural areas in the early 1980s, very few one-child families could be found above the kindergarten level in the outlying areas of Beijing. Thus, the sampling decision was made to select just kindergarten level only children in the suburban areas. Certain parts of the data analysis were done by geographical areas. Little variation appeared in individual and family characteristics between urban and suburban areas.

7. The timing of the data collection in 1984 and 1985 was critical in that it allowed the researcher to obtain adequate samples for both only and non-only children. Now such data collection is not possible because such a large majority of Chinese families have become only-child that very few non-only child families exist, especially in Beijing proper.

8. The study has built-in validity and reliability checks to insure data quality. Split-half reliability for major attitude measures ranges from .65 to .80. The test-retest reliability of the whole questionnaire is .89 (based on two tests over a one-month interval, n = 30). Two coders were used to achieve intercoder reliability. For problematic questions and missing information, coding was done by agreement between the coders. The estimated error rates in coding range from 0.23 percent to 1.65 percent (based on a random selection of fifty cases for 230 variables). The overall evaluation indicates that this data set is highly valid and reliable.

9. Five percent of the households, because they were headed by grandparents who cared for grandchildren, were excluded from the analysis. These children actually belonged to their parents' households.

10. The data set does not provide a detailed breakdown of household chores with the duties performed by wife or husband specified. Because we are primarily concerned with comparison of spousal participation and sharing in household work and childcare, chores done by grandparents (only 4.2 percent) were excluded from the analysis.

11. These figures by gender were a result of sampling procedures rather than the actual sex distribution in the Chinese population in which male children outnumber females.

12. The mean score of 12.10 of mother's child-centeredness ideology is affected by the skewed distribution of mothers who scored highly in this variable.

References

Aird, John S. 1983. "The Preliminary Results of China's 1982 Census." *China Quarterly* 97:613–640.

Andors, Phyllis. 1983. *The Unfinished Liberation of Chinese Women, 1949–1980*. Bloomington, IN: Indiana University Press.

Baker, Rod. 1987. "Little Emperors Born of a One-Child Policy." *Far Eastern Economic Review* 137:43–44.

Banister, Judith. 1984. "Population Policy and Trends in China, 1978–83." *The China Quarterly* 100:717–741.

Bian, Yianjie. 1986. "A Preliminary Analysis of the Basic Features of the Life Style of China's Single-Child Families." *Social Science in China* 8:189–209.

Bongaarts, John, and Susan Greenhalgh. 1985. "An Alternative to the One-Child Policy in China." *Population and Development Review* 11:585–617.

Charlton, Sue Ellen M., Jana Everett, and Kathleen Staudt, eds. 1989. *Women, the State, and Development*. Albany, NY: State University of New York.

Chen, Charles H. C., and Carl W. Tyler. 1982. "Demographic Implications of Family Size Alternatives in the People's Republic of China." *China Quarterly* 96:65–73.

Chen, Pi Chao, and Adrienne Kols. 1982. "Population and Birth Planning in the People's Republic of China." *Population Reports*, Series J, No. 25. Baltimore, MD: Johns Hopkins University Press.

Chen, Xianming. 1985. "The One-Child Population Policy, Modernization, and the Extended Chinese Family." *Journal of Marriage and the Family* 47:193–202.

Cheung, Fernando Chiu Hung. 1988. "Implications of the One-Child Family Policy on the Development of the Welfare State in the People's Republic of China." *Journal of Sociology and Social Welfare* 15:5–25.

Ching, C. C. 1982. "The One-Child Family in Chian: The Need for Psychological Research." *Studies of Family Planning* 13:208–212.

Chodorow, Nancy. 1978. *The Reproduction of Mothering*. Berkeley, CA: University of California Press.

Chow, Esther Ngan-ling. 1976. "Family Egalitarianism in the People's Republic of China." Unpublished paper presented at the Annual Meeting of the American Sociological Association, Chicago, Illinois.

Coale, Ansley J., Wange Feng, Nancy E. Riley, Lin Fu De. 1991. "Recent Trends in Fertility and Nuptiality in China." *Science* 251:389–393.

Croll, Elisabeth. 1985. "Introduction: Fertility Norms and Family Size in China." Pp. 1–36 in *China's One-Child Family Policy*, edited by Elisabeth Croll, Delia Davin, and Penny Kane. New York: Macmillan.

Croll, Elisabeth, Delia Davin, and Penny Kane, eds. 1985. *China's One-Child Family Policy*. London: Macmillan.

Dalsimer, Marilyn, and Laurie Nisonoff. 1987. "The Implications of the New Agricultural and One-Child Family Policies for Rural Chinese Women." *Feminist Studies* 13:583–607.

Davin, Delia. 1987. "Gender and Population in the People's Republic of

China." Pp. 111–129 in *Women, State, and Ideology*, edited by Helen Afshar. Albany, NY: State University of New York Press.

Davis-Friedmann, Deborah. 1985. "Old Age Security and the One-Child Campaign." Pp. 149–161 in *China's One-Child Family Policy*, edited by Elisabeth Croll, Delia Davin, and Penny Kane. London: Macmillan.

Falbo, Toni. 1987. "Only Children in the United States and China." *Applied Social Psychological Annual* 7:159–183.

Freedman, M. 1970. *Family and Kinship in Chinese Society*. Stanford, CA: Stanford University Press.

Goode, William J. 1963. *World Revolution and Family Patterns*. New York: Free Press.

Hochschild, Arlie. 1989. *The Second Shift: Working Parents and the Revolution at Home*. New York: Viking.

Hong, Lawrence K. 1987. "Potential Effects of the One-Child Policy on Gender Equality in the People's Republic of China." *Gender & Society* 1:317–326.

Hsu, F. L. K. 1959. "The Family in China: The Classical Form." Pp. 123–145 in *The Family: Its Function and Destiny*, edited by R. A. Anshen. New York: Harper.

Huang, Lucy Jen. 1982. "Planned Fertility of One-Couple/One-Child Policy in the People's Republic of China." *Journal of Marriage and the Family* 44:775–784.

Johnson, Kay Ann. 1986. "Women's Rights, Family Reform, and Population Control in the People's Republic of China." Pp. 439–462 in *Women in the World*, edited by Lynne B. Iglitzin and Ruth Ross. Santa Barbara, CA: ABC-Clio, Inc.

Kandiyoti, Deniz. 1988. "Bargaining with Patriarchy." *Gender & Society* 2:274–89.

Levy, M. J. 1949. *Family Revolution in Modern China*. Cambridge, MA: Harvard University Press.

Mandle, Joan D. 1987. "Comment on Hong." *Gender & Society* 1:327–331.

O'Brien, Mary. 1981. *The Politics of Reproduction*. London: Routledge, Kegan Paul.

People's Daily. Overseas edition. October 31, 1990.

Poston, Dudley L., and Mei-Yu Yu. 1985. "Quality of Life, Intellectual Development, and Behavioral Characteristics of Single Children in China: Evidence from a 1980 Survey in Changsha, Hunan Province." *Journal of Biosocial Science* 17:127–136.

Qian, Xinzhong, and Zhengyu Xiao. 1983. "An Analysis of the One in One Thousand Sample Survey of Fertility." *Renkou Yu Jinji (Population and Economics)*. Special Issue. Beijing: Beijing Economic College.

Robinson, Jean C. 1985. "Of Women and Washing Machines: Employment, Housework, and the Reproduction of Motherhood in Socialist China." *China Quarterly* 101:32–57.

Shanghai Preschool Education Study Group. 1980. "Family Education of Only Children." *Chinese Woman* 5:16–17.

Stacey, Judith. 1983. *Patriarchy and Socialist Revolution in China*. Berkeley, CA: University of California Press.

State Statistical Bureau of the People's Republic of China. 1988. *China Statistical Yearbook.* Hong Kong: International Centre for the Advancement of Science and Technology.

Sun, Lena H. 1990a. "China Failing to Curb Births." *The Washington Post.* December 28, 1990, pp. A21 and 26.

———. 1990b. "China Seeks Ways to Protect Elderly." *The Washington Post.* October 21, 1990.

———. 1993. "China Lowers Birth Rate to Levels in West." *The Washington Post.* April 22, 1993, A1 and A34.

Sun, Yuesheng, and Zhangling Wei. 1987. "The One-Child Policy in China Today." *Journal of Comparative Family Studies* 18:309–325.

Tien, H. Yuen. 1983. *China: Demographic Billionaire.* Population Bulletin 38 (2). Washington, DC: Population Reference Bureau.

Wang, Jichuan. 1988. "Determinants of Fertility Increase in Sichuan, 1981–1986." *Population and Development Review* 14:481–488.

Wang, Yalin, and Jinrong Li. 1982. "Urban Worker's Housework." *Social Sciences in China* 3:147–65.

The Washington Post. 1987. "Only-Child Family." July 26.

Wolf, Margery. 1972. *Women and the Family in Rural Taiwan.* Stanford, CA: Stanford University Press.

Wong, Siu-lun. 1984. "Consequences of China's New Population Policy." *The China Quarterly* 98:220–240.

Wu, Naitao. 1986. "Dealing with the 'Spoiled Brat'." *Beijing Review* 29:26–28.

Yang, H., H. Kao, and W. Wang. 1980. "Survey of Only-Children in Educational Institutes of Beijing City Districts." *China Youth Daily* 2 (October).

Chapter 4

Working without Wages in Australian Welfare

Cora Vellekoop Baldock

Introduction[1]

A number of themes that have been discussed so far will reappear in this chapter. The chapter applies what Chow and Berheide call the "system interdependence model" to the relationships among work, family, and welfare as the three major systems of production, reproduction, and redistribution. It focuses on women's position of relative economic dependence in the Australian family, and women's marginality in paid work—factors which have facilitated their availability for unpaid work in the Australian welfare system. I will draw attention to the effect of government policies that reinforce the relations among work, family, and welfare, as well as women's position within them. These government policies are written in the context of a separate sphere model which assumes a strict separation between work and family, public and private spheres, paid and unpaid work, and work and welfare.

Conclusions drawn from my Australian study are in line with the trends in other countries discussed in this book. However, I argue that certain specific circumstances combined with particular government policies have given the Australian situation a unique character. Most important in this context has been the development of a unique system of welfare, i.e., one dependent on the delivery of welfare services through volunteer labor in the non-government sector.

I aim in this paper to analyze the features of Australian society which have led to the development of this unique welfare system, with

Working without Wages in Australian Welfare

its strong dependence on the work of female volunteers. I hope to demonstrate that the delivery of welfare through volunteer labor has evolved in Australia because of a) the marginality of women to paid work and b) the low priority given to welfare provision. I will argue finally that the system of Australian welfare need not be determined wholly by economic and political constraints, but that women may have an important role to play in exploiting its contradictions for the benefit of positive social change.

Data and Methodology[2]

The data reported in this chapter were collected between 1983 and 1987 as part of a study on Western Australian welfare organizations employing volunteers (Baldock 1990).[3] The research started with a year-long pilot project, during which I (with thirty other women) participated in a volunteer training course. The main study consisted of four phases: an initial interview with one representative (usually the chief administrator) of 61 welfare organizations; a questionnaire completed by 482 workers in these organizations; an in-depth interview with a sub-sample of 61 of these workers; and a final brief follow-up questionnaire with 179 workers who had answered the first questionnaire. Respondents to the first questionnaire included 85 paid staff and 392 volunteers. Eighty percent of the volunteers and 78 percent of the paid workers who answered the questionnaire were women. The sample of 61 welfare organizations represented about 16 percent of the total number of welfare organizations in metropolitan Perth, Western Australia. It was a stratified sample, based on size of organization and type of clientele (Baldock 1990, pp. 148–52).

For my study I defined a volunteer as someone who regularly contributes her or his time and energy to a community welfare organization without being paid for this, other than in some instances through the payment of out-of-pocket expenses. I used the term "volunteer" rather than a more neutral term such as "unpaid worker" because in Australia women and men who carry out unpaid work within welfare organizations generally use the term volunteer to describe their own role.

Women, Work, and Welfare in Australian History[4]

Historically, government policies have reinforced the primary role of women as homemakers. The landmark decision in Australia's industrial relations, the so-called Harvester Judgment of 1907, which established the notion of a family (basic) wage to be paid to a worker so he could sustain himself, a wife, and two or three children, enshrined the idea that women are housewives (Ryan and Conlon 1989, pp. 89–91). The family wage was accompanied by strict divisions between men's work and women's work, with women receiving on average about 50 percent of the male wage rate. The family wage was paid to men whether or not married, but women in paid work were presumed to be single, without dependents, and awaiting marriage (Matthews 1984, p. 60).

Women's proper place, then, was seen to be in the sphere of reproduction, economically dependent on a male breadwinner, and caring for home and family.[5] Indeed, throughout this century the perception of women's role as homemakers has not changed. During the Second World War, for example, when some women took on "men's work" and received male wages, this was seen as temporary—a caretaker role for the men who were away (Beaton 1980, pp. 69–70). After the war, women were removed from men's work, with accompanying wage reductions. The ideology of domesticity came back in force and there was considerable pressure on women to return to their proper place in the home. Ironically, however, many continued to work (albeit in lowly paid, part-time "women's work") in order to help pay for the mortgages and consumer items that the suburban dream of the 1950s created (Game and Pringle 1979).[6]

It was not until 1966 that married women attained permanent positions in the Public Service, mainly because at that time the Public Service was expanding and experienced a severe shortage of workers (Deacon 1984). And it was not until 1972 that the principle of equal pay was established (Gaudron and Bosworth 1979, p. 169)—a principle, however, which was never fully implemented (Ryan and Conlon 1989, p. xxi). Federal anti-discrimination legislation did not come into place until 1984, while affirmative action policies were not introduced until 1986 (Baldock and Cass 1988, pp. 42–43). Maternity leave has been generally available since 1979, but it remains unpaid in most cases and the return to a comparable job after such leave is guaranteed only to women who work in large public and private enterprises (O'Donnell and Hall 1988, pp. 63–64). There is no provision for parental leave in case of children's illness, and government provision of childcare facilities is thoroughly inadequate (Cox 1988, pp. 197–204). Compared to many European countries, Australia is still well behind in the introduction of the various legislative changes which allow motherhood and paid work to be combined (Glezer 1988).

Further, those legislative changes which *have* been implemented have made little difference to women's position. Equal pay, equal employment opportunities, or affirmative action policies, for example, have not brought much improvement in women's employment situation because Australia remains a country with a heavily sex-segregated labor force right up until this day.[7] As O'Donnell and Hall (1988, p. 25) point out, "four industries—community services (26 percent), the wholesale and retail trade (23 percent), finance and business (14 percent) and manufacturing (12 percent)—account for three-quarters of women's employment."

Women continue to be employed in these industries in "women's work" without promotion or career prospects (Ryan and Conlon 1989, p. xxiv; Franzway, Court, and Connell 1989, Ch. 5). When women do gain access to "non-traditional" jobs, they are seldom treated as equals; and the specific work they take up becomes devalued as soon as it is carried out by women (Game and Pringle 1983; Eveline 1989). Such inequality of opportunity even applies to professional women with tertiary educations (Currie 1989).

Given this marginalization of women from the sphere of production, it may not be surprising that the sphere of reproduction is also highly sex-segregated.[8] In other words, men show very little inclination to share in housework or childcare (Baxter, Gibson, and Lynch-Bosse 1990; Bryson 1984), and women are held solely responsible by the community for their children's (and husband's) behavior and well-being (Broom 1986 and 1988).[9] This sexual division of labor occurs even in professional households where the woman defines herself as a feminist (Thiele 1990). Employers' attitudes do not help: There are virtually no arrangements for jobsharing in Australia, and employers have argued that paternity leave would be detrimental to a man's career.[10]

As in other western countries, the overall participation rate of women in the paid labor force has increased steadily since the Second World War. The participation rate of Australian women over the age of 15 is now 50.5 percent, as compared with 75 percent for men (Australian Bureau of Statistics 1990). Increased participation, however, has not reduced marginality because most of the growth in women's paid employment is only in part-time, casual work: Women comprise the overwhelming majority (83.7 percent) of the part-time workforce, with married women accounting for 53.8 percent of all part-time employees (Australian Bureau of Statistics 1990). For mothers, working part-time is by choice and by necessity: Women's primary responsibilities in the sphere of reproduction and the lack of adequate childcare make full-time work practically impossible while their children are young (Young 1990, p. 32). It is common in many western nations for women with children to work part-time (see, for example Acker's account in this volume), but in Australia women who work part-time do so under poor conditions. Many women without children who work part-time do so not as an alternative to full-time work but to unemployment (O'Donnell and Hall 1988, p. 22).

The history of women's role in paid work in Australia, then, is based on a stringent sexual division of labor and public policies which follow a separate sphere model, prescribing that women's primary responsibility is to the sphere of reproduction, not production. The ideology of domesticity continues to identify women as suitable only for work which is an extension of their presumed domestic, and above all caring, labor—work to be done intermittently and part-time so as to ensure it does not interfere with women's homemaking responsibilities. This ideology extends to all women, regardless of marital and/or motherhood status.

Welfare in Australian History

At the beginning of this century, Australia was called the "social laboratory of the western world" (Roe 1976, pp. 4–5) because of its advanced welfare policies. It was one of the earliest countries to introduce old age and invalid pensions, and its family wage was also lauded throughout the world. It is important to remember, however, that these welfare benefits were not universal. They were not available to the indigenous people, the Aboriginals, or to Asians living in Australia; the pensions were heavily means-tested (that is, available only to people below a certain level of income), and the family wage was available only to men.

In fact, it can be argued that throughout most of its history Australia's system of redistribution through social security payments has been a residual one. In other words, welfare payments have always been low, granted as a last resort, and never sufficient to lift their recipients out of poverty. Thus, receiving social security benefits is not seen as a right, but as a privilege (Edwards 1988, p. 200; Tomlinson 1989, pp. 35–36). One Scandinavian observer described Australia as a country "where large and persistent poverty gaps have not been closed and appear in fact to have widened, where levels of benefits have been undermined by inflation without being sufficiently adjusted, and where welfare rights have not been established for the population at large" (Oyen 1980, p. 2). This is illustrated by the fact that Australia's overall expenditure for social security relative to GDP (Gross Domestic Product) is well below that of most European countries, including Greece, Portugal, and Spain (Saunders 1987, p. 411). The most recent estimate of people within Australia living below the poverty line is 17.7 percent (Harris 1989, p. 11).[11]

Low-level welfare provision and lack of welfare rights have been accompanied, predictably, by a stratification of social security recipients into deserving and non-deserving. This is shown in stringent eligibility requirements, work tests reinforcing the work ethic, sexist policies regarding de facto relationships, and extensive surveillance of clients (Tomlinson 1989, pp. 22 passim). The eligibility requirements have been tightened rather than relaxed in recent years. Since 1989, for example, single parents receiving supporting parents' pensions have had to complete a detailed questionnaire at regular intervals with the aim of exposing de facto relations (Cox 1988, pp. 33–36).[12]

Direct government provision of welfare *services* has also been quite limited. For most of the 19th century, charitable organizations had been responsible for the delivery of welfare, providing clothing, food, cash, or institutional care to the destitute, the sick, the aged, and orphaned or neglected children (Kewley 1973, pp. 11–13; Roe 1976, p. 13; Dickey 1980). After Federation, the federal government took charge of social security payments, but government social welfare services in the British mold, as in healthcare, housing, and personal services, did not develop until the 1970s; up until that time the preoccupation was mainly with cash benefits. Whatever limited personal welfare services were offered throughout most of this century remained the responsibility of non-government welfare organizations. This included institutional care of orphans, sick and elderly people, and emergency relief in the form of food parcels, second-hand clothes, and occasional cash hand-outs.

The Federal Labor Government which took office in 1972 introduced a range of important welfare measures and vastly increased its expenditures in the areas of personal services, education, and health, as well as social security. However, subsequent conservative *and* Labor governments, faced with considerable cost increases and with a more hostile climate to central government control over welfare, retreated from a number of these policies. An important feature of this retreat has been the resurgence of the non-government welfare sector. In fact, during the late 1970s, when Australia experienced a severe recession and unemployment soared, voluntary agencies again became the safety net for the destitute as they had been early in Australia's welfare history. There was a dramatic increase at that time in demands for emergency relief, ranging from urgent requests for blankets and food to the pressing need for financial assistance from people who could no longer afford to pay their mortgage or electricity bills. Federal and state governments subsidized voluntary agencies in their efforts to deal with these demands, but it was the non-government sector which became the actual welfare provider for many needy Australians (Baldock 1983, p. 284).

Central to the increased role of the non-government sector in the 1980s have been *systematic* government policies designed to transfer responsibility for welfare services from federal and state governments to the non-government welfare sector (Yates and Graycar 1983, p. 150). One policy—the contracting-out of services from governments to community welfare organizations—has become a major approach to emergency relief, the care of the elderly and disabled, and in the development of programs for the training and support of the unemployed. Upon application, governments provide funds in each of these areas to eligible community welfare organizations, which then take on the entire responsibility for the administration and delivery of services.

Governments' transfer of responsibility for these services to community organizations has added to the residual and selective nature of welfare services. This happens because privatization lessens the accountability of governments for welfare provision (Baldock 1983, pp. 286–289): Funding privileges can be given or withdrawn from agencies without the government having to answer to the electorate. When funds are insufficient, welfare organizations, not governments, are left with the unpleasant task of turning clients away (Wainwright 1988).

Furthermore, welfare services carried out by community organizations are removed from public scrutiny and criticism. Community organizations have an inevitable tendency to provide services only to a selected clientele. They typically cater to a local community, or may be sponsored by religious organizations, and are, therefore, not readily accessible to geographically and socially isolated people who have no access to information via churches, social workers, doctors, community centers and the like. As I found in my Western Australian study, some volunteers had difficulty interacting with Aboriginal clients, non-English-speaking migrants, or people with severe physical or mental handicaps. However, where voluntary agencies are involved, the sheer aura of altruism surrounding the provision of services reduces the likelihood of a critical examination of the effectiveness of such services by members of the public: Welfare clients who are dissatisfied with service delivery lack the means of having their voices heard.

Welfare, Women, and Volunteers

Throughout Australia's history, volunteers have had an important role to play in the system of redistribution. Nineteenth century social work was the domain of middle-class ladies who visited the poor in their homes, offering material support and spiritual guidance (Roe 1988, pp. 1–2). Given the definition of home and family life as private, such philanthropic work, as an extension of domesticity, was seen as the only activity suited to these ladies (Godden 1982). Professionalism eventually developed and paid social work appeared (Marchant and Wearing 1986), but charitable activities remained the domain of volunteers.

At the beginning of the 1980s there were more than a million volunteers in Australia (in a population of about 16 million) working for non-government welfare organizations (Milligan, Hardwick, and Graycar 1984, p. xi). The combined work effort of these volunteers, most of whom provided services, added up to the equivalent of 160,000 full-time paid jobs (Yates and Graycar 1983, p. 159).[13] This is a unique feature of Australian volunteerism, in contrast to the United States and Europe (Abrams, Abrams, Humphrey, and Snaith 1986; Boolsen and Holt 1988, pp. 13–18; Oyen 1986, p. 14; Yates and Graycar 1983, p. 159).

Recent policies of privatization which led to the contracting out of welfare services to non-government welfare organizations have vastly increased the need for volunteers. Federal and state governments assumed that volunteers carry out a substantial portion of the administrative and service work; funding allows for the appointment of a volunteer co-ordinator, and (sometimes) the payment of volunteer insurance and training, but generally not for the hiring of paid workers to deliver the services. Administrators view the contracting-out arrangement as one which increases their costs, and they use volunteers as a means of containing such costs.

I found that most welfare administrators who responded to my survey recognized the use of volunteers as a cost-saving device. Nearly two-thirds of all organizations would have liked more paid staff but could not afford to hire them. They used their volunteers for administration, fund-raising, and especially for service delivery. Although there are no current figures, if anything the use of volunteers has increased since the early 1980s.[14]

The sheer volume of the tasks to be performed has led many non-government organizations to an ever-increasing search for more volunteers. Volunteer Centers provide referral services for volunteers as well as agencies; and the provision of volunteer badges and the celebration of Volunteer Recognition Day are means of expressing recognition for volunteer effort, and also function as a recruiting technique. These efforts to increase the pool of volunteers are accompanied by attempts to boost the image of volunteers, from "high socioeconomic groups to all groups, from unskilled to skilled, from reactionary to pace setters, and from submissive to assertive."[15] These attempts are meant to attract young and male volunteers, and effectively conceal the ongoing volunteer work of older women.

That most volunteers working in welfare service delivery in Australia are *women* (Hardwick and Graycar 1982; Marchant and Wearing 1986) is of special significance in the context of this paper. In my study the majority of the volunteers involved in service delivery on a day-to-day basis were women: 80 percent of the volunteers who responded to my survey, for example, were women. Although men volunteer for some areas of service delivery, these are generally "men's work" such as transport or home repairs (Hardwick and Graycar 1982; Wheeler 1986), whereas women are typically engaged in volunteer tasks which are extensions of their domestic caring labor. I found that women acted as hospital visitors, delivered "meals on wheels," packed and distributed food parcels, answered the telephone, carried out typing and clerical duties, or made the tea. They were in many respects, like the women in the secondary paid labor market, involved in repetitive caring labor, without prospects or rewards. Like their sisters in paid work, many had not received formal education beyond the age of 14 or 15; when employed, they had been in low-paid and unskilled women's work.

Some well-educated, married women with young children were also among the volunteers in my study; their financial situation allowed them to remain outside the paid labor force, but they planned to return to paid work once their children reached high school age. Most of these well-educated women volunteers performed professional tasks such as counselling, thereby emulating paid professional workers. Nonetheless, their preoccupations remained with caring labor.

Conclusion and Evaluation: Toward Empowerment of Women?

Four central issues have been established so far. First, women are marginal to the paid labor force in Australia, and their access to paid work is not seen as a right. Second, welfare provision is residual in Australia, with income maintenance and the provision of welfare services seen as a privilege, not as a right. Third, the central role given to non-government welfare organizations within this residual system of welfare has led to a high degree of reliance on volunteers. Finally, women are the core of volunteer effort in Australian welfare.

Clearly these four central issues are closely connected. There is a relationship between the marginality of women to paid work and their availability for volunteer labor on the one hand, and the residual nature of welfare, coupled with the demand for volunteer labor, on the other. Given the dearth of funding in an economic and ideological climate which defines welfare as a privilege, welfare organizations can only maintain their assigned role in welfare service delivery if they have access to a pool of workers willing to dedicate their time and skills without remuneration. So far this has been possible because of the availability of female volunteers who combine and intersperse volunteer labor with other unpaid work, or with paid work on the margins of the wage economy. In Australia these women have been available because of the sexual division of labor with its ideology of caring labor, which has produced women's marginal attachment to the sphere of production. Both volunteer work and the marginality of women's paid work can thus be seen to depend on the continuation of the ideology of domesticity which presumes that women's primary responsibility is to home and family.

Only in a context where welfare, as the system of redistribution, is seen as residual can such extensive reliance on non-government agencies and on volunteers be justified. Were welfare provision taken seriously and given adequate resources, this work would be in the hands of fully qualified, well-paid professionals, and not the responsibility of a myriad of local agencies with poorly paid staff and unpaid volunteers.

The scenario that I have described so far contains a number of interesting contradictions. First, the new emphasis on the importance of non-government welfare has produced an increased demand for volunteers at the very time that economic pressures force ever-growing numbers of women to look for paid work.

The scarcity of volunteers has led to extensive recruitment drives aimed at attracting, motivating, and keeping volunteers in what is effectively a sellers' market. At the same time, funding conditions insist that welfare organizations be selective in their choice of volunteers, and, generally, ensure a high-quality volunteer performance. This combination of scarcity and selectivity, then, forms the second contradiction.

There is, however, another more crucial contradiction. Increased government regulation of volunteers and the emphasis on professionalism, as a condition of contracting-out arrangements, has in effect contributed to an awareness among volunteers of the importance of their contribution, and thereby to their empowerment. In my study this showed in three important ways: in insistence on volunteer rights, in demands for meaningful volunteer work, and in the search for paid employment.

As to volunteer rights, the emphasis on professionalism and its implicit message that volunteer work is of value to the community, led the majority of volunteers in my study to the realization that they *deserved* accident insurance, payment of out-of-pocket expenses, decent working conditions, and recognition. In 1988 it led Western Australian welfare organizations to demand a Charter for Volunteers, which specified, among other things, volunteers' rights to equal opportunity and non-discriminatory practices, the right to appeal, the right to promotion and appropriate training, and recognition of services rendered.

The training provided to volunteers as part of the push toward professionalism led to demands by a number of volunteers for more interesting volunteer work. As I mentioned earlier, many female volunteers in my study were women engaged in fairly menial volunteer work. Among these were many who had missed out on education when they were young, and whose paid work had been uninteresting and menial. Some had left employment when they could afford to do so, because it did not give them any job satisfaction. When volunteer training was made available to these women, they were eager to take advantage of it, with the goal of engaging in work which would provide interest and challenge.

Volunteers who received this training lost interest in doing repetitive support work, and searched for more meaningful activities in counselling or other face-to-face interactions with clients. Some became quite assertive in their objections to doing support tasks such as typing, telephone answering, or domestic cleaning, arguing that this should be done by a paid worker. Others argued that volunteer work should be different from what women are expected to do in the home. It appears, in fact, that many of these women were looking for volunteer work which would give them the job satisfaction and recognition which they had lacked in their roles as housewives and paid workers.

It is an irony that the entry of these women into volunteer work, and the training provided as part of it, gave them an opportunity for self development and growth, and to "do something for themselves"— an opportunity which they had not had before in domestic *or* in paid work. It appears that some women saw the opportunity to engage in volunteer work and training as a break from "compulsory altruism" (Land and Rose 1985). They in fact saw their volunteer work as part of the public sphere of production, quite distinct from the "natural" obligations attached to caring for their own family. They chose to do volunteer work, sometimes against the wishes of their husbands, as an activity which took them away from what they saw as the private sphere of reproduction and toward community service in the public domain.

The training provided to ensure a greater professionalism among volunteers also had enabled volunteers to compete for paid work. As mentioned, among the volunteers in my study were a number of well-educated younger women with small children who had taken time out from paid work. They also took full advantage of the opportunities for training offered by their welfare organizations and used such training as an avenue to future careers. This, then, forms another contradiction: Volunteer training, rather than creating a more skilled volunteer work force, ultimately creates a depleted one.

What is the future, then, for volunteerism in Australia? If the pressure continues on the voluntary sector to perform essential welfare services, and at the same time professionalism remains as an incentive and as a requirement for responsible service, the inevitable outcome may be an increased demand by women for financial remuneration and entry into paid work. For those women who, due to lack of job opportunities or family responsibilities, are unable to take up paid work and who therefore remain volunteers, the outcome may be a rejection of repetitive service work, and a channelling of skills and experience into more meaningful volunteer tasks. These may include working for social action and lobby groups with a focus on social change.

What is happening, then, is that women, through their appropriation of volunteerism as an avenue to further training, paid work, or self-fulfillment, are subverting that cluster of social structures and assumptions that led them to be available for volunteer labor in the first place, because of their marginal attachment to the full-time paid work force. The future of volunteering in Australia is uncertain, but it would appear that women themselves are a powerful force in shaping its destiny.

No other western country relies on volunteers for service delivery in welfare to the extent Australia does. Nonetheless, throughout the world, unpaid work in caring labor is seen as the responsibility of women (Waring 1988). In Western Australia women now realize the important contribution they make to the welfare of their society through their unpaid work and have been empowered by this. It may well be the case that women across the world are gaining a similar sense of empowerment through their own re-evaluation of their unpaid caring labor.

Notes

1. This is a revision of a paper I presented in a joint session of Research Committees 19 and 32 at the 12th World Congress of Sociology, Madrid, 1990. I

am indebted to Victoria Rogers for her critical comments and editorial corrections.

2. I was supported financially by the Australian Research Grants Committee and Murdoch University.

3. Not all community welfare organizations in Australia employ volunteers, but many have no paid staff at all, and are kept alive solely by volunteer effort (Yates and Graycar 1983, p. 159). Thirteen out of 61 organizations in my study had no paid staff.

4. I focus in this account on the period since Federation (which took place in 1901). Prior to Federation, government was in the hands of individual states.

5. From 1891 onwards the Australian colonies adopted a census classification which divided the population into breadwinners and dependents. Thus women who previously had been defined as productive workers (e.g., as farmers' wives) now became classified as dependents (Deacon 1985).

6. This included a large number of non-English-speaking migrant women who had come to Australia in post-war years and worked in the factories which produced the consumer items necessary for the suburban dream. They did so generally without the benefit of proper childcare, and the ideology of domesticity, so heavily emphasized for Anglo-Saxon women, did not appear to apply to them (Bottomley and de Lepervanche 1984; Power 1976).

7. Comparative studies have shown that Australia has the most occupationally segregated labor force of the OECD (Organization of Economic and Cultural Development) countries (O'Donnell and Hall 1988, p. 24).

8. It is ironic, however, that women do not receive much reward for their work in the sphere of reproduction. Family allowances, paid by government to mothers to help reduce the cost of children, are not indexed and their value has eroded over time (Cass 1988, p. 85) and single-parent households headed by women are among the poorest in the country (Cass and O'Loughlin 1985; Harris 1989, p. 11).

9. In recent years, law enforcement agencies have blamed "broken homes," that is, single parent families headed by women, as the cause of juvenile delinquency; in some drug and alcohol rehabilitation programs women are held responsible for their husband's addiction; and commercial advertisers urge women to keep their families on healthy diets (see, e.g., Broom 1988, pp. 270-71).

10. The Australian Council of Trade Unions recently mounted a test case for paternity leave; employers were most unsympathetic to the proposal for this reason.

11. People below the poverty line are those whose incomes are so low that they are unable to purchase the most basic necessities (Harris 1989, p. 2).

12. This questionnaire asked detailed questions regarding jointly owned household appliances, shared household duties, and shared childcare as indications of de facto relations; same-sex sharing, however, is not considered relevant.

13. In addition, many volunteers work for statutory authorities in the field of welfare, e.g., hospitals, local councils, and government departments.

14. Costs are kept down also by the low wages of paid staff in the nongovernment welfare sector (Garde and Wheeler 1985; Mowbray 1982). The inability of paid staff in welfare organizations to gain better wages may well be caused by the presence of so many volunteers.

15. The Western Australian Minister of Community Services made this statement at the 1989 Annual General Meeting of the Western Australian Volunteer Centre.

References

Abrams, P., S. Abrams, R. Humphrey, and R. Snaith. 1986. *Creating Care in the Neighbourhood*. London: Neighbourhood Care Action Programme.

Australian Bureau of Statistics. 1990. *The Australian Labour Force, Australia*, January 1990. Catalogue No. 6203.0. Canberra: Australian Government Publishing Service.

Baldock, C. V. 1983. "Volunteer Work as Work." Pp. 278–296 (reprinted in 1988 2nd ed.) in *Women, Social Welfare and the State.*, edited by C. V. Baldock and B. Cass. Sydney: Allen and Unwin.

————.1990. *Volunteers in Welfare*. Sydney: Allen and Unwin.

Baldock, C. V., and B. Cass, eds. 1988. *Women, Social Welfare and the State*. 2nd edition. Sydney: Allen and Unwin.

Baxter, J., D. Gibson, and M. Lynch-Bosse. 1990. *Double Take: The Links between Paid and Unpaid Work*. Canberra: Australian Government Publishing Service.

Beaton, L. 1980. "The Importance of Women's Paid Labour." Pp. 67–75 in *Second Women and Labour Conference*, edited by The Convenors. Melbourne.

Boolsen, M. Watt, and H. Holt. 1988. *Voluntary Action in Denmark and Britain*. Copenhagen: The Danish National Institute of Social Research.

Bottomley, G., and M. de Lepervanche, eds. 1984. *Ethnicity, Class and Gender in Australia*. Sydney: Allen and Unwin.

Broom, D. 1986. "The Occupational Health of Houseworkers." *Australian Feminist Studies* 2:15–34.

————. 1988. "In Sickness and in Health: Social Policy and the Control of Women." Pp. 262–277 in *Women, Social Welfare and the State*, edited by C. V. Baldock and B. Cass. 2nd edition. Sydney: Allen and Unwin.

Bryson, L. 1984. "The Australian Patriarchal Family." Pp. 113–70 in *Australian Society*, edited by S. Encel and L. Bryson. Melbourne: Cheshire.

Cass, B. 1988. "Redistribution to Children and Mothers." Pp. 54–88 in *Women, Social Welfare and the State,* edited by C. V. Baldock and B. Cass. 2nd edition. Sydney: Allen and Unwin.

Cass, B., and M. A. O'Loughlin. 1985. "Single Parent Families and Social Policies in Australia 1974–1982." *Australian Journal of Social Issues* 20:247–267.

Coombs, E. 1989. "Community Care and the Social Construction of Work: The Case of the Home Care Services in New South Wales." Unpublished Ph.D. thesis. Sydney: University of New South Wales.

Cox, E. 1988. "Pater-patria: Child-rearing and the State." Pp. 190–205 in *Women, Social Welfare and the State,* edited by C. V. Baldock and B. Cass. 2nd edition. Sydney: Allen and Unwin.

———. 1989. "De Facto, Dependency and Destitution." *Refractory Girl* 33:33–36.

Currie, J. 1989. "Tertiary Graduates and the Labour Market: Analysing Class and Gender Effects." Paper presented at International Colloquium Gender and Class. Belgium: University of Antwerp.

Deacon, D. 1984. "The Employment of Women in the Commonwealth Public Service." Pp. 132–150 in *Australian Women and the Political System,* edited by M. Simms. Melbourne: Longman.

———. 1985. "Political Arithmetic: The Nineteenth Century Australian Census and the Construction of the Dependent Woman." *Signs* 11:27–47.

Dickey, B. 1980. *No Charity There, A Short History of Social Welfare in Australia.* Melbourne: Nelson.

Edwards, A. R. 1988. *Regulation and Repression.* Sydney: Allen and Unwin.

Eveline, J. 1989. "Patriarchy in the Diamond Mines: Women's Work, Research and Affirmative Action." Unpublished honours thesis. Perth: Murdoch University.

Franzway, S., D. Court, and R. W. Connell. 1989. *Staking a Claim: Feminism, Bureaucracy and the State.* Sydney: Allen and Unwin.

Game, A., and R. Pringle. 1979. "Sexuality and the Suburban Dream." *Australian and New Zealand Journal of Sociology* 15:4–15.

———. 1983. *Gender at Work.* Sydney: Allen and Unwin.

Garde, P., and L. Wheeler. 1985. *Hard Labour: The Community Services Industry.* New South Wales Council of Social Services Issues Paper 5, November.

Gaudron, M., and M. Bosworth. 1979. "Equal Pay?" Pp. 161–169 in *In Pursuit of Justice: Australian Women and the Law 1788–1979,* edited by J. Mackinolty and H. Radi. Sydney: Hale & Iremonger.

Glezer, H. 1988. *Maternity Leave in Australia: Employee and Employer Experiences.* Monograph No. 7. Melbourne: Institute of Family Studies.

Godden, J. 1982. "'The Work for Them, and the Glory for Us!' Sydney Women's Philanthropy, 1880–1900." Pp. 84–102 in *Australian Welfare History,* edited by R. Kennedy. Melbourne: Macmillan.

Hardwick, J., and A. Graycar. 1982. *Volunteers in Non-government Welfare Organisations in Australia: A Working Paper.* SWRC Reports and Proceedings, No. 25 (September). Sydney: Social Welfare Research Centre, University of New South Wales.

Harris, P. 1989. *Child Poverty, Inequality and Social Justice.* Child Poverty Policy Review 1. Melbourne: Brotherhood of St. Laurence.

Kewley, T. H. 1973. *Social Security in Australia 1900–72.* Sydney: Sydney University Press.

Land, H., and H. Rose. 1985. "Compulsory Altruism for Some or an Altruistic Society for All?" Pp. 74–99 in *In Defense of Welfare,* edited by P. Bean, J. Ferris, and D. Whynes. London: Tavistock.

Marchant, H., and B. Wearing. 1986. *Gender Reclaimed: Women in Social Work.* Sydney: Hale and Iremonger.

Matthews, J. J. 1984. *Good and Mad Women.* Sydney: Allen and Unwin.

Milligan, V., J. Hardwick, and A. Graycar. 1984. *Non-Government Welfare Organisations in Australia: A National Classification.* SWRC Reports and Proceedings, No. 51. Sydney: Social Welfare Research Centre, University of New South Wales.

Mowbray, M. 1982. "Localism and Austerity." Paper presented at Sociological Association of Australia and New Zealand. Sydney, August.

O'Donnell, C., and P. Hall. 1988. *Getting Equal.* Sydney: Allen and Unwin.

Oyen, E. 1980. "Who Is Afraid of the Welfare State?" ABC Guest of Honour Programme, July 27. Sydney: Australian Broadcasting Company.

———. 1986. "Identifying the Future of the Welfare State?" Pp. 1–19 in *Comparing Welfare States and their Futures,* edited by E. Oyen. Aldershot: Gower.

Power, M. 1976. "Cast-off Jobs: Women, Migrants, Blacks May Apply." *Refractory Girl*: 27–31.

Roe, J., ed. 1976. *Social Policy in Australia: Some Perspectives 1901–1975.* North Melbourne: Cassell Australia.

———. 1988. "The End Is Where We Start From: Women and Welfare Since 1901." Pp. 1–19 in *Women, Social Welfare and the State,* edited by C. V. Baldock and B. Cass. Sydney: Allen and Unwin.

Ryan, E., and A. Conlon. 1989. *Gentle Invaders: Australian Women at Work 1788–1974,* 2nd ed. Ringwood, Vic.: Penguin.

Saunders, P. 1987. "An Agenda for Social Security in the Years Ahead." *Australian Journal of Social Issues* 22:409–423.

Thiele, Beverley. 1990. "Negotiating the Domestic Division of Labour." Pp. 129–152 in Proceedings of Inaugural National Women's Conference. Canberra: Rewrite Press.

Tomlinson, J. R. 1989. "Income Maintenance in Australia: The Income Guarantee Alternative." Unpublished Ph.D. thesis. Perth: Murdoch University.

Wainwright, R. 1988. "Welfare Agency Shuts Its Doors." *Western Australian,* 13 April, p. 7.

Waring, M. 1988. *Counting for Nothing.* Sydney: Allen and Unwin.

Wheeler, L. 1986. *Close to Home: The Community Services Industry, New South Wales.* New South Wales Council of Social Service Issues Paper 7, December.

Yates, I., and A. Graycar. 1983. "Non-governmental Welfare: Issues and Perspectives." Pp. 149–170 in *Retreat from the Welfare State,* edited by A. Graycar. Sydney: Allen and Unwin.

Young, C. 1990. *Balancing Families and Work: A Demographic Study of Women's Labour Force Participation*. Canberra: Australian Government Publishing Service.

☙ **Chapter 5** ☙

Women's Work, Wealth, and Family Survival Strategy: The Impact of Guatemala's ALCOSA Agribusiness Project

Rae Lesser Blumberg
with the assistance of
Maria Regina Estrada de Batres
and
Josefina Xuya Cuxil

Introduction[1]

Setting the Stage

The "quadruple overlap" of gender, family, economy, and the state has profound consequences for women in the Third World. In general, the way state ruling elites conceive of the family and gender can buttress a legal, ideological, religious, political, and economic system in which women may be valued or devalued, as well as encouraged or discouraged from seeking paid work. In turn, women's relative control of income and other economic resources relates directly to their position within the family.

State economic policies can have a powerful impact in and of themselves. From the 1950s until the early 1980s, most Third World states promoted "import substitution industrialization" (ISI). This policy benefits a small number of firms run by politically favored industrialists. These firms can afford to pass along costs, including paying a small unionized labor force a locally good wage and legally mandated fringe benefits. Such an ISI labor force is almost invariably disproportionately male.

Beginning in the early 1980s, the debt crisis and economic stagnation in much of the Third World elicited pressure from the international donor/financial agencies (World Bank, International Monetary Fund, U.S. Agency for International Development) for "structural adjustment." Such adjustment involves reducing state employment, "floating" the currency, cutting subsidies and tariffs of the ISI era, and "getting the prices right." For a decade, the new orthodoxy of the mainstream development paradigm has stressed export-driven growth of labor-intensive manufacturing, especially in Export Processing Zones (EPZs), and Non-Traditional Agricultural Exports (NTAEs: labor-intensive flower, vegetable, and fruit crops). Competing in a cutthroat international market with other Third World countries has led the non-traditional industrial and agricultural exports to a disproportionately female (and cheaper) labor force (see, e.g., Blumberg 1989a).

The present case study examines how a highly repressive state, a multinational corporation (MNC), and a development project in support of NTAE broccoli and cauliflower grown by poor Mayan Indians affect women and their position within the family. It is a restudy of 1980 research (Kusterer et al. 1981) on a Guatemalan agribusiness project. The 1980 research covered three villages where poor peasants, mainly Cakchiquel-speaking Mayan Indians, grew broccoli, cauliflower, and snow peas on contract for ALCOSA, a wholly-owned subsidiary of a U.S. MNC, Hanover Brands. The Ladina (mestiza) women workers at the ALCOSA plant who processed, froze, and packed ALCOSA's vegetables for export to the U.S. market were also studied. I restudied these same four sites in 1985 because I discovered (Blumberg 1983) that they formed a "natural experiment" of what happens to the individuals, families, and communities and to the project itself when planned development affects the gender division of labor and/or resources.

In 1980 the project was floundering in the only village (Patzicia) where women didn't labor on the agribusiness contract crops, but was very successful in the village where women not only worked but also shared in cash returns for the family's crops (Santiago Sacatepequez). Productivity in the processing plant—where women worked long hours, earned high wages, and controlled their own income—was exceptional. In addition, the processing workers' income brought them greater self-esteem and their families greater well-being. Thus, the 1980 research showed that the more women worked on and received benefits from the ALCOSA agribusiness project the greater the success of that project. Moreover, dealing women into the rewards of a planned development project helped not only the project (Carloni 1987) but also the women themselves and their families (Blumberg 1989a).

Taking Exception to the "Black Box" Model of the Household

If these patterns reemerged in 1985, then the data would cast empirical doubt on the model of the household common to two otherwise very dissimilar development paradigms—the conservative/"mainstream" and the radical/dependency/World Systems (Wallerstein 1974) approaches. Both share a "black box" model of the household: that it is a monolithic and unitary pooling entity united in a common survival strategy. Indeed, the "mainstream" development paradigm adopts the neo-classical economics approach of describing the household by a single production function (Becker 1981). In this common "black box" model, it doesn't matter who does the work, who gets the information, or who gets the rewards; somehow, everything is pooled. Differences in power and privilege between male and female, senior and junior, are ignored.

But as women in development (WID) researchers are increasingly emphasizing, this model does not describe the empirical reality of households in much of the world (see, e.g., Blumberg 1988, 1989a, and 1989b; Dwyer 1983; Dwyer and Bruce 1988; Staudt 1987). I argue that rather than a universal "single production function" model of the household, a worldwide continuum exists along which one can identify the extent to which an "internal economy of the household" based primarily on gender and age prevails. At one end of this continuum is the unitary household where there is no internal economy since everything is pooled, typically under the direction of the (male) head. At the other end are households where the internal economy is very pronounced: Virtually nothing is pooled, and men's, women's, and older children's relative power and independently controlled resources must be taken into account.

This "black box/single production function" model of the household fits worst in Africa (e.g., Blumberg 1988, 1989a, and 1989b), where men and women tend to keep at least partially separate purses, especially where polygyny and/or marital instability are high. I extend this argument to two peoples whose "family survival strategy" and household are popularly held to epitomize the monolithic, "patriarchal and pooling" household: Ladinos (mestizos) and Mayan Indians from

Guatemala. The research presented here show that in Guatemala, too, the monolithic "black box" model of the household obscures more than it reveals: The model neglects important aspects not only of gender stratification but also of how "family survival strategies" function.

Guiding Hypotheses

A series of hypotheses from my theories of gender stratification (Blumberg 1984) and gender and development (Blumberg 1988, 1989b, and 1991) guided the research. They deal with three issues: (1) economic independence and power (hypotheses 1–5); (2) women's and their family's well-being (hypotheses 6–7); and (3) how development policy affects women's status (hypotheses 8–9). Though the data collection methodology did not permit a definitive test of these hypotheses, they illuminated and focused the research.

H1:   For women, control of economic resources is the most important, although certainly not the sole, variable affecting gender stratification and numerous other consequences for women's lives.

H2:   Independently controlled income is the most readily accessible form of economic power open to women (vs. control of land or other property).

H3:   Therefore, women's independently controlled income is associated with their greater leverage in: (a) fertility decisions; and (b) household economic and domestic decisions.

H4:   Women's unpaid work (i.e., subsistence and reproductive activities that do not result in independently controlled income) is *not* associated with their greater leverage in family fertility and economic decisions.

H5:   When income under women's control falls, they lose household power more precipitously than they gain it when their income rises.

H6:   Women's independently controlled income is associated with their greater sense of efficacy and self-esteem.

H7:   Women are more likely than men are to spend income under their control on family expenditures, especially children's nutrition and necessities.[2]

H8: When scarce development resources are targeted to poor, powerless groups such as women, the landless, etc., those resources tend to be distributed in terms of "power and privilege" (Lenski 1966), which is manifested in a "trickle up" of benefits.

H9: Vulnerable groups (e.g., women) may be shut or pushed out of project benefits unless (a) barriers to the group's receiving of benefits are reduced by deliberate selection procedures and appropriate delivery mechanisms, and (b) oversight of project benefit allocation continues.

What follows is a background profile of the research setting and methodology. Then the 1985 findings are compared with the earlier data. Finally, the last two sections synthesize what has been learned from theoretical, empirical, and policy standpoints.

The Guatemalan Context and Research Methodology

The Socioeconomic and Gender Setting

The Mayan Indians of Highland Guatemala generally adopt a "family subsistence strategy" (what some have termed a "peasant mode of production") to survive. Rather than pooling all earnings into a "common pot," the male household head and grown children who are still participating members of the household (even though they may not live there year round) contribute some proportion of labor and/or earnings. Wives also tend to engage in income-generating ventures (e.g., weaving, market trading), but they devote virtually all their income to household subsistence expenses ("el gasto").[3] Women's involvement in fieldwork varies from village to village, although they usually raise chickens and small animals and tend kitchen gardens. They also usually sell the family's surplus production, their own weaving, or other products. Men, in addition to farming, often migrate seasonally to coastal plantations or the city. In short, an "internal economy of the household," differentiated by gender and age, can be perceived within the Mayan "family subsistence strategy."

A Brief Sketch of the Methodology

I attempted to use Kusterer's research team and parts of the 1980 questionnaires (for farmers and plant workers). Moreover, whenever possible, 1980 respondents were reinterviewed. The methodology employed was Rapid Rural Appraisal (RRA), which involves the "triangulation" of diverse data gathering approaches, from interviews with key informants to analysis of records, to group meetings, to small surveys.[4] Other RRA techniques employed included participant observation and meetings in which people with varying perspectives on the project and on Guatemala (e.g., officials of the Latin American Agribusiness Development Organization and the Guatemalan Mission of the U.S. Agency for International Development[5]) discussed preliminary findings.

Counting only the ALCOSA female plant employees and present and former ALCOSA growers of both sexes, a total of 101 people were interviewed (mostly in their homes, in order to better measure material well-being). Among the plant workers interviewed, one-half had been there since the previous study and one-half had been hired in the last couple of years. In the villages, we also attempted to split our interviews among recently contracted ALCOSA growers, those who had contracts since the previous study, and those who no longer were ALCOSA growers. The breakdown of respondents by gender and location is shown in Table 5.1.

The 1985 Findings

Patzicia: Women Begin Working but Don't Control Income

In their 1980 interviews, Kusterer et al. found no females working on the ALCOSA crops, even though these crops require more labor than traditional agriculture. Moreover, ALCOSA has very exacting standards for produce they will accept, which further increases the labor

Table 5.1 Interviewees by Location and Gender

Interviews	Men	Women	Total
Patzicia	13	10	23
Chimachoy[6]	8	10	18
Santiago Sacatepequez	13	17*	30
San Jose Pinula	—	30	30
	34	67	101

*11 were interviewed at a group meeting

burden. Kusterer et al. also found the project floundering for lack of sufficient labor. Given the depths of Guatemala's economic crisis between 1980–1985, I predicted that necessity would erode cultural taboos on women doing field work.

Indeed, in 1985, we found a considerable degree of female involvement in the single most labor-intensive, time-sensitive operation: harvesting. About half of the twenty-three people we interviewed were 1980 ALCOSA grower families; the other half were newer people. Although newer families seemed a bit more likely to claim the wife participated in agriculture, in thirteen of the twenty-three cases either the woman or her husband described her as working in the fields. Of the ten women, five said they did. Of the thirteen men, eight said the wife worked in the fields; one man was a bachelor; and three men said no, as did a fourth man, by far the most prosperous man interviewed. But his wife, in a separate interview, told a very different story. As my field notes report:

> Her first response to the question was to deny that she did field work. But under further probes (what about during the broccoli harvest: Do you *ever* help out with the cutting (*el corte*)?), she said that she did. Three days a week, in fact—and for both the broccoli and cauliflower harvest—i.e., for a total of over four months a year. Her children also helped when they weren't in school. And no, field work was something she had never done before they began growing the ALCOSA vegetables. Yes, it was a good deal of extra work, but household income had increased. . . . She was wistfully optimistic that her husband would spend (some of) the extra income on family well-being.

In contrast to 1980, in over half the 1985 interviews, thirteen out of twenty-two married women did ALCOSA field work. Five people (three men and two women) *explicitly* said that the woman's involvement in field work had occurred since they had begun growing ALCOSA vegetables, thus allowing economic considerations to override cultural convention. Thus, women added a double day of fieldwork without receiving *direct* benefits, but they seemed hopeful that their efforts would aid family well-being.

Patzicia also provided support for another hypothesis (#H3b). In twelve cases—including nine of the ten women respondents (the tenth woman was an unmarried farmer who had an ALCOSA contract in her own name) and three of the thirteen men—respondents described a relationship between women's independent income and the men's consulting with women on household decisions. If women had such income (often from selling in the market), men typically consulted with them; if they had no earnings of their own, men typically did not. The income in most instances merely contributed to *"el gasto"*—the household subsistence expenses deemed to be women's domain. But if women made some material contribution to this subsistence budget, the contribution earned them some degree of "consultation."

Overall, we encountered no cases of women too timid to voice an opinion, as had been the norm in the 1980 research. The women of Patzicia are now more open and less submissive.

My field notes on the case of a Ladina woman whose family had arrived in Patzicia only nine months before confirm the importance of women's independent income:

> Her husband had lost his job (working in surveying) in Guatemala City, inherited a small plot of land in Patzicia from his father, and moved the family there to try their luck growing vegetables for ALCOSA on a farm near the Pan American Highway. She had always worked in the city (usually as a domestic) and felt that there her income gave her more independence and household power (*voz y voto*—"voice and vote"). Previously he had given *her* money for "el gasto" and decisions had been mutual. Here, although the initial decision to plant for ALCOSA was mutual, it was the last such joint decision. So she works three days a week in the fields, has no outside income, and now *he* makes the decisions.

This vignette indicates: (a) that woman's independently controlled income is more important than her unpaid work in production in determining her degree of household power and decision-making leverage (as per H4), and (b) how quickly a woman's status can erode when her own income drops (as per H5).[7]

Santiago Sacatepequez:
The Cooperative Thrives but Policy Changes Hurt Women

In 1980, this village had the most successful project, and women had the highest participation in field work as well as the most direct access to cash benefits. Only Santiago had a cooperative to organize farmers and administer the ALCOSA contract. The co-op thrived economically. In 1984, it sold a million dollars worth of produce.

The co-op had become a large employer with thirty permanent employees and, from July to February, 100–125 additional people as packers. Of these, two-thirds were women and one-third were men. Then, disturbed by the "constant talking" and "romances" of the women employees, the co-op directors replaced them with men. Production nose-dived so sharply that they fired the men after only one week and hired back the women—who continued to be both productive and talkative. The directors now viewed packing as "women's work" because of the women's allegedly greater manual dexterity and tolerance of the boring routine.

A 1983 policy change essentially eliminated women's access to direct benefits, a change with repercussions for female autonomy and welfare. After an incident in 1983,[8] the co-op had strongly requested that the person who comes for the weekly payoff be the co-op *member*. The number of women co-op members in 1985 was somewhere between two and eight out of 580. Furthermore, since early 1984, the payoff usually has been by check made out exclusively to the *member*. Based on their typical three to four days a week of field work, could women be made co-op members in their own right, along with their husbands? Unthinkable, according to the head of the co-op "social program." In his opinion, the men would never allow it. But he admitted that he had never asked them.

As a result, women no longer received direct payment if they delivered the produce. Most women did not know how much their husbands received, thereby weakening their ability to claim a share. Co-op professional staff agreed that the position of the women had deteriorated to one in which they were more dependent on their husbands.

Co-op families no longer devoted as much time and space on their small parcels in 1985 to grow the traditional crops which Santiago women have long sold (at least partly for their *own* gain) in Guatemala City's terminal market. Because of encroaching suburbanization from the ever-growing capital, land is at a premium. The men would rather grow more ALCOSA-type vegetables for guaranteed sale to the co-op rather than grow horticultural crops women can sell in the city. Since the co-op has ended women's direct access to the income benefits despite their heavy involvement in all phases of ALCOSA vegetable production, they are now doubly disadvantaged, while working at least as hard as ever.

However, women's position had begun to erode before the 1983 incident: As their labor burden increased with the co-op vegetable crops, women had both less time and less reason to sell their traditional crops. Before ALCOSA, several women informants told me, wives used to divide their time between farm work (roughly three days) and selling in Guatemala City markets (usually three days).

Now they had to add an additional day's farm work per week, on average, at a cost of one day's market selling and its income.

Although interview data from men and women of Santiago indicate that the women still had *some* voice in agricultural decisions, the two home economists thought it less than before the policy change. My field notes indicate that they felt that:

> Before, women in Santiago's outlying hamlets (whose access to the market has been more curtailed than the women of the town of Santiago itself) were more independent and sold surplus crops in the market. They had a voice in what to plant because they knew what sold best. Now that the co-op buys, the men make the economic decisions.

The head of the "social program," concurring with this assessment, added that women had "lost a certain independence and the making of household decisions."

Tulio Garcia, the co-op founder, shared the view that women's position had deteriorated. He noted that home and "basic human needs" purchases, including diet/nutrition, had improved less than male-decided purchases. As women's income and household decision-making power declined, we would predict that men's spending priorities would be more fully realized.

Co-op staff and men farmers interviewed both as a group and individually all stated that many men save for scarce and ever more expensive land, since additional land means additional income. As noted, however, they are in increasing competition with the developers, who view Santiago Sacatepequez as not too far from the capital for suburban subdivisions.

Second, men regard transport, especially big-ticket items such as pickup trucks, as high priorities.[9] Tulio Garcia suspected that malnutrition still existed. At minimum, he felt that the increase in nutrition/well-being was lagging relative to the increase in men's favored spending targets.[10]

Co-op staffers were concerned enough about both "the problem with women" and "the problem with health and nutrition" that they began special programs targeted at both, but these programs involve the most traditional home economics and do not seem to be having the desired effects. In keeping with the "trickle-up" (H9) hypothesis, though, the three people chosen by the village leaders to be trained by the co-op as health/nutrition promoters were relatively well-off young men, on the grounds that they could get away more easily for the four-week training.

At a women's group meeting in Pachalí, one of Santiago's seven outlying villages, eleven females, mostly well-dressed adolescent girls, attended a cake-baking demonstration. The home economists baked the cake in the community center in a modern stove donated by a U.N. agency. None of the families have anything like it. As my field notes report:

> An elderly widow who is a co-op member (one of two she knows about) said that a previous women's group started with 22 members, but soon only six were left. They had many domestic arts demonstrations, but the women wanted something with more economic potential, so they stopped coming.

Married women with more obligations and less time needed income. Both the home economists and the head of the social program wanted to find a more income-oriented program, but such economic activities are not easily found. Meanwhile, attendance at their meetings was low: The women in Santiago's outlying villages, whose relative position had dropped off more sharply, had now to ask *permission* of reluctant husbands even to attend meetings; the women of Santiago itself, who still carry a crushing burden of heavy farm work and more frequent marketing trips to Guatemala City, had no time for such meetings.

Aside from a tiny bakery project that the women of one of the outlying hamlets had launched, the only idea that had surfaced was a bee-keeping project. Originally, the co-op was investigating bee-keeping for men but decided they were too busy. Since the co-op leaders' understanding was that bee-keeping takes only one morning a week (an underestimate when hives are in full production), they felt that this could be added to the women's schedules. Then, the co-op would market the honey. This would give the women direct access to income and, perhaps, the boon of co-op membership in their own right: as bee-keepers on a part-time basis.

My interviews with the men showed their support for an activity that provided income to their wives. The women claimed that although their hours worked in agriculture had gone up since the co-op, most had always cultivated. Nevertheless, co-op technical assistance was directed solely to the male members, thereby confirming that even where women are traditional farmers, it's overwhelmingly the men who get the training and extension help (see, e.g., Ashby 1981; Berger, DeLancey, and Mellencamp 1984; Blumberg 1992; Saito and Weidemann 1990; Staudt 1978 and 1985).

In sum, the co-op had grown substantially, while the position of women had deteriorated. The Santiago experience indicates: (a) the importance of project delivery channels as "gatekeeper mechanisms" affecting women's access to benefits; (b) how fast the balance can tip against women when someone is not continuously "riding herd" on institutional policies and procedures as they differentially affect each gender; and (c) that benefits—especially valuable ones—have a tendency to be distributed on the basis of relative power and privilege, i.e., to "trickle up" over time. Where the initial target group consists of those on the bottom of the class pyramid, as these women are, they find it difficult to retain valuable benefits.

San Jose Pinula:
Women's Control of Income Benefits Them and Their Families

The situation of the women ALCOSA plant employees remained at least as strong in 1985 as it had been in 1980. Income remained high, due to long shifts (twelve hours or more during the eight to nine month "high season," for which ALCOSA paid the widely ignored minimum wage), and not one woman claimed that she was less than satisfied with the work. Much of their satisfaction was due to the economic benefits, which, in keeping with the hypotheses, continued to have strong positive repercussions for the women's power and decision-making leverage at home. The proportion of married women had gone up since 1980, but still not one woman turned over all of her pay to her husband. The data show that 93 percent of the sample (87 percent of the veterans and 100 percent of the newer workers) wanted to continue indefinitely with ALCOSA (83 percent even if they have more children).

Only 3 percent (one person) did all her housework; the others had delegated it to paid or unpaid other women or to their own children. Despite the standard seventy-two-hour workweek (that often exceeds eighty hours), only 20 percent consider their *total* workload "excessive." In contrast, 47 percent find it "supportable" and 33 percent find it "comfortable." (Total workload includes both ALCOSA and household labor.) Specifically, hours worked at ALCOSA are more than at their last job in 66 percent of the cases, equal in 14 percent, and *less* in 19 percent—the latter all having worked as domestic servants.

None of the women's income was less than 25 percent of total household income; 23 percent of the women's income was 25–50 percent; 40 percent of the women's income was 50–75 percent; and 37 percent of the women's income was more than 75 percent. In 83 percent of the cases, the woman herself decided how she wanted to spend her income, without consulting anyone. Although only 30 percent of the women failed to give some of their income to their parents (66 percent give to the mother), in only two cases of newlyweds did the women pool *any* of their income with their husbands. (Of nine cases of pooling income—two with the husbands and seven with parent(s)—only one woman pooled it all. The others put in only part.) But all with children used their earnings to support them (in keeping with H7). Thus, even for married women with children, the "single production function" model of the household would have been wrong: These women kept control of most or all their income.

ALCOSA income changed their economic situation. Previous to ALCOSA, 37 percent reported that their economic situation was *desperate;* 26 percent that their situation was *difficult;* and 37 percent that their situation was *comfortable.* Now, however, 70 percent had been able to make purchases beyond subsistence-level needs (e.g., furniture, appliances). Eighty-seven percent reported that their lives had changed. Economic/income was the overwhelming response, with greater liberty mentioned second most often. Confirming this, 87 percent reported that their economic situation had improved, and 13 percent stated that it had stayed the same; not one person reported a decline.

ALCOSA income changed their self-perception and perception by others. Eighty-two percent reported greater self-confidence than before, in keeping with H6. Many offered economic reasons, e.g., "I have the money to back me up." Eighty percent report greater independence (53 percent gave explicitly economic reasons). Sixty-seven percent report receiving greater respect from family members—again, economic reasons were often offered spontaneously.

Since the plant employed nearly 300 women during most of the year (75–85 percent of the labor force), wages earned there had a spread effect. Not only did the women pay for childcare, but a somewhat smaller proportion also paid for housework and/or laundry. Local women sold foods to the ALCOSA workers. There was now a rental market for rooms—one that had been only in the most rudimentary stage during the 1980 research.

By U.S. standards, ALCOSA's labor practices, working conditions, and minimum wage would not be particularly favorable. But for Guatemalan women, especially in a town caught between farming and urban/industrial growth during hard times, ALCOSA's jobs were a rare opportunity. Supervisors could afford to be very strict about "the right attitudes" (although this emerged as an implicit rather than an explicit demand in the interviews),[11] since many local women would be all too pleased to work for ALCOSA. A number of parents (mostly mothers) who sat in on their daughter's interview introduced younger daughters, mentioning hopes that they might also find employment at ALCOSA. Before the economic crisis, some parents viewed these jobs more ambivalently because of the "fast" reputation of the well-dressed and quite independent young women. But by 1985, economic need had proven more important than traditional cultural constraints.

Kusterer et al. found that the women's independence extended to their domestic arrangements: About one-fourth of the 1980 sample had changed their household more to their own liking, and only a fifth of the sample was married. In 1985, 27 percent of the thirty women interviewed were female household heads, but the proportion of "1980 veterans" married had risen considerably (to 47 percent from 21 percent). This marriage increase counters what could be a very powerful argument against allowing women to take jobs offering an ALCOSA level of return in double-standard Guatemala: that economic improvement for women leads them to forswear married life.

Fertility seems strongly curbed by ALCOSA employment. In 1985, almost half (14 out of 30) said they did not intend to have more children, and they had only an average of 2.6 at the median age of 33.5. In fact, the entire sample of thirty women (ages 18 to 39) averaged only 1.8 children. The median age of the fifteen women who are "1980 veterans" was 32.5 years. They had an average of 2.2 children each. Ten of the fifteen had given birth to a total of thirteen children since 1980 (three women had two children each and seven had one child each). Seven of the fifteen said that they would not have any more children.

By Guatemalan standards, these figures reflect a remarkably low level of childbearing. Compare these figures, for example, with those for Patzicia, the only village studied which had a substantial Ladina population. There, data were collected on the fertility of twenty women (including one single woman of 36 who was a childless full-time farmer with her own ALCOSA contract). Their median age was 33.5 (vs. 32.5 for the fifteen women ALCOSA "veterans"). But whereas the fifteen ALCOSA workers in San Jose Pinula averaged 2.2 children each, the twenty Patzicia women averaged 5.2 (5.5 excluding the woman ALCOSA contractor). The costs vs. benefits of children diverge sharply for female factory workers toiling long shifts vs. rural farm women, Table 5.2.

Furthermore, a total of nine of the thirty processing plant women are both single and childless: one (age 30) of the fifteen who were 1980 veterans and eight of the fifteen newer employees. Their median age (30 percent of the thirty) was 24 years, an extraordinary statistic by Guatemalan standards.

TABLE 5.2   Fertility Patterns among Women of ALCOSA and Patzicia

| Fertility Comparisons | ALCOSA Employees (N=30) | | | 20 Patzicia Women |
	1980	Newer	Total	
Median age	32.5	26.0	29.0	33.5
Mean Number of Children	2.2	1.5	1.8	5.2
Won't Have More	47%	47%	47%	No Info
Median Age	37.0	31.0	33.5	No Info
Mean Number of Children	2.3	3.0	2.6	No Info

A comparison of the 1985 data with the 1980 data for marital status provides another perspective on fertility patterns of the female ALCOSA plant workers, Table 5.3. Table 5.3 shows that women who had remained with ALCOSA (the "1980 veterans," the key group) had indeed been "at risk." A much higher proportion were married: 47 percent vs. 21 percent of the Kusterer 1980 sample and 20 percent of the newer employees. Only 7 percent of the veterans remained childless. The big news is that although these women were reproducing, they were doing so in moderation. Not one woman had more than two children under five, and, of course, five out of fifteen had none. The veterans were young enough (25 to 39) to have had considerably more children. The median age for the ten who had babies since 1980 is 30 versus 34 for the five who had not.

The quite low fertility of these women factory workers is related to the high cost of children—both financial and personal. For example, ten of the twenty-one women who had children mentioned that they paid for childcare (six paid relatives and four paid employees). In fact, all the women who gave reasons for intending not to have more children mentioned economic costs as a factor. As a mother of three almost wailed in response to the question of having more babies: "Aaaay, how much these children have cost me!"

In addition, single or married, these women had considerably more leverage to realize their fertility preferences than the average farming women (as per Hypothesis 3a). A frequent complaint from women with many children (who were economically dependent on their husbands) was that she did not want more but he did, so she would have to continue having babies. The only case among the

TABLE 5.3   Marital/Fertility Status of ALCOSA Women Workers

		1985 Data (%)		1980 Data (%)
	1980 Vets (N=15)	Newer Group (N=15)	Total (N=30)	Total (N=42)
Married w/Children	47	20	33	21
Single, No Children	7	53	30	38
Single, Widowed, Divorced w/Children	46	27	37	40
	100	100	100	100
Single w/Children	27	7	17	
Divorced w/Children	13	7	10	
Widowed w/Children	7	13	10	
	46	27	37	

ALCOSA factory women that seems initially similar reveals some significant differences. As my field notes report:

> The 32-year-old mother of seven had more children than anyone else interviewed (only one other had more than four children, in fact). Her youngest were three and two. More children? "I don't want to but because my husband wants them I have to continue." Do you use any birth control methods? "No, I am afraid of them." This was also the woman whose husband was most strongly opposed to her working. Yet she has steadfastly refused to quit. (She began in 1980.) She gives her husband nothing from her pay. Her money has given her independence: "Before I worked I wasn't allowed to go anywhere and he used to humiliate me." Now he just gives her children.

In sum, these women earned an income high enough to support their families on their own, if they so chose. They kept independent control of that income (only two newlyweds even pooled any part of their income with their husbands). Their income seemed to empower them in their personal relationships with spouses, parents, and children. It also gave them more leverage in household decision-making: not only in economic matters but also in fertility decisions and in domestic affairs (see Hypotheses 3a and 3b). In particular, the data lend support to Hypothesis 3a that independently controlled income from production gave them decision-making power over their reproduction. The decision to have further children was the woman's alone in 65 percent of the cases with data (thirteen out of twenty), primarily hers in another 5 percent, mutual in a further 10 percent, never discussed in 5 percent, and principally the male's in only 15 percent.

The economic basis of these women's household power came out repeatedly in the interviews. For example:

> One 37-year-old woman's common-law husband is an agricultural day laborer who therefore earns very little. She has been with ALCOSA since its beginning in 1975, and three of her four children are "ALCOSA babies" (ages seven, four, and two). A servant does the housework and childcare. She makes well over 75 percent (the top category) of total family income and pays not only for the household expenses (*"el gasto"*) and the servant but also for some of her husband's agricultural expenses. However, she gives nothing of her salary to him, controlling it all herself. She feels more independent and self-confident and receives more respect from her husband because she works for ALCOSA. She also has more power in the household as a result: "One has one's resources and says 'I can buy and do.'" Most tellingly, she now feels superior to the man—and at any rate: *"I am superior: I bring in the money and he takes me into account. If he wants to do something, he consults me first."*

While the final quote is more blatant than others were in asserting a woman's money-based power, the same patterns described above are found in much of the sample. Rather than disintegrating families, ALCOSA employment produces families where women have more say, especially over how income is spent, and where they play a key role in the "family survival strategy."

By the standards of women's work in Guatemala, the women of ALCOSA had a very positive situation.[12] By the standards of the research sites, this was the only one that provided direct benefits to women in 1985, and the consequences seemed, if anything, to be more positive than in 1980.

WID Lessons Learned

The situation in the research sites in 1985 proved very different from 1980. Patzicia revealed the substantial incorporation of women into cultivation. What had been a stubborn cultural tradition had been rapidly breached. On the positive side, this change indicates that "the dead hand of tradition" will not long sustain a restriction on women's productive activity that has become economically counter-productive in a time of economic crisis.[13] On the negative side, the change indicates that women's control of resources and benefits is a fragile thing in a society where they are subordinate, and their control may be quickly undermined. Such undermining can come from unplanned or very macro-level economic transformations and trends. Or, as per H9, it can occur as the unintended consequence of institutional policy shifts and/or choice of project delivery channels (e.g., what happened in Santiago Sacatepequez). Either way, the relative position of women vis-a-vis men, work, and resources is much more malleable than is often thought the case.

A second point is that (as posited in H4) work per se provides few benefits. Slaves, workers, and peasants have long labored without inheriting the earth or much of anything else. The women of Patzicia are unlikely to find that their harvesting work brings them much more leverage in major household economic decisions or much more status so long as they derive no income from their increased toil.[14]

Meanwhile, many of the women of Patzicia are working harder then ever before but are justifying it (vs. bemoaning their "double day" load) on the grounds that it should enhance family welfare. Except for the woman who lost her entire independent income (the woman who moved from Guatemala City to Patzicia), and unlike the women of Santiago Sacatepequez, Patzicia wives did not complain about lower earnings from market selling and correspondingly reduced household leverage. Rather, they saw themselves as contributing more, thus altering what seemed to be an immutable cultural tradition. As a result, they seemed to feel good—and a bit more important. Work in production does seem to be a first step on an often long and problematic journey whereby women gain a share in productive resources (or at least that universal solvent, income).

The data from all the various sites indicate support for the propositions that women's relative degree of independent control of economic resources/income (a) is more important than unpaid work in affecting their degree of control over their own lives (H4), and (b) seems to affect their family's as well as their own well-being (H3, H6, H7). This finding has relevance to the broader context of gender stratification theory (see, e.g., Blumberg 1984, 1991; Chafetz 1984 and 1990). In all the research sites, evidence indicated a direct connection between women's control of resources and their level of self-confidence, independence, and decision-making power.

However, women's loss of direct returns in Santiago Sacatepequez reveals that keeping benefits channeled to a subordinate population (ethnic, gender, class, etc.) requires commitment from administrators and project staff (see H8 and H9). If the subordinate population does not have an advocate who can assess the impact of even ostensibly "mere procedural" changes, their chances of keeping such benefits over time probably are not good. Apparently innocuous policy and procedural changes can turn out to be anything but (e.g., the shift in payment policy and procedures in the Santiago cooperative). Furthermore, there may well be some outright attempts to co-opt or coerce resources out of the hands of the subordinate population.

The ideal situation is one where it is in the interest of the dominant population to keep certain benefits among the more vulnerable group; for example, to head off social explosion. But women are rarely perceived as constituting an immediate and violent threat. More likely, women will be hired as at the ALCOSA plant (or *re*hired, as at the Santiago co-op) because they are more productive, as well as cheaper and more tractable, in doing certain tasks.

Breaking into the "Black Box" of the Household: Implications of the Findings

The data clearly show the existence of an "internal economy of the household" based on gender among the households included in the research. Among the Guatemalan Ladinos, as among most mestizo groups in Latin America, the norm that women are supposed to be economically dependent is fairly strong, even if practice is far different than official ideology. The norm manifests itself when asking a rural Latin American woman her occupation, or asking her husband what she does, a question which overwhelmingly elicits the answers of "housewife" or "domestic chores."

Although the dominant Ladino ideology holds that women should be economic dependents of men (among Indians, the prevailing ideology is more one of male-female partnership), when the ALCOSA women did, indeed, manage to earn income, they did not just hand it over to their husbands. The ALCOSA women were very explicit about keeping control of all or part of their income. Just how a woman allocates those monies is, de facto, her business if she earns income.

In the case of female market vendors (a predominant occupation for poor Guatemalan women), the woman's conversion of some of her own merchandise and profits into the best array of goods she can get is part of her entrepreneurial skill. Her husband would not have similar expertise, and she is not under his control when in the market. Indeed, a wife often also sells her husband's agricultural produce, and what she brings home to him may already have been spent first to enhance her own trading and purchasing.

The research also revealed the opposite side of the coin—the constriction of a woman's household power, decision-making input, and control over her own and her children's welfare—when she no longer has independently earned (and controlled) income. Only in cases such as that of the Ladina woman who became her husband's dependent when they moved, or where women were complete economic dependents of their husbands, could one legitimately speak of a unitary, pooling, "single production function" household.

Women who earned/controlled some income did contribute most of it to "family survival strategy." In all research sites, women emphasized that their ALCOSA-related work was done for their children and/or other family members. Women clearly received more leverage when at least some of the income and benefits went directly to them. In summary, a basic lesson of the present research is that when women create wealth and benefit from it, in a broader sense, we all gain. Especially in light of the evidence that income passing through women's hands has a more direct impact on family well-being (see, e.g., Blumberg 1988), it would seem that any paradigm concerned with any but the narrowest "Gross National Product/capita" definitions of development must take these intrahousehold effects into account.

So too, must the sociology of the family. Up until now, family sociology has been quite concerned with differential male/female power and has generally recognized women's earnings as a determinant of greater marital power (see, e.g., Blumberg and Coleman 1989; Blumberg 1991). But with few exceptions (e.g., Pahl 1989; Whitehead 1981), family sociology also has neglected the differential welfare consequences of how much income and power within the family are on the female vs. the male side.

In most of the Third World, economic necessity, rather than enlightenment, will be the driving force behind any shifts in state policy and practice that affect the treatment of gender and the family. As noted at the start of this paper, most Third World countries are relying increasingly on labor-intensive non-traditional exports—both industrial and Non-Traditional Agricultural Exports (NTAE) such as ALCOSA's broccoli and cauliflower. These countries tend to have large female labor forces, especially in processing operations. Hence, the probability is that the proportion of women doing work counted as productive—and income-generating—will continue to increase (Sivard 1985). Women's resultant gains may be slow and may be slowed further by backlash. But every new dollar under a woman's control represents one additional drop of solvent, slowly eating away at the economic foundation of patriarchy.

Notes

1. The editing aid of Catherine W. Berheide, Elaine Stahl Leo, Esther N. Chow, Huma Ahmed Ghosh, Lorna Lueker and Suzanne L. Willis is gratefully acknowledged.

2. This hypothesis was only in rudimentary form in 1985. Accordingly, data speaking to this proposition were collected only sparingly and qualitatively. Blumberg (1988 and 1989a) develops it more.

3. These women are rarely classed as economically active in Guatemalan data. Female activities are typically undercounted in Latin American national statistics (Wainerman and Recchini de Lattes 1981).

4. For a fuller description of RRA methodology and bibliography, see Beebe (1985) and Blumberg and Revere (1989).

5. Two bureaus of the U.S. Agency for International Development (A.I.D.) funded the research: (1) the Bureau for Latin America and the Caribbean (LAC); and (2) the Bureau for Program and Policy Coordination. It is also reported in Blumberg (1989c).

6. The 1980 and 1985 results for a third village, Chimachoy, are not reported in this paper because Chimachoy was a victim of the 1981–1982 peak of counterinsurgency violence. We found 40 widows among the 100 original families; most survivors had been moved to a "pacification village." Some 30,000–50,000, mostly poor Indians, died from 1979–1984 (Krueger and Enge 1985).

7. Blumberg (1984) and Blumberg (1989b) discuss these hypotheses in greater detail.

8. A woman claimed to have been shorted Q200 (about $200). The co-op paid, alleging that she was mistaken (her husband threatened to call in all authorities, including military). Despite a reorganization and resignations among accounting personnel the following year amid rumors of irregularities, the rationale for requiring husbands to pick up the money was that women are illiterate (although, as skilled market sellers, women's numeracy is not in doubt).

9. In a study of the coming of cash-crop sugar cane to a Belize village, Stavrakis and Marshall (1978, p. 158) found that the new income went for

men's priorities ("spent on drink, trucks, travel, and purchased female companionship"), and they saw little benefit to women and children.

10. Kennedy and Cowgill (1987), Kumar (1978), Senauer (1988), Stavrakis and Marshall (1978), and Tripp (1981) empirically document that children's nutrition is more closely associated with women's, not men's, income in Kenya, India, the Philippines, Belize, and Ghana respectively.

11. One control device involved the slack season. Some experienced workers worked "short weeks;" the rest were laid off. The supervisors recalled only the hard workers with "the right attitudes," a spur to both productivity and docility.

12. The standard of comparison used by these women must be kept in mind. Not only does ALCOSA pay the rarely honored minimum wage and benefits—thereby permitting women to make 150–300 percent of average female income (as market vendors, maids, etc.) by working long shifts—but the appearance of its facilities is attractive, with modern-looking plant buildings and well-tended grounds. However, hard work and long hours were required.

13. If the constraint on women's economic activity results only in less production/income, and the people have enough of a cushion of surplus to tolerate some inefficiency for the sake of preserving the gender status quo, the constraint will probably survive (e.g., women still aren't allowed to work with men—or even to drive—in Saudi Arabia, but in Kuwait, many economic restrictions on women were dropped during the desperate months of the Iraqi occupation).

14. See Acharya and Bennett (1983) for strong empirical support.

References

Acharya, Meena, and Lynn Bennett. 1981. *Women and the Subsistence Sector: Economic Participation in Household Decision-Making in Nepal.* Washington, DC: World Bank. Working Paper No. 526.

Ashby, Jacqueline. 1981. "New Models for Agricultural Research and Extension: The Need to Integrate Women." In *Invisible Farmers: Women and the Crisis in Agriculture*, edited by Barbara C. Lewis. Washington, DC: U.S. Agency for International Development, Office of Women in Development.

Becker, Gary. 1981. *A Treatise on the Family.* Boston: Harvard University Press.

Beebe, James. 1985. "Rapid Rural Appraisal: The Critical First Step in a Farming Systems Approach to Research." Networking Paper No. 5. Farming Systems Support Project. Gainesville, FL: University of Florida.

Berger, Marguerite, Virginia De Lancey, and Amy Mellencamp. 1984. *Bridging the Gender Gap in Agriculture Extension.* Washington, DC: International Center for Research on Women, U.S. Agency for International Development, Office of Women in Development.

Blumberg, Rae Lesser. 1983. "To What Extent Have Women Been Taken into Account in U.S. Foreign Aid in Latin America and the Caribbean? Clues from the 'Paper Trail' of Agency for International Development Projects." Washington, DC: Agency for International Development, Bureau for Latin America and the Caribbean.

———. 1984. "A General Theory of Gender Stratification." In *Sociological Theory 1984*, edited by Randall Collins. San Francisco: Jossey-Bass.

———. 1988. "Income Under Female vs. Male Control: Hypotheses from a Theory of Gender Stratification and Data from the Third World." *Journal of Family Issues* 9(1):51–84.

———. 1989a. *Making the Case for the Gender Variable: Women and the Wealth and Well-Being of Nations.* Washington, DC: U.S. Agency for International Development.

———. 1989b. "Toward a Feminist Theory of Gender and Development." In *Feminism and Sociological Theory*, edited by Ruth Wallace. Newbury Park, CA: Sage.

———. 1989c. "Work, Wealth and a Women in Development 'Natural Experiment' in Guatemala: The ALCOSA Agribusiness Project in 1980 and 1985." In *Women in Development. A.I.D.'s Experience, 1973–1985. Vol. II. Ten Field Studies*, edited by Paula O. Goddard. Washington, DC: Agency for International Development, Center for Development Information and Evaluation.

———. 1991. *Gender, Family, and Economy: The Triple Overlap.* Newbury Park, CA: Sage.

———. 1992. "African Women in Agriculture: Farmers, Students, Extension Agents, Chiefs." Morrilton, AR: Winrock International Institute for Agricultural Development. Development Studies Paper Series.

Blumberg, Rae Lesser, and Marion Tolbert Coleman. 1989. "A Theory-Guided Look at the Gender Balance of Power in the American Couple." *Journal of Family Issues* 10(2):225–250.

Blumberg, Rae Lesser, and Elspeth Revere. 1989. *Guatemala's Urban Microenterprise Multiplier System (SIMME): 1989 Program Appraisal.* Washington, DC: Management Systems International, USAID/Guatemala.

Carloni, Alice Stewart. 1987. *Women in Development: A.I.D.'s Experience, 1973–1985. Vol. I. Synthesis Paper.* Washington, DC: Agency for International Development. A.I.D. Program Evaluation Report No. 18.

Chafetz, Janet Saltzman. 1984. *Sex and Advantage: A Comparative, Macro-Structural Theory of Sex Stratification.* Totowa, NJ: Rowan and Allenhold.

———. 1990. *Gender Equity.* Newbury Park, CA: Sage.

Dwyer, Daisy Hilse. 1983. "Women and Income in the Third World: Implications for Policy." New York: Population Council. International Program Working Paper No. 18.

Dwyer, Daisy Hilse, and Judith Bruce, eds. 1988. *A House Divided: Women and Income in the Third World.* Stanford, CA: Stanford University Press.

Kennedy, Eileen T., and Bruce Cowgill. 1987. *Income and Nutritional Effects of the Commercialization of Agriculture in Southwestern Kenya.* Washington, DC: International Food Policy Research Institute. Research Report No. 63.

Krueger, Chris, and Kjell Enge. 1985. *Security and Development Conditions in the Guatemalan Highlands.* Washington, DC: Washington Office on Latin America.

Kumar, Shubh K. 1978. "Role of the Household Economy in Child Nutrition at Low Incomes: A Case Study in Kerala." Occasional Paper No. 95 (December). Ithaca, NY: Cornell University, Department of Agricultural Economics.

Kusterer, Kenneth C., Maria Regina Estrada de Batres and Josefina Xuya Cuxil. 1981. *The Social Impact of Agribusiness: A Case Study of ALCOSA in Guatemala.* Washington, DC: U.S. Agency for International Development, Bureau for Program and Policy Coordination, A.I.D. Evaluation Special Study No. 4.

Lenski, Gerhard E. 1966. *Power and Privilege: A Theory of Social Stratification.* New York: McGraw-Hill.

Pahl, Jan. 1989. *Money and Marriage.* London: Macmillan.

Saito, Katrine, and Jean Weidemann. 1990. "Agricultural Extension for Women Farmers in Africa." Washington, DC: World Bank, Policy and External Affairs Working Papers, Office of Women in Development.

Senauer, Benjamin. 1988. "The Impact of the Value of Women's Time on Food and Nutrition." Minneapolis-St. Paul: University of Minnesota, Department of Agricultural and Applied Economics. Draft.

Sivard, Ruth. 1985. *Women—A World Survey.* Washington, DC: World Priorities.

Staudt, Kathleen A. 1978. "Agricultural Productivity Gaps: A Case Study of Male Preference in Government Policy Implementation." *Development and Change* 9:439–457.

———. 1985. *Agricultural Policy Implementation: A Case Study from Western Kenya.* West Hartford, CT: Kumarian Press.

———. 1987. "Uncaptured or Unmotivated? Women and the Food Crisis in Africa." *Rural Sociology* 52(1):37–55.

Stravrakis, Olga, and Marion Louise Marshall. 1978. "Women, Agriculture and Development in the Maya Lowlands: Profit or Progress." Tucson, AZ: *Proceedings* of the International Conference on Women and Food, University of Arizona.

Tripp, Robert. B. 1981. "Farmers and Traders: Some Economic Determinants of Nutritional Status in Northern Ghana." *Journal of Tropical Pediatrics* 27:15–22.

Wainerman, Catalina H., and Zulma Recchini de Lattes. 1981. *El Trabajo Femenino en el Banquillo de los Acusados: La Medicion Censal en America Latina.* Mexico: The Population Council.

Wallerstein, Immanuel. 1974. *The Modern World System.* New York: Academic Press.

Whitehead, Ann. 1981. "I'm Hungry, Mum: The Politics of Domestic Budgeting." In *Of Marriage and the Market*, edited by Kate Young, Carol Wolkowitz, and Roslyn McCullagh. London: CSE Books.

Part II

Strategic and Practical Gender Interests,
Families, and Policies

❦ Chapter 6 ❦

Controlling Less Land, Producing Less Food: The Fate of Female-Headed Households in Malawi

Catherine White Berheide
and
Marcia Texler Segal

Many people regard patriarchy as a form of relationship between men and women within a household. Increasingly, though, scholars see patriarchy as a form of relationship among people of various gender, age, race, and class categories within institutions beyond the household as well (Reskin and Roos 1990; Tinker 1990). The state and the economy are critical locuses of patriarchal control throughout the world, particularly over female heads of households (Walby 1990). Thus, the state and the economy as well as the family and gender relations determine the fate of female-headed small-holders in Malawi.

As Walby (1990, p. 197) notes, while female heads of households "lose their own individual patriarch, they do not lose their subordination to other patriarchal structures and practices. . . . Their income and standard of living are . . . determined . . . either by the patriarchal state . . . or the patriarchally structured labor market." Public patriarchy substitutes for private patriarchy in controlling female heads of households. Specifically, in Malawi, women-peripheral state policies which favor rural development and inhibit urban migration place limits on the economic opportunities of small-holder households, especially female ones. Furthermore, state policies determine that access to credit and extension services varies by gender. Finally, virtually exclusive domination of the cash economy, both formal and informal, by males and the relative lack of educational opportunities afforded to females further reduce the alternatives available to women.

The economy and the state, both of which are highly gendered macro-level institutions, shape the division of labor at the micro-level within small-holder households. Worldwide households do not view labor as an impersonal commodity, nor do they view the labor of different family members as interchangeable. Studies of farm households in the United States (for example, Simpson, Wilson, and Young 1987) find that the demands of integrating off- and on-farm activities produce different divisions of labor by gender. These new arrangements vary with, among other variables, the demands of different crops. Further, divisions of labor in farm households are dynamic, changing in response to altered structural and economic conditions, as the changing role of women in cash crop cultivation in Patzicia, Guatemala, illustrates (see Blumberg, preceding chapter). The differences in men's and women's work and family activities socially construct gender in any particular society.

Class differences create further variations. Garrett (1984, p. 2) argues that how "smallholders organize their enterprises for commodity and subsistence production varies by social strata." In Ecuador, Garrett identifies three strata among small-holders: peasants who produce primarily for subsistence, use mainly family labor, and sell only their surplus; petty commodity producers who use more hired labor and produce primarily for sale; and semi-proletarians for whom household production is supplementary to income earned through off-farm employment. Peasants rely more heavily on the productive labor of women and children. Petty commodity production uses hired male labor which implies the semi-proletarianization of other households. Hiring male labor may free the women in these households for other activities such as craft production, and free children for formal education. Semi-proletarian families depend upon the sale of labor to substitute for home production. If the labor sold can produce more resources this way, this pattern may be an efficient adaptation. However, semi-proletarianization may shift the burden of farm production almost entirely to women and children or even create a situation where some or all family members must engage in both paid labor and subsistence crop production to ensure family survival. Thus these class differences may have positive consequences for women in petty commodity households but negative ones for those in peasant and semi-proletarian households.

Malawi offers an opportunity to examine the relationships among the family, the economy, the state, and gender under conditions which are not widely replicated. It is a capitalist economy influenced by British colonial rule. As in most sub-Saharan African nations, women traditionally participate extensively in farming. Malawi is ethnically diverse; significantly, about a third of its population has matrilineal and matrilocal traditions. The government discourages permanent rural to urban migration and industrialization. National policy emphasizes rural development through expanding production on both small-holder and estate farms of cash crops such as tea, coffee, tobacco, and maize.

Incorporation into the global economy is transforming the social structures of Malawi and other former colonial societies. To understand the process and patterns of that transformation, both the former structures and the emergent ones must be viewed as gendered. The gendered nature of the economy, the family, and the state produces significant differences in the lived experiences of women and men, including institutionalized differences in their access to resources. In other words, these societies were and are stratified, and the older forms of resource allocations, including patriarchy, shape those just coming into being (Awe, Geiger, Mba, Mbilinyi, Meena, and Strobel 1991).

Some Background

This chapter compares the approximately one-third of Malawi's small-holder households headed by women with those headed by men. The systematic differences suggest that distinct small-holder strata similar to those Garrett identifies for Ecuador are emerging in Malawi. Whether a household adopts the peasant, petty commodity, or semi-proletarian pattern is, at least in part, a function of its gendered division of labor and of gendered opportunity structures created by the economy and the state.

In Malawi, as elsewhere, small-holders are independent farmers who produce both subsistence and cash crops on their own land. Geographical location influences the crops they can cultivate. Malawi reserves certain areas for small-holder farming; therefore, the state does not confine small-holders, as a class, to marginal land. People cannot buy land in these areas; family heads, village heads, or traditional courts accord usage rights in a manner consistent with pre-colonial traditions.

Normative definitions of "household" and "family" vary from one culture to another. Given a pre-colonial mix of matrilineal and patrilineal traditions and the influences of Christianity, Islam, and British colonial rule, multiple normative patterns exist in Malawi. Traditionally, in matrilineal areas, men control the resources but those resources are vested in mothers' or wives' family lines. In such communities, the wife's family or the husband's mother's brother gives a married couple land to farm. In other communities, control of resources and residence are patrilineal and patrilocal. Both matrilineal and patrilineal traditions have continued into the colonial and postcolonial periods, but where people live today is often a matter of convenience or of access to land.

Research Methods and Concepts

To provide adequate data bases for planning and evaluating projects involving women, the Malawian government has begun to disaggregate some of its statistics by gender, including by gender of head of household (see Spring 1983, 1984). This chapter uses data from the 1983–1984 Sample Survey of Agriculture, which is based on a representative sample (N = 3,749) of the more than 1,100,000 small-holder households in Malawi.[1]

The households enumerated by the Annual Sample Survey of Agriculture (ASSA) are residential units, either single dwellings or compounds, that control specific segments of agricultural land. The land may be broken into several plots, all of which are controlled by the same unit. Unit members define who the permanent residents are, but some may be away at work or school at any given time. The core of the residents are parents and children. A polygynous man is defined as a member of the household of each of his wives.

The Status of Female-Headed Households

Women headed 31.6 percent of Malawi's small-holder households in 1983–1984 (see Table 6.1). However, headship is, in part, a product of government land registration and agricultural support policies requiring or favoring households headed by men (Rogers 1980; Spring 1986). In some instances, enumerators may also have assumed that resident adult males were the heads of households. Thus, the survey may be undercounting female-headed households.

Farm Club Membership

The Malawi government initiated farmer clubs as a means of organizing farmers for participation in state and donor agency-sponsored pro-

Table 6.1 Club Membership by Gender of Household Head in 1983–1984

Type of Household	Gender of Household Head		
	Male	Female	Total
% of All Households	68.4	31.6	100.0
% of Club Households	85.9	14.1	100.0
% Club Member	20.9	7.6	
% Non-member	79.1	92.4	
Total	100.0	100.0	

grams. Membership brought access to important resources and information, including increased support from agricultural extension services (Spring 1986) and better access to credit and agricultural inputs (i.e., fertilizer and seed), in part because the state thought farm club members were better risks.

Only 20.9 percent of male-headed households (MHHs) and 7.6 percent of female-headed households (FHHs) belonged to farm clubs. The smaller proportion of female-headed club households was, at least in part, a legacy of a policy in effect at that time: A household's land had to be registered in a man's name (that is, the household had to have a de jure, if not de facto, male head) to be eligible to participate in a club (Spring 1984).[2] While men might obtain credit individually or through a club, women needed club membership to obtain credit or to gain entry into some development projects. Thus the state's policy restricted their opportunities for moving beyond subsistence-level farming by channeling the necessary resources to a select group of men.

Land, Livestock, and Labor

In addition to differing by the gender of the head of the household and by membership in farmer clubs, small-holder households also differed by the size of their land and livestock holdings, the size and gender ratio of their membership, their labor capacity, their hiring of non-family labor, and their allocation of time to productive activities on- and off-farm. FHHs farmed less land than MHHs (see Table 6.2). Their mean holding size was .91 hectares or 2.27 acres compared to 1.32 hectares or 3.30 acres for male-headed households. Thus, females' holdings averaged 68.9 percent of males'. Lack of sufficient land is one

Table 6.2 Selected Economic and Demographic Characteristics of Small-Holder Households by Type of Household in 1983–1984

	Household Head		Club Membership			All Households
Characteristic	Male	Female	Non-Member	Member	FHH Member	
% All Households	68.4	31.6	82.9	17.1	2.2	100
Holding Size*	1.32	.91	1.07	1.80	1.34	1.16
Annual Income**	K254	K166	K203	K347	K263	K225
% Calories Met	74.8	67.7	67.2	97.0	87.6	68.7

   * In hectares.

  ** In Kwachas. At that time K1.00 = $.60 U.S.

factor that leads men to leave their household to seek work elsewhere (UNICEF 1987). As Table 6.2 indicates, female-headed club households farmed larger land holdings (1.34 hectares) than the average small-holder household (1.16 hectares), but not as large as the average club household (1.80). Farm club membership policies favor the female-headed households with the most land.

Similarly, FHHs generally owned less livestock (predominantly cattle and goats) than male-headed households. The male average was 3.54 head compared to 1.85 head of livestock for females (see Table 6.3). By contrast, female-headed club households generally had more livestock (6.90 head) than any other type of household because they often specialized in raising livestock. Although women generally had less access to club membership, in some instances special clubs were created for them. For example, in the Ngabu Agricultural Development District, they were virtually the only farmers in the country raising pigs, and they also had sizable herds of cattle and goats. In Liwonde District, female-headed club households raised sheep. Tinker (1990, p. 43) argues that such women-only programs isolate and marginalize women. In contrast to farm clubs designed for men which concentrated on cash crop production, the state was more likely to direct female farm clubs toward subsistence crop or small livestock production, thereby actually limiting this group of women's potential for upward mobility. Thus development programs may increase gender inequality as men move into the market economy and women are left behind in the labor-intensive subsistence economy (see also Acosta-Belen and Bose 1990; Boserup 1970; Fernandez Kelly 1989).

Table 6.3   Livestock Ownership by Type of Household in 1983–1984*

Type of Livestock	Household Head		Club Membership			All Households
	Male	Female	Non-Member	Member	FHH Member	
Cattle	1.34	.70	.99	1.61	2.37	1.16
Sheep	.10	.06	.14	.19	.35	.09
Goats	1.56	.88	1.24	2.14	2.63	1.36
Pigs	.54	.21	.37	.79	1.55	.45
Total	3.54	1.85	2.68	4.94	6.90	3.05

*Mean number of each type of livestock owned.

Differences in household structure and composition also produce differences in family well-being. Table 6.4 shows that while the average rural household contained almost five members, FHHs were, on the average, smaller than MHHs (3.9 members compared to 4.9). Both households averaged 2.5 female members, but FHHs, not surprisingly, included fewer male members (1.4 males compared to 2.7). Female-headed club households tended to have more males and slightly more females than the average FHH—2.6 males and 2.9 females. In short, female-headed farm club households had both more land and more people than did other female-headed households.

FHHs, as a direct consequence of their smaller size, had less family labor available than MHHs (1.65 "man equivalents" compared to 2.35 "man equivalents"), and women and children contributed more of the labor capacity in FHHs.[3] Club households generally had more labor capacity than non-club ones largely as a result of state policy favoring households with more resources, a policy which disproportionately disadvantaged female-headed households.

When a household had more members than it needed to farm its land, that household had unused labor capacity. At first glance, Malawi's small-holder sector appeared to have a great deal of surplus labor. Overall, the state considered around 60 percent of the potential rural labor unused. However, because farm work is seasonal, even households with a net surplus of labor may have experienced labor shortages during planting and harvesting seasons. Time not needed for cultivation is available for other pursuits. Women's and children's unused time could most readily be rechanneled into reproductive tasks, formal education, or leisure. Men's could be rechanneled into

Table 6.4   Size and Labor Capacity by Household Type in 1983–1984

Characteristic	Household Head		Club Membership			All Households
	Male	Female	Non-Member	Member	FHH Member	
Household Size						
Male	2.7	1.4	2.1	2.9	2.6	2.2
Female	2.5	2.5	2.3	3.0	2.9	2.4
Total	4.9	3.9	4.5	5.1	4.2	4.6
Labor Capacity*						
Male	1.51	.75	1.22	1.59	1.13	1.26
Female	.83	.89	.84	.89	.88	.86
Total	2.35	1.65	2.07	2.48	2.06	2.13
% Unused Labor Capacity*	57.9	66.9	63.4	43.2	52.6	63.5

*Labor capacity is expressed in "man-equivalents."

non-agricultural production, agricultural production at other locations, or leisure. (See Clark 1975 and Mueller 1985 for estimates of time allocation by different age and gender categories in Malawi and neighboring Botswana respectively.)

Small-holder farming created few opportunities for paid farm work. On the average, the farm households in this sample used very little hired labor, suggesting that most fell in the peasant class. Aggregate data, however, obscure the extent to which farmers with larger holdings did hire labor. As Table 6.5 indicates, FHHs hired less non-family labor (12 workdays per year compared to 21), so that they fell disproportionately in the peasant class.

Off-farm labor by resident members of households included work on neighboring farms as well as paid work in the formal and informal non-farm sectors. Table 6.5 reveals little difference in the amount of off-farm labor done by women in male- and female-headed households (21 workdays per year compared to 15), but a considerable difference in the amount of off-farm labor done by men. Males from FHHs worked 14 days on the average while those from MHHs worked an average of 81 days. Males in male-headed households were much more likely to work off-farm than were females, whose sources of employment were more restricted and who generally faced additional

Table 6.5   Sources of Income by Gender of Household Head in
1983–1984*

	Household Head	
Sources of Income	Male	Female
Gross Annual Income	K254	K166
Cash Value of Crops	K194	K136
Cash Value of Livestock Turnovers	K23	K13
Income from Remittances	K7	K9
In Cash	K6	K8
In Kind	K1	K2
Off-Farm Income	K19	K8
Paid Labor		
Off-Farm "Mandays"/Year		
Male Household Members	81	14
Female Household Members	21	15
On-Farm Hired Labor ("Mandays"/Year)	21	12

*All income data rounded to the nearest kwacha, which at this time was equal
to $.60 U.S.

responsibilities such as housework and childcare. Furthermore, the
larger MHHs contained more individuals available for outside
employment. These MHHs have moved closer to a semi-proletarian
class position. Thus FHHs are relatively disadvantaged in terms of
land, livestock, and labor, which helps to explain their extreme disadvantage in terms of income.

Income

In each of the three types of off-farm labor, female-headed households
earned less than male-headed households. They earned K4 compared
to K8 in self-employment, K4 compared to K11 in agriculture, and K7
compared to K18 in non-agricultural labor. As a result, MHHs reaped
the benefits of more days of off-farm labor. Although both FHHs and
MHHs earned only modest amounts off-farm, FHHs earned less. The
MHHs earned an average of K19 each year from local off-farm labor of

household members while FHHs earned an average of K8. These income data are another indicator that MHHs have moved a little closer to the semi-proletarian class than have FHHs.

Additional sources of income for rural households included remittances from family members working elsewhere. Even though the labor migration of adult males is responsible for creating rural households headed by females, the benefits to FHHs for male labor migration appeared to be minimal. Remittances, in cash or in kind, constituted a very minor portion of household incomes perhaps because over time, many men lose contact and "eventually the marriage ends in separation or divorce" (UNICEF 1987, p. 64). While FHHs averaged slightly higher remittances than MHHs from relatives working elsewhere (K7 for MHHs and K9 for FHHs), the difference was insignificant compared to the differences favoring MHHs from other sources of income. Most remittances were in cash (K6 out of K7 in MHHs and K8 out of K9 in FHHs) and the remainder in kind, such as food.

The majority (70 percent) of female household heads were unmarried, perhaps explaining why FHHs averaged about the same income from remittances as did MHHs. Married FHHs who had husbands engaged in migrant labor may, in fact, have received substantial income from that source. Since only about three in ten had non-resident husbands and the income they received was averaged over the entire group of FHHs, the contributions may have been obscured. The real effect of labor migration can only be measured by controlling for the existence of non-resident male members employed off-farm. Aggregation of data may have also obscured the importance of remittances in kind as sources of income in some households, particularly those in heavily matrilineal areas (cf. Hirschmann and Vaughan 1983).[4]

Because crop sales accounted for the bulk of gross income, holding size was a major determinant of income (M. T. Segal 1986b). FHHs realized, on the average, less income both from crops and livestock than did male-headed ones (see Table 6.5). The average cash value of the crops of FHHs was K136 compared to K194 for MHHs. Their livestock turnovers averaged K13 compared to K23 for MHHs. Not surprisingly, therefore, the FHHs had lower average gross annual incomes than MHHs (K166 or about $100 per year compared to K254 or about $152 per year). Table 6.2 also shows that the gross annual incomes of club FHHs were higher than those of other non-club FHHs (K263) and higher than those of male-headed ones as well, but not as high as the average club household (K347).

Another measure of the economic well-being of farmers was the ability to meet the household's caloric needs through agricultural production. As Humphrey's (1975) survey indicated, most families did not buy food. If subsistence crops proved inadequate, they would consume cash crops and slaughter livestock for food as well. Rather than use what little cash was available to buy food, they were more likely to use it to satisfy individual and household needs such as clothing and school fees. In 1983–1984, FHHs, with their smaller holdings, met a lower proportion of their caloric needs (67.7 percent) through their own crops than MHHs, who met 74.8 percent (see Table 6.2). By meeting 87.6 percent of their caloric needs, female-headed club households fared better than the average household regardless of sex of head, but not as well as the average club household (97 percent). While both types of FHHs faced food and cash shortages, the situation of non-club households was especially severe; they faced serious malnutrition. Thus in Malawi even the most successful female heads of households struggle and often fail to meet their families' basic needs.

Summary

In short, compared to those headed by males, female-headed households had fewer members, fewer male members, less family labor available, but more unused labor capacity because they farmed less land, less livestock, fewer off-farm work days, and less total income and income from off-farm work, crops, and livestock. Although these women control resource allocation, they have few resources to allocate. In contrast, with their larger holdings, FHHs that belonged to farmer clubs fared better economically than both the average FHH and the average MHH. Only 7.6 percent of FHHs belonged to clubs (see Table 6.1); the average club FHH did not have as much land or labor nor did it do as well economically as the average club household. Some club FHHs were either participating in projects designed specifically for them or had become club farmers as a condition for participation in particular projects.

Agricultural Experience and Participation in Extension Services

According to the National Statistical Office (1984, Table 1.9), 35.9 percent of male and 72.3 percent of female household heads had never attended school while only 8.4 percent and 1.8 percent respectively had completed the eight year primary school sequence. Female heads were also less likely to have received other types of training and experience. Less than one percent (0.7 percent) of female heads and 8.3 percent of male heads had formal vocational training, while 79.9 percent of male heads and 12.7 percent of their female counterparts had worked away from the farm for wages for at least one year (National Statistical Office 1984, Table 1.9). In particular, 24.6 percent of MHHs and 6.8 percent of FHHs had a year or more of experience as a farm worker on an estate farm, at an agricultural research station, or in the employ of a club or project small-holder.[5] Presumably these farmers acquired knowledge and skills which they can put to use on their own land (National Statistical Office 1984, Tables 1.9, 1.16).

As Bourque and Warren (1990, p. 84) note, "European colonial adminstrators, applying their own notions of appropriate gender roles, made men the preferred recipients of training by Western technicians, even in areas where women were the primary agriculturalists. As a result of the differential access of each sex to new technology, women's status declined." These data suggest that this pattern continues today. Table 6.6 indicates that FHHs had less contact with agricultural extension services than male heads (19.4 percent compared to 34.3 percent for MHHs). Surprisingly, female heads of club households were more likely than other club operators to have participated in some extension activity (81.5 percent compared to 70.9 percent for all club households). They were more likely to have received a personal visit from an extension agent (26.6 percent) or to have attended a meeting (62.3 percent), but less likely to have attended a day-long workshop (5.5 percent). Despite the fact that the state generally targeted development projects and extension services toward men, female heads of club households were more likely than any other category of household head to have had contact with these services.

Table 6.6 Contact with Extension Services by Type of Household in 1983–1984 (in percentage form)

	Household Head		Club Membership			All Households
Type of Contact*	Male	Female	Non-Member	Member	FHH Member	
Personal Visit	12.6	6.5	7.1	26.6	29.0	10.9
Meeting	28.1	15.9	16.1	62.1	62.3	24.7
Day Course	4.8	1.8	2.0	12.2	5.5	3.9
All Types*	34.3	19.4	21.3	70.9	81.5	30.2

*Multiple responses were permitted.

Other data indicated that nearly a quarter (23.2 percent) of male heads of households, 10.7 percent of the wives of male heads, and 8.4 percent of female heads had attended a training course (National Statistical Office 1984, Table 1.10). The fact that the wives of MHHs were more likely than FHHs to have attended a farm course may have reflected the greater difficulty a lone adult experiences, particularly a woman, in arranging to be away from the home and farm for one or more days. It may also have reflected the fact that men were repeatedly urged to encourage their wives' participation in certain kinds of activities (E. Segal 1986). Extension courses directed exclusively toward women featured a high proportion of homecraft content while those open to men and women focused more on crop or animal husbandry (Hirschmann 1984).

Spring (1984, p. 39) examined the content of advice given to male and female household heads and the wives of male heads in one project area. She found that extension services exposed men to more topics and that women were less likely than men to receive advice on any topic except home economics. Moreover, apart from home economics, wives were less likely than FHHs to receive advice on any given topic. Thus, for example, 76 percent of male heads, 63 percent of female heads, and 47 percent of wives received advice on crop husbandry while 64 percent of male heads, 43 percent of female heads, and 33 percent of wives received advice on credit. Mere access to education and training is insufficient for improving the lives of women and their families; the gendered content of the programs also needs to be transformed (Bourque and Warren 1990).

In short, the data show that female household heads had less education and training (especially agricultural) than their male counterparts. They were also less likely to receive information and advice about farming from agricultural extension services. Yet, the extent to which female heads of farm club households participated in extension activities shows that women were interested in the full range of information available. That these women were also among the most successful farmers suggests that the wives of MHHs as well as other female heads might also benefit from greater access to the advice given to club farmers. The patriarchal nature of state and donor agency projects rather than women's lack of interest and participation in them has intensified gender inequality in Malawi. Increasing women's access to these vital resources is necessary for improving their position. The expansion of services to women may occur whether planned or not. The World Bank notes that with the increase of de facto female-headed farms, more than 60 percent of actual extension contacts in Kenya are now with women (Gettinger 1990, p. 28).

Discussion and Conclusions

This chapter described the situations of male- and female-headed small-holder households, highlighting some of the conditions that limit women's lives. Generally, FHHs are disadvantaged relative to MHHs, and state policies, such as those regarding farm clubs and extension services, further disadvantage them. They lack education and training; they have less land and help available. Because they have responsibility for children and housekeeping, women cannot engage in regular or seasonal off-farm labor as easily as men, even if work were available. Their incomes from all sources are lower, and remittances from absent members appear to be insignificant sources of income for most. Their lack of resources limits their membership in farm clubs which would give them access to the credit and training that would in turn increase their productivity and their resources.

Malawi is becoming increasingly more stratified, with substantial differences between those rural households with larger land holdings and those with smaller ones. State and donor sponsored farmer clubs and programs designed to increase the quantity and the quality of produce favor larger land holders, thereby enabling them to become petty commodity producers. When these households, which are more likely to be male-headed, exhaust their already greater supply of family labor, they have the resources, including credit provided through farm clubs, to hire others. Households which can supply such labor are able to adopt the semi-proletarian pattern, retaining their own land for food, but working for pay to meet at least some non-food needs. Households that contain both male and female adult members and that control limited amounts of land can exercise this option; those with only a female adult are forced to continue to rely almost exclusively on the yield of their land.

Unless they are among the tiny proportion of women who have relatively large land holdings, female-headed households have little alternative but to follow the peasant pattern of subsistence production. There is only minimal demand (and that primarily on tea estates in the south) for female agricultural labor; and there is virtually no demand for female labor in Malawi's very small industrial and service sectors. In Malawi men dominate all paid labor, including domestic service. No unskilled jobs exist for which women are preferred. While jobs requiring education are not officially closed to women, nursing is the only profession reserved for them. Teaching in the lower primary grades is the only other profession with a substantial proportion of women. Therefore, peasant women have no realistic alternatives for improving their economic well-being except through agricultural and compatible pursuits.

To care for their members adequately, FHHs have to find ways to supplement crop production which are consistent with the other work and family demands. These could include selling or trading produce to acquire other necessities (something most peasants already do), as well as marketing handicraft items or prepared food (see Tinker's chapter on street food trade in this volume). Small business is an option for those who have sufficient capital. In areas where maize is the dietary staple, women often operate profitable grinding mills. Very small shops, often in people's homes or in lean-tos, sell everyday necessities such as sugar, salt, and soap. In addition, women who belong to farmer clubs have been experimenting with raising poultry and other small animals for sale. Women are now eligible to participate in cattle projects as well. Cattle can not only be marketed, they can also be used, and rented out, as draft animals. Everett (1989) warns, however, that involving women in development projects might meet their basic survival needs without changing the structural conditions which perpetuate gender inequality.

In summary, a comparison of male- and female-headed smallholder households in Malawi demonstrates that genderless concepts such as surplus labor and size of holding do not adequately describe the dynamics of households nor the economic opportunities open to them. Small-holders are no longer a single class of independent peasants. They are becoming differentiated into those who produce for sale as well as subsistence, those who supplement subsistence production with paid labor, and those who remain peasants. The probability of remaining a peasant household is higher for those households headed by women because their household divisions of labor are less flexible and their opportunities for paid work are more limited. Malawi's state policies give FHHs some access to land but deny them sufficient access to farm clubs and extension services. The gendered nature of development in Malawi affects male and female heads of households differently, even when both engage in agricultural production. Favoring men in development projects and in virtually all forms of work in the formal and informal economy relegates female-headed households to subsistence-level or even below subsistence-level standards of living, thereby ensuring women's continued subordination.

The patriarchal state and the patriarchally structured labor market that Walby (1990) describes limit women's opportunities in Malawi. Public patriarchy makes female-headed households "the poorest of the poor, exemplifying the phrase 'the feminization of poverty'" (Tinker 1990, p. 5). In Malawi as in the other least developed countries, if state and donor agencies are to ameliorate the living conditions of the poor, they must implement more women-centered projects that increase women's economic opportunities. More women-centered policies would promote the well-being of women and their families by enhancing both their practical and their strategic interests (Molyneux 1985; Staudt 1990).

Notes

1. Special thanks for helping us locate and process the ASSA data analyzed in this chapter are due A. T. Matemba, Malawi Commissioner for Census and Statistics, and S. V. Bussche, C. Machinjiri, W. R. Muelenbeld, and R. J. Wigmore of the National Statistical Office. M. T. Segal (1986a and 1986c) reports some of the data; the rest are unpublished.

2. The assumption behind this requirement was that male-headed small-holder households were more stable and would be more likely to produce cash crops than female-headed ones.

3. Malawi measured labor availability or capacity in "man days" or "man equivalents." This approach almost certainly under-valued the agricultural labor of women while ignoring the constraints posed by their other role obligations. This measure made several important assumptions. It assumed that when present, everyone—children and adults, females and males—contributed to household agricultural production. However, the calculations imputed rather than empirically demonstrated limitations imposed by strength and skills as well as by other role obligations. This measure estimated the agricultural productivity of adult female household members to be about 70 percent of that of adult male household members. It estimated adult males who were regularly employed off-farm to contribute 30 percent of the labor they would provide if they were full-time farmers, school children to contribute 10 percent of the labor of an adult male, and children not in school, 30 percent. It estimated polygynous males to contribute 50 percent of their labor to each household (Planning Division, Ministry of Agriculture, unpublished). Thus, the government counted two households of the same size but with different age and gender compositions as having different amounts of available labor. This approach assumed that those households consisting primarily of women and children, typically the situation in FHHs, had less available agricultural labor than households of the same size which included both sexes and a higher proportion of adults as was characteristic of MHHs. It is likely that when they are engaged in agricultural labor on their own holdings, women contribute as much, if not more, productive labor per given period as men. Their nonagricultural, reproductive labor is most likely performed in addition to, not instead of, productive labor. Men, largely free from family demands, can perform productive labor at more times and places.

4. Independent matrilocal FHHs receive food and similar in-kind remittances from parents and other relatives who live nearby. The pattern described

by Hirschmann and Vaughan is similar to American and Caribbean urban patterns that Stack (1974) and others report.

5. Estate farms are owned by individuals or corporations and are exclusively devoted to cultivating cash crops, such as tea or tobacco, primarily for export.

References

Acosta-Belen, Edna and Christine E. Bose. 1990. "From Structural Subordination to Empowerment: Women and Development in Third World Contexts." *Gender & Society* 4:299–320.

Awe, Bolanie, Susan Geiger, Nina Mba, Marjorie Mbilinyi, Ruth Meena, and Margaret Strobel, eds. 1991. *Women, Family, State, and Economy in Africa.* Chicago, IL: University of Chicago Press.

Boserup, Ester. 1970. *Woman's Role in Economic Development.* London: George Allen and Unwin.

Bourque, Susan C., and Kay B. Warren. 1990. "Access Is Not Enough: Gender Perspectives on Technology and Education." Pp. 83–100 in *Persistent Inequalities*, edited by Irene Tinker. New York: Oxford University Press.

Clark, Barbara A. 1975. "The Work Done by Rural Women in Malawi." *East African Journal of Rural Development* 8(1&2):80–91.

Everett, Jana. 1989. *The Global Empowerment of Women.* Washington, DC: Association for Women in Development.

Fernandez Kelly, M. Patricia. 1989. "Broadening the Scope: Gender and International Economic Development." *Sociological Forum* 4:611–635.

Garrett, Patricia. 1984. "Agricultural Research and Development: Variable Objectives for Smallholder Programs." Paper presented at Farming System Research Symposium. Kansas State University, Manhattan, KS, October.

Gittinger, J. Price. 1990. "Household Food Security and the Role of Women." World Bank Discussion Paper No. 96. Washington, DC: The World Bank.

Hirschmann, David. 1984. *Women, Planning and Policy in Malawi.* Addis Ababa: U.N. Economic Commission for Africa.

Hirschmann, David, and Megan Vaughan. 1983. "Food Production and Income Generation in a Matrilineal Society: Rural Women in Zomba, Malawi." *Journal of Southern African Studies* 10(1):86–99.

Humphrey, David H. 1975. "Socio-Economic Aspects of Rural Development in Malawi: A Report of Some Survey Findings." *East African Journal of Rural Development* 8(1&2):45–60.

Molyneux, Maxine D. 1985. "Mobilization without Emancipation? Women's Interests, State, and Revolution in Nicaragua." *Feminist Studies* 11:227–254.

Mueller, Eva. 1985. "The Value and Allocation of Time in Rural Botswana." Pp. 27–76 in *The Household Economy of Rural Botswana: An African Case.* World Bank Staff Working Paper No. 715. Washington, DC: The World Bank.

National Statistical Office. 1984. *National Sample Survey of Agriculture 1980/81.* Zomba, Malawi: The Government Printer.

Planning Division, Ministry of Agriculture. Unpublished. "Scheme for Calculating Labour Availability by Assigning a Coefficient by Comparison with a Fully Available Adult Male." Zomba, Malawi.

Reskin, Barbara F., and Patricia A. Roos. 1990. *Job Queues, Gender Queues: Explaining Women's Inroads into Male Occupations.* Philadelphia, PA: Temple University Press.

Rogers, Barbara. 1980. *The Domestication of Women: Discrimination in Developing Societies.* New York: St. Martin's Press.

Segal, Edwin S. 1986. "Women, Children and Families: Public Ideology in Malawi." Paper presented at the North Central Sociological Association Meetings, Toledo, OH, April.

Segal, Marcia Texler. 1986a. "Work-Family Systems of Malawi's Small-Holder Households: An Analysis of Data from the 1983–1984 ASSA." [Malawi] *Journal of Social Science* 13:104–123.

———. 1986b. "Women as Progressive Farmers: A Malawi Example." Paper presented at the African Studies Association Meetings, Madison, WI, October.

———. 1986c. "Land and Labor: A Comparison of Female- and Male-Headed Households in Malawi's Small-Holder Sector." WID Forum X. East Lansing, MI: Michigan State University.

Simpson, Ida Harper, John Wilson, and Kristina Young. 1987. "The Sexual Division of Farm Household Labor: A Replication and Extension." Paper presented at the American Sociological Association Meeting, Chicago, IL, August.

Spring, Anita. 1983. "Disaggregating National Agricultural Data by Sex in Malawi: Progress to Date and a Proposal." Paper presented at the Association for Women in Development Conference: A Decade of Experience, Washington, DC, October.

———. 1984. *Profiles of Men and Women Smallholder Farmers in the Lilongwe Rural Development Project, Malawi.* Final Report of the Women in Agricultural Development Project in Malawi. Submitted to the Office of Women in Development, USAID, Washington, DC.

———. 1986. "Men and Women Smallholder Participants in a Stall-Feeder Livestock Program in Malawi." *Human Organization* 45(2):154–161.

Stack, Carol. 1974. *All Our Kin: Strategies for Survival in a Black Community.* New York: Harper & Row.

Staudt, Kathleen, ed. 1990. *Women, International Development, and Politics: The Bureaucratic Mire.* Philadelphia, PA: Temple University Press.

Tinker, Irene. 1990. *Persistent Inequalities: Women and World Development.* New York: Oxford University Press.

UNICEF and Government of Malawi. 1987. *The Situation of Women and Children in Malawi.* Lwongwe, Malawi.

Walby, Sylvia. 1990. *Theorizing Patriarchy.* Cambridge, MA: Basil Blackwell.

❦ Chapter 7 ❧

The Urban Street Food Trade: Regional Variations of Women's Involvement

Irene Tinker

Selling ready-to-eat food along the streets is a ubiquitous activity in cities around the world. Women visibly dominate this street food trade in such diverse countries as Nigeria, Senegal, Thailand, and the Philippines where they sell local varieties of breakfast porridge, or tea with sweets, or meals of noodles, rice, or cornmeal topped with vegetable and meat sauces. In contrast, men sell the fried soybean cakes to school children in Indonesia, hawk lentil-rice snacks at Bangladesh bus stops, or provide falafel to hungry Egyptians.

It is hard to visualize an urban center in the developing world without these colorful vendors; what is more, they are an established presence even in "developed" cities such as Los Angeles, New York City, or Washington, DC. The pervasiveness of street food vendors clearly suggests their crucial role in feeding the urban populace. What may be less obvious, however, is that the street food trade is also a critical element in the survival strategies of the urban poor, and especially of women.

The study of the urban street food trade described in this chapter has provided important comparative data on how women and their families secure their livelihood, and the extent to which government policies or development programs assist or impede this enterprise. More specifically, this study illustrates the varied influences of culture and patriarchy on women's economic responsibility for, and power

163

within, their families. This study has also shown how the confusing tangle of urban policies which formally and informally regulate street food vendors replicates the contradictions within both development theory and practice with regard to these micro-entrepreneurs. Thus, this study makes clear how both the structures of the family and the policies of government affect the functioning of the trade and the implementation and outcomes of programs designed to increase incomes among the urban poor.

The first section of this chapter sets the context for examining women's roles in the street food trade by examining the family setting for these women entrepreneurs and then by reviewing the development theories and policies that have treated micro-entrepreneurial activities such as the street food trade as marginal and dispensable. The second section presents data drawn from the Street Foods Project of the Equity Policy Center (EPOC) which initiated studies in provincial cities in seven developing countries in Asia and Africa between 1982 and 1985: Iloilo, Philippines; Bogor, Indonesia; Chonburi, Thailand; Manikganj, Bangladesh; Minia, Egypt; Ile-Ife, Nigeria; and Ziguinchor, Senegal. A brief overview of the street food findings is followed by an analysis of women's involvement in preparing and selling street foods, and the impact of government policy on street vendors. Utilizing these findings, I will argue that the theories both about family and economic development have obscured reality. As a result, the importance of women's economic activities for family survival and the impact they have on intra-household dynamics have been denigrated and undervalued.

The Context

Family

Both culture and history influence the gender relationships observed by the street vendor families and help explain the wide variations in women's involvement in the seven countries EPOC studied. The explanatory power of class differences within any given country are more problematical, especially where social stratification is weak. Together culture, history, and class combine to produce distinct patterns in the distribution of power and responsibility within the family. These patterns predict how the street food enterprise in each country is established and run.

The seven countries under discussion represent three widely different types of gender relationships: Bangladesh and Egypt are part of the patriarchal belt that extends across North Africa and encompasses

West, South, and East Asia; Senegal and Nigeria reflect the separate-budget culture of Africa south of the Sahara; the remaining three countries, Thailand, Indonesia, and the Philippines, depict a Southeast Asian pattern that is distinct from the other two categories.

Some feminist theoreticians might consider all these systems "patriarchal" because, in the ideal, the husband acts as head of the intact family while divorced, widowed, or single women are controlled and protected by male relatives. Such an over-generalization, however, would mask clear differences among these types of gender systems as to women's autonomy, economic responsibilities, and physical freedom. Using the term "patriarchy" to apply to any form of male dominance "obfuscates rather than reveals" intrahousehold dynamics, according to Kandiyoti (1985). She suggests that "women strategize within a set of concrete constraints that reveal and define the blueprint of what I will term the 'patriarchal bargain' of any society" that women strike "to maximize security and optimize life options . . . " (1988, pp. 274–275).[1] Essentially, Kandiyoti argues that women under patriarchy negotiate a balance between economic and physical security and greater autonomy.

This trade-off between protection and freedom is challenged by Egyptian scholar Sarah Loza. She maintains that women have *more* autonomy within a benevolent patriarchal family than they would living and working independently in the unfriendly urban streets (see Tinker 1990, p. 12). This opinion is reflected by many young middle-class Egyptian women who are choosing to wear that symbol of patriarchy, the veil, which they insist gives them both greater protection and freedom of movement. Such diverse views simply illustrate the complexity and variety of patriarchal bargains.

What does seem to be common across cultures, however, is the relationship between the material basis of the family and the amount of protection it can offer to women. The more that women contribute to the economic support of the family, the stronger their bargaining power. The phenomenal rise of women-headed households worldwide indicates both women's economic prowess and the collapse of family support systems. At what point does family disintegration take place? Is there a difference among types of patriarchal systems that predicts the point in time when the "bargain" breaks down? Are women vendors independent heads of households or do they function within some type of exploitative patriarchal family system? Would development program support to women vendors result in their working longer hours for no obvious benefit, an outcome that in fact happened when improved fertilizer increased men's crops and required more time weeding by their wives (Agarwal 1985; Kandiyoti 1985), or when women's new income simply has meant that their husbands contributed less to the household budget? Or would women be able to utilize their added income to improve the nutrition or living standards of their family members (Dwyer and Bruce 1988; Senauer 1990)? Thus, family composition as well as the control of labor and income within the family become critical aspects of the study.

Development Theory

For years the street food trade, like other micro-enterprises, was generally dismissed as insignificant economic activity by development economists. Both Marxist and liberal economists believed that such petty trading was a holdover from earlier economic systems and would disappear as development proceeded. Instead, vendors are in fact increasing in variety and numbers as rural migrants flood the cities of the developing world. As a result, scholars began to rethink and redefine the myriad of economic activities that take place outside the formal sector, particularly in urban areas. The impetus to undertake studies of the informal sector came from the International Labor Organization (ILO) which realized from its projections for global industrialization that the goal of the World Employment Program of 1969 for full employment could not be attained solely through work in the formal sector.

These early studies provoked a heated scholarly debate between proponents of Marxism and of liberal economics who saw the informal sector respectively as exploitative or as opportunity.[2] Further, since according to both perspectives the informal sector was expected to disappear in the wake of modernization, scholars were forced to reinterpret both theories to account for the persistence of these economic activities.[3] Today there is widespread recognition that informal sector enterprises are not only a permanent feature of contemporary economies but that the increasing informalization of existing formal sector firms has added to their numbers. While the scholarly debate continues about the desirability of such trends, industry continues to adapt to changes in the global economy by inventing new forms of relationships between formal and informal enterprises.[4]

The new respectability of the informal sector did not, however, extend to micro-entrepreneurs. These tiny enterprises were largely excluded from the ILO research because, as one-person or family activities, they were judged as too small to grow and employ others. ILO economists often characterized such entrepreneurs as the "community of the poor" (House 1984). Thus women entrepreneurs, who tend to be clustered at the smallest end of the informal sector, remained invisible.

Parallels to the invisibility for planners of women's work in rural areas are obvious. Women's work in subsistence agriculture was reflected neither in definitions (Beneria 1980) nor in statistics (Dixon 1983). As a result of women's statistical invisibility, stereotypes of women's lack of economic contribution were perpetuated and development programs were designed that focused on men, undercutting and undervaluing women's work (Boserup and Liljencranz 1975; Tinker 1976). During the 1970s, stimulated by the second wave of the women's movement and given legitimacy by the U.N. Decade for Women: 1976–1985, scholars documented women's economic roles in developing countries (Boserup 1970; Sullerot 1971; Wipper 1972), advocates translated these data into policy (Tinker 1983), and practitioners began to redesign women's programs to recognize women's roles in agriculture and crafts. Together they created the field of women in development (Tinker 1990).

The legacy of these beliefs about the informal sector continues to influence policies toward micro-entrepreneurs in many ways. The wide variety of economic pursuits classed under the vague terminology were ignored for many years; yet even after scholars began to study these enterprises, women's work continued to be overlooked. Today, literature on women's work as micro-entrepreneurs both in home-based industry and in street vending is growing. It is written primarily by women and not yet well integrated into mainstream thinking (Banerjee 1991; Beneria and Roldan 1987; Grown 1989; Otero 1990; Singh and Kelles-Viitanen 1987). This lack of attention to micro-enterprises reinforced stereotypes of these activities as low-paying, dead-end jobs of trivial economic importance and so masked the contribution they made to income and food distribution for urban populations in developing countries.

Development Policy

Without data to justify programming, planners for many years left micro-enterprise development out of their projections. Attitudes began to change as the development community became increasingly concerned with the growing disparity of incomes in developing countries and shifted the priorities of assistance programs during the Second Development Decade from infrastructure projects to the provision of basic needs. Many international non-governmental organizations (NGOs) began to move beyond the provision of food aid by setting up programs to help the poor earn an income. These programs often focus on "income-generating" activities for women's groups. Lacking an understanding of economic forces, however, many of these income-generating programs suffered from middle-class stereotypes concerning women's "appropriate" activities, that is, knitting, weaving, or sewing.[5] Such an approach narrowed the available occupations and often resulted in a glut on the market of Bangladesh jute bags, Kenya baskets, or Peruvian alpaca sweaters. Because economic considerations such as demand for the goods produced or the method and cost of marketing were seldom researched, this type of project became identified with welfare, not income.

Gradually, information began to circulate about innovative poverty programs devised by indigenous NGOs: SEWA (Self-Employed Women's Association) in Ahmedabad, India, instituted a bank for women employed as street vendors or in home-based enterprises; the Grameen Bank in Bangladesh originated a system to offer loans to landless women and men with no business experience. Donors began to replicate these credit programs for the poor, even in the United States (Sirola 1991). Critics continue to argue that such programs create dependence through welfare attitudes and are much too costly to replicate. Rather, they advocate lower cost programs that provide training, technological advice, and loans to small enterprises in order for such enterprises to grow and compete in the free market.

This debate does not merely reflect the question of welfare versus investment; it revolves around basic values and goals of both the entrepreneur and the donor. For example, is the objective of the support program solely to increase profits? Or are such considerations as exploitation of employees, pollution of the environment, or cornering the grain market to be deplored or forbidden?[6] If the programs emphasize growth, they are likely to be focused on small (usually male) entrepreneurs rather than on the micro-entrepreneurs (predominantly female). Many advocates of free market economics emphasize efficiency: They claim that loans to existing enterprises have a higher cost-benefit ratio because their growth increases labor demand; further, the larger the size of the loan the cheaper the overall cost per dollar of the loan program.

Essentially, the argument is between the supporters and challengers of classic hard-edged economic values. The challengers question the basic tenet of classic economics: That all individuals only seek to maximize their own happiness. Rather, they applaud the actions of many women micro-entrepreneurs who invest in their families instead of their enterprises and propose that such family and community values become the basis of a more human and humane economics (Hyden 1980; Tinker 1987b).

The effect of this debate on women in the street food trade has been two-fold. First, women's work in the informal sector remained invisible even as data were collected on both owners of and workers in the small and medium enterprises because women's "pre-entrepreneurial" enterprises tend to cluster at the smallest end of the scale among the community of the poor. Secondly, since many economists have tended to dismiss micro-entrepreneurial activity *a priori* as non-economic because these enterprises are not likely to create a surplus in order to grow, they argue that any assistance given to micro-entrepreneurs would have a negligible effect on economic development. Growth is the only measure of success; family survival and investment in the nutrition and schooling of children are not considered adequate outcomes for extending support to micro-entrepreneurs in a free market climate when resources are scarce (Tinker 1987a, pp. 38–50).

EPOC's Street Foods Project

The EPOC Street Foods Project was conceived in the midst of these debates. Instead of evaluating artificially introduced income-generating activities, the project would first undertake an in-depth study of an existing micro-enterprise. Instead of subscribing to the idea that poor women do not know how to run a business, the project would analyze existing practice and constraints and suggest interventions that could facilitate the enterprise. Customers would be interviewed to assess the demand. Because the focus was both on micro-enterprise and on women's ability to earn a living as entrepreneurs, the study would collect data on both women and men in order to compare the extent and type of involvement in the enterprise.

The selection of street food vending was a logical choice for the in-depth study. Women are charged with the provision of food in all societies; their move to the marketplace appeared to be a relatively easy one in most countries. Anecdotal evidence of women selling prepared food is frequently included in both travel notes and scholarly articles. Yet, while market women have been widely studied in many parts of the world, the selling of prepared foods throughout the city by either women or men had not been a focus of research in these studies. As noted above, scholars studying the informal sector did not include micro-enterprise activities.

Research Design

EPOC began the Street Foods Project in 1982, studying provincial towns[7] in Senegal, Nigeria, Egypt, Bangladesh, Philippines, Indonesia, and Thailand.[8] Each country study took between one and a half and two years to complete. While EPOC coordinated the research, we had a resident director in only four of the countries; in Nigeria, Egypt, and Thailand local research groups directed the study with EPOC providing a consultant.[9]

During the process of selecting a city site in each country, local administrators and scholars were interviewed about their views of the importance and utility of the study and their knowledge of relevant scholarly literature and government documents. These interviews provided country-specific information on family structure, existing development programs, and governmental regulations regarding street food vendors. Those individuals expressing interest in the project were invited to join an advisory committee along with leaders of women's organizations, community-based NGOs, and vendor organizations (where they existed).

The committee members provided important local support for and legitimacy to the study. They were asked to assist in finding staff to do the surveying and interviewing, to suggest issues to be studied, to review the results of the surveys and questionnaires, and to help interpret the overall findings. Committee members presided over each final briefing held for a broad array of NGOs, municipal bureaucrats, and scholars, and led the discussion to identify possible interventions or programs that would help vendors improve their surroundings, increase their income, or enhance the quality and safety of the food sold.

The lack of basic data on street foods necessitated a research design that avoided assumptions about who made, sold, and ate prepared food on the street. The first step in each town was to map the streets and locate all vendors selling at various times during the day. This census was repeated two or three times during a year to reflect seasonality. A 10 percent sample of vendors was selected, based on location and type of food sold, for the administering of both a social and an economic questionnaire. These vendors were frequently observed in order to verify who was actually selling, making decisions, preparing the food, cleaning up. In addition, calculations were made about the costs of the food the vendors sold in order to check their responses to the questionnaires about profits and operating costs.

A customer survey identified who eats the food, where and when; a household survey of food consumption indicated the importance of food bought on the street in the total diet of the customers. Samples of foods were tested for contamination; also, cleanliness habits in preparation, serving, and cleaning up were observed both in the homes and at the point of sale.

To refine our knowledge about the division of labor both at the point of sale and at home where preparation of many foods took place, fifteen vendors were observed for at least a week each, at home and while selling. This intense involvement with the lives of vendors provided an opportunity to compare questionnaire results with observed behavior. These case studies provide an insight into the motivations and goals of the people who prepare and sell food on the streets.

The ultimate objectives of the project were practical: First, to design interventions that enhanced income and improved the quality or safety of the food. Second, to utilize this information from one existing economic activity to improve programs that assist women microentrepreneurs in general and so challenge assumptions and theories about them that had previously impeded assistance.

Street Food Trade

The diversity of towns included in the Street Food Study is illustrated in Table 7.1. Population size of cities studied varied from Manikganj, a district office center whose commercial importance as a river town was declining, to a rapidly modernizing Bogor, satellite city to Jakarta. Minia excepted, these data support the intuitive assumption that the number of street food enterprises increases with, and faster than, the increase in city size. A possible explanation for the exception of Minia lies in the types of food eaten at home and that eaten on the street. In most countries traditional foods eaten at home take a long time to prepare, so busy housewives or employed women will avoid this effort by feeding their families street foods. In Egypt, however, the basic diet of cheese and bread is served cold so that meals require a minimum of preparation, especially if bread is purchased. Supporting this explanation is the fact that the favorite street foods in Minia are bean-based *foul* and *tamia*, foods that take considerable time to prepare.

Figures in Table 7.1 are only for the season when the largest number of vendors were on the streets. The seasonal variations were primarily due to women-headed firms and reflected women's roles in agriculture. In Ziguinchor the total of vendors in the rainy season, 748, were less than half of the 1,534 vendors recorded in the dry season; the town itself is semi-rural with agricultural lands interspersed with commercial strips and modern buildings.[10] The decline was less precipitous in Chonburi where the 1,370 dry season vendors were reduced to 948 in the rainy season. In contrast, the total number of vendors dropped only by 5 percent in Bogor during the prime agricultural season. These seasonal variations suggest that for some women vendors selling street foods is only one of several survival strategies.

Table 7.1   Street Food Enterprises by City

City	Urban Population	Enterprises (High Season)	Population per Enterprise	% Outside Commercial Area
Manikganj Bangladesh	37,996	550	69	8
Chonburi Thailand	46,000	1,370	34	36
Ziguinchor Senegal	86,295	1,534	56	59
Ile-Ife Nigeria	135,000	2,603	52	87*
Minia Egypt	200,000	784	255	52
Iloilo Philippines	244,827	5,100	48	74
Bogor Indonesia	248,000	17,760	14	85

*23% of foods are sold in completely residential areas; 64% in mixed residential and smaller commercial areas.

In Iloilo and Manikganj the seasonality was based on religious holidays rather than on agriculture. Christmas brought extra vendors out in Iloilo but this increase was balanced by other vendors who stopped selling for a time, perhaps returning to their natal villages. In Manikganj, the Islamic month of fasting alters eating habits. Special types of street foods for breaking the fast after sundown and for eating during the night replace the foods sold throughout the rest of the year.

The street food vendor census revealed that relatively few sellers actually move constantly. Rather, the vast majority of vendors, even those selling from wheeled carts, sell from a single definite place every day, though some had two daily spots while others moved on weekends (to the botanical gardens, etc.) or changed on market days. Even women selling from baskets carried on their heads tended to squat in the same place every day: in front of a school in the morning, outside the court, or near a cinema in the afternoon. By custom, good places are reserved and jealously guarded; their rights may even be sold. The really mobile vendors follow regular routes. Bicycle carts are used to pedal breads or *sate* (i.e., shish kebab) or ices. Vendors using shoulder poles provide table and food: On one end of the pole they hang a stool and tiny table to balance a brassier on the other end which is used for heating water for tea or for grilling sate. These mobile vendors account for perhaps a quarter of all sellers in Ife, 18 percent in Chonburi, and 10 percent in Ziguinchor.

An important finding of the study is the large percentage of street vending establishments located outside of major commercial areas. Because more complaints are registered about vendors blocking sidewalks and streets in downtown areas, city planners overlooked the street vendors near bus stops, cinemas, schools, and hospitals as well as in both poor and middle-class residential areas. In fact, it is logical that food is sold where people congregate; fast food establishments in the United States are more often outside than inside urban centers. Further, selling food in their own neighborhoods is an obvious advantage to women, who must usually balance their home responsibilities with their vending.

Patriarchal Context of the Trade

The cultural and religious traditions of each country influence the patriarchal bargain women make as they reduce their autonomy in return for protection. These traditions also dictate women's roles in the street food trade. In Minia, Egypt, and in Manikganj, Bangladesh, patriarchal control is re-enforced by religion, which is predominantly Islamic in both countries; women's expected behavior differs little among the Coptic Christians in Egypt or the Hindus in Bangladesh. While purdah (complete seclusion) is no longer widely practiced and veiling in public is a political statement now, women are expected to be modest and retiring. Therefore, vending in public places is an economic alternative of the last resort. These two cities also had the smallest percentage of women among the total number of vendors enumerated: 1 percent for Manikganj, 11 percent for Minia. Women vendors were absolved of their non-conformity to the social norms applied to most women on the grounds of necessity: They had to work to survive because they were widows without family able to support them; or, in one case, the woman's husband was a drunkard. In Minia the social restrictions seemed less severe; only slightly more than half (57 percent) of the women vendors were either widowed or married to men who did not work. Other women in the Minia sample became vendors to support large families.

With her husband's permission and approval from the building owner, Sanaa sells *foul* (stewed beans) in front of the apartment building where her husband works as a porter; the family lives in a room under the stairs. His monthly salary of 15 LE (Egyptian pounds) could not feed a family of ten, four children each from previous marriages. Sanaa now earns around 2.5 LE per day, nearly four times as much as her husband's salary if she works twenty-four days a month.

The women vendors in Ziguinchor, Senegal, and Ile-Ife, Nigeria, come from a very different cultural tradition than the women described above; as in most areas of sub-Saharan Africa, the family does not function as a unit. Instead, women and men operate in separate spheres, have differing responsibilities, and keep separate budgets. Islam seems to have moderated this system marginally in Ziguinchor, but there is no observable difference in that city between the Muslim vendors (93 percent) and the Catholic vendors. More significant was tribal origin: Nomadic men and women dominated the meat and yoghurt trade respectively. Men are expected to supply the staple food for the family; however, a majority of the women vendors (59 percent) were the primary support for their families (an average of 9.5 persons) because they were divorced or widowed or had husbands who did not contribute (the husbands were absent or unemployed). Even in families where the man supplied a monthly bag of rice, his expenditure was about equal to the woman's spending on millet and ingredients for the vegetables and meats eaten as sauce.

In Ile-Ife, about 70 percent of the vendors followed some form of Christianity: Protestants were the largest, 47 percent; Catholics, 14 percent, and Aladura (African Christians), 10 percent. One-quarter of the vendors followed Islam while the remaining 3 percent said they adhered to an indigenous religion. As in the other areas, the overall cultural pattern seems unrelated to religious belief. Almost none of the women were widowed or divorced, yet all were the major provider for their children. Three-quarters of the women also supported one or more other children who lived with them.

In Southeast Asia the family system is distinct from those described above; women exhibit much of the autonomy characteristic of African women but maintain a more interrelated relationship with their spouses. Before marriage, young women often assisted their mothers, stopped vending when their children were small, then returned to work to earn money for school fees. In Indonesia and the Philippines, many enterprises were jointly run.

Islam has had some effect in Indonesia; although the country is technically 90 percent Muslim, various islands have experienced Islam's penetration differently. In east and central Java the former animistic and Hindu beliefs have been intermingled with Islamic ones, while in the western part of the island a purer form of Islam predominates. Bogor, the city studied, lies on the borderline between the resulting cultural patterns. This variation helps explain the lower percentage of female street food vendors in Bogor than found in Jogjakarta in central Java only some 200 miles away. Instead of selling on the streets, many women in Bogor earned income in "invisible street foods," that is, by informal contracts to supply meals to offices or dormitories, or by marketing sweets through shops.

In Catholic Philippines divorce is not allowed. Women and men both contribute to the family; indeed, jointly run street food enterprises were by far the most profitable. In Buddhist Thailand, where divorce is not common, five percent of the vendors were separated. Women vendors in Chonburi were of both Thai and Chinese origin, but no Thai men were found in the trade. In both Philippines and Thailand, many of the male spouses worked at lower paying but higher status government jobs. The importance of income was illustrated in Iloilo where one-fifth of all vendors had some college education.

In these seven countries, then, three distinct family patterns influence women and their enterprises: classic patriarchy of Egypt and Bangladesh, separate spheres and budgets of Africa, and the intermediary Southeast Asian pattern. Women are independent vendors in Africa and Southeast Asia; men and women work together in Southeast Asia as well as in Bangladesh and Egypt. In all countries, culture and history are more important than religion in influencing women's behavior.

Where the patriarchal bargain values seclusion for women, poverty may both force women to work and excuse them for doing so. But in other areas, women of all classes are expected to work and do so. Because street vending is relatively lucrative, this activity is often selected by middle-class women as well as by poorer ones. In all the countries the idea of men protecting the women of the family seems to hold; in none of the countries was harassment of women sellers by men mentioned as a problem in contrast to women vendors in Washington, DC, for whom this is a major problem.[11]

Women in the Street Food Trade

As Table 7.2 indicates, the percentage of women selling street foods varies across the towns studied from a mere one percent in traditional Muslim Manikganj to 94 percent in Ile-Ife with its history of market women and traders. In Ziguinchor and Chonburi about three-quarters of all vendors are women; in both countries, as in Ile-Ife, women and men sell separate types of food and do not work together. This commonality may trace its origins to the more strict sexual division of labor typical of slash and burn farming systems that continue to be practiced in parts of Africa and in the hills of Thailand. Separate budgets and the mother's responsibility for feeding her children are part of the female farming system (Boserup 1970 and 1990). It may also reflect the fairly low status of commerce versus warriors or rulers that is embedded in their cultural traditions.

Women's involvement in the trade, however, is not synonymous with being women vendors. In Manikganj and Minia a significant number of women played some role in street food vending. In Manikganj, 26 percent of the male vendors have unpaid help from their wives; another 10 percent buy from women neighbors on a regular basis. Thus, 36 percent of the male vendors in Manikganj had female help in their businesses, a figure which raises women's involvement in street food vending from one to thirty-seven. In Minia, the town with the second lowest percentage of women vendors, women were either the sole or major vendor in 17 percent of the enterprises. In addition, 14 percent of the male vendors were assisted by females, either in food preparation or in washing up; this assistance brings women's involvement to 31 percent, the lowest figure overall of the cities studied.

Table 7.2   Street Food Entrepreneurs by Women's Involvement (in percentage form)

| City | Operators | | | Female Assists | Total Women's Involvement |
	Women	Men	Couple		
Manikganj Bangladesh	1	99	—	36	37
Chonburi Thailand	78	22	—	—	78
Ziguinchor Senegal	77	23	—	—	77
Ile-Ife Nigeria	94	6	—	—	94
Minia Egypt	17	83	—	14	31
Iloilo Philippines	63	10	27	—	90
Bogor Indonesia	16	60	24	—	40

In Southeast Asia, the traditionally strong role of women is mitigated by religious custom to produce three distinct patterns. In both Iloilo and Bogor, about one-quarter of all vending establishments are operated by couples, a finding that reflects strong family values. As noted above, Bogor's women vendors are fewer in number than have been found in other Javanese towns where Islamic influence is less intense. It appears that the women reported as part of a couple were often assistants to their husbands, although in some instances each made and sold foods complementary to each other. For example, one man would sell noodle soup and his wife would sell herbal drinks; in another couple the woman sold fritters and her husband sold ice drinks.

Iloilo exhibits the reverse pattern. The traditional dominance of Southeast Asian women in commerce continues; Christianity requires monogamy and permanent marriage so that couples indeed see themselves as permanent entities. Women operate about two-thirds of the firms alone, but when a woman becomes successful she is often joined by her husband, who may assist *her* in selling. Husbands also may help by obtaining or buying a truck and going out into rural areas to buy ingredients at a lower cost. Thus, women in Iloilo run some 90 percent of all vending establishments.

This strong female commercial role is evident in Chonburi as well, but (as in the African cities) women vendors operate independently from men. This contrasts with the cooperative patterns of Bogor and Iloilo, where women and men assist each other in both the selling and preparation phases of operating the enterprises. In Minia and Manikganj, spouses help each other in preparing street food but not in selling it. In Manikganj, family members helped widows construct their selling kiosks but did not appear to play a regular supportive role. In Minia, however, 17 percent of the female vendors received help from their spouses.

Thus, the results of the street foods study identify only two types of vending systems: separate sex and family enterprises. In Ile-Ife, Chonburi, and Ziguinchor, women dominate the trade; most of the foods they sell are different from those sold by men. In the other four countries, the enterprise is a family business. In Bogor and Iloilo couples work together in the selling as well as the making of the foods. In Minia and Manikganj, wives prepare foods in the home; but women alone or those without an 'earning' husband will sell on the street and may receive help from their spouse or other male family members. The impact of patriarchal bargains on women's autonomy to choose to trade is evident; the configuration of the enterprise is influenced by additional factors that need further research.

Income and Its Use

Street food vendors do not usually keep written records, but most have clear memories for expenses and income. However, few are willing to confide such details to interviewers. Therefore, we cross-checked answers given on the questionnaires by estimating daily costs and observing daily sales. These findings were once again checked during the in-depth study of selected vendors and their families. In all of the towns, return on the street food trade was generally higher than income derived from entry-level jobs in government, industry, or domestic service, but the variation is wide between countries and within the occupation.

In Iloilo average vendor profits were above the minimum daily wage; in Bogor they were higher than the wage for construction workers. In Manikganj vendor income was more than twice the wage of an unskilled agricultural worker, more than that of a mason, and about the equivalent of a carpenter. In Minia the vendors' average monthly income was 35 percent higher than minimum wage. Women vendors in Ziguinchor made more than housemaids. The Chonburi study indicates that even the lowest reported income is sufficient to support a family of four or five. The Ile-Ife study was conducted in the midst of a recession; data reveal that only a quarter were making a good income; half were only making a meager income. It is likely that these vendors represent casual sellers who gave up after the "street cleaning" exercise of the government.

Overall, male vendors made a higher income than female vendors. One reason seems to be that women sell foods that take longer to prepare (two to three hours), as compared to men's preparation time of one hour. Shorter preparation time and no household tasks to do means that men generally spend more hours actually selling street foods. Thus, women make less money than men except in Bogor, where women often sell medicinal beverages which are very profitable. Where couples work together, as in Iloilo and Bogor, their income is higher than either sex working alone.

Women's income from street foods is essential to household survival. Our data indicate that in Ziguinchor, 59 percent of the women vendors are the sole support of their families. In Minia, 55 percent of the women vendors are primary household providers, as are 70 percent of the men vendors. Data from Chonburi show the importance of women's income to their extended families: While 20 percent of the women vendors provide the main source of income to their nuclear family, another 21 percent, all unmarried, are the primary support for parents or siblings. In Manikganj the women, all widows but one, were vendors because they had no other source of income; the woman who sold fruit from her garden had to beg as well. The data from Iloilo indicate that 75 percent of all vendors derive their primary income from street vending; since women run 90 percent of the firms, this means that they are the primary earner in 68 percent of the households. In Ile-Ife, two-thirds of the vendors have no other source of income; further, 92 percent report that they also fed their families from their street foods.

These data suggest that whether the enterprises are run by women alone or by family cooperation, the street food trade is an important source of livelihood. Further, the poorer the family, the more critical are women's roles, a finding that echoes studies done in rural areas (Stoler 1977). Bangladesh and Egypt, the most conservative countries studied, relaxed restrictions on women's freedom of movement in the face of economic need. The Street Foods Project did not attempt to find out whether the income earned by women actually altered the intrahousehold dynamics. However, women's ability to earn income from street foods does improve the nutritional status of the family. In Nigeria the family fed on the street foods. In Senegal, where local Islamic custom dictates that men supply the basic staple to the family, the study found that 84 percent of the men provided their households with a large bag of rice each month. Women's daily expenditure on vegetables and meat to use as sauce equalled the cost of a bag of rice over a month. Yet neither the women nor the men realized their costs were equal and continued to say that men fed their families. Without street food income, the women would have been unable to buy the sauce ingredients.

Policy and the Street Food Trade

Governmental policies toward street vending are generally hostile around the world: Conventional wisdom is that street vendors clog the streets and produce congestion, pollute the air with their fires, produce waste, and sell contaminated food. These indictments underscore the widely held belief that vending and other micro-enterprises are old-fashioned remnants of tradition or symbols of underdevelopment that are embarrassing to modern municipalities and should be regulated or even expunged. These indictments also reflect the assumption that street foods are a marginal economic activity.

Regulations

All the cities studied had some form of required registration, and certificates were required by the health departments. Procedures for registration are generally onerous and costly, so that most vendors did not, or could not, comply with the law. Enforcement of these regulations was uneven. Although there was some indication of corruption, fees were sometimes not charged because the police knew the profits for the day were low. In Los Angeles, street food vendors are illegal but usually ignored in face of more pressing and destructive crimes (Sirola 1991). The majority of street food vendors were illegal, or at best extra-legal. Indeed, the primary difficulty they faced, according to the street food vendors themselves, was this lack of legitimacy, a condition that allowed them to be harassed by police and protectionist groups. Most feared was the periodic clearing of the streets by police or army, a fact of trade that discouraged vendors from improving their carts or stalls or otherwise investing in their enterprise.

One such government sweep occurred in the final days of the study in Ile-Ife. The new military government decided to enforce laws against vending. Six weeks after the streets were cleaned, the project staff scoured the city in search of as many vendors as they could find. This special survey suggests that the military action pushed out the more casual of the vendors but the women with the largest sales and longest experience had reappeared.

Such harassment is inconsistent with the economic importance of street vending to the municipality and the importance of street foods in the urban diet. In Bogor, the average household spent 25 percent of the daily food budget on street foods; the figure is 30 percent in Iloilo. In Chonburi an amazing 47 percent of the average household expenditure is on street foods with a slightly higher percentage of the budget being spent by the poorest income group. In fact, in Thailand where multiple dishes are the traditional diet, 70 percent of households in Chonburi do not cook food for every meal and 13 percent of the families surveyed *never* cook at home. In Ile-Ife 83 percent of all households surveyed buy breakfast from vendors between four and seven times a week. These data prove that street foods are indeed the fast foods of developing countries. Translated into labor force participation, we find that even in Manikganj some 6 percent of workers are directly or indirectly involved in the street foods trade; the figure rises to 25 percent of all workers in Bogor! Aggregate yearly sales, expressed in 1985 U.S. dollars, contributed two million dollars to the economy of the small district town of Manikganj and an amazing sixty-seven million in the booming city of Bogor.

When presented with these data during the EPOC briefings, municipal authorities realized that their policy of harassment was illogical, that they should not disrupt as important a trade as street foods. As a result, representatives of vending groups and governmental agencies have met in several towns to seek new solutions to the problems inherent in vending, and to try to improve the trade, not obliterate it. In at least three towns, the EPOC study encouraged NGOs to offer credit and support programs to vendors (Tinker 1987a) and in Bogor, the Dutch government is funding a training program for food vendors (Biljmer 1991).

Food Policies

Other national policies also affected the street food vendors; while pricing policies for foodstuffs affect enterprises all along the food distribution system, the tendency of governments to ignore traditional foods is of greater concern to vendors whose food reflects indigenous diets. In Senegal, imported rice was subsidized but local millet was not. Women selling a millet-based breakfast food often diluted it with the rice— which should have been more expensive—when millet prices rose! Also in Senegal, large quantities of milk powder imported under food aid programs affected traditional yoghurt production. Nomadic women used to have a monopoly on yoghurt; male market traders, unlike these women, had sufficient capital to buy the large bags of powdered milk and began to produce yoghurt in competition. In Indonesia, nutritionists on the street food project staff created an improved *kropok* (puffed rice chips) by adding subsidized imported soy flour. The new product went off the market when the subsidy was withdrawn. Imported wheat promoted bread as a substitute for traditional staples in several countries.

Findings of the EPOC study precipitated a change in the manner in which nutritional surveys are conducted. Previously, the usual method was to gather data on food prepared and consumed at home; clearly such data are invalid in light of data showing that perhaps one-fifth of all food is eaten outside the house. Agricultural policy was altered in the region around Iloilo because the study showed a demand for different foods than originally planned. Pricing policies for rice versus millet were also challenged by street food findings of millet use by food vendors. Such policy implications of this micro-study underscore the interrelationships among women and their families to such major social institutions as the economy and the state.

In all these instances, the move from traditional to modern food has had several significant implications. Agricultural products less suited to the environment are favored; modern food is often less nutritionally balanced; and production of the newer commodity shifted from female to male. In the future, government policy needs to consider these effects when subsidizing food.

Conclusion

Three pertinent assumptions widely held both by theorists and practitioners are challenged by the findings of the street foods study: (1) that the income from such enterprises are trivial; (2) that street foods are snacks with marginal nutritional value; and (3) that women's involvement in the trade represents economically unimportant "pin money."

Theories that denigrate the importance of income derived from vending, referring to the operators as the "community of the poor," are clearly dismissing these entrepreneurs without investigating their income. While municipal administrators are adapting some policies to the needs of vendors, the planners in development agencies continue to hold onto unrealistic assumptions about economic trends and values that would offer support only to enterprises that grow to employ more workers. They overlook the critical contribution that income from vending plays for the poor. For casual vendors, who indeed make a meager income, selling is only one of many activities utilized to survive. For all vendors, their income from street vending is essential to the household. The fact that three-quarters of the enterprises are owner-operated should not mean that they are not worthy of credit programs and other types of support from NGOs and the donor community so that they are able to improve their productivity and income.

Use of income for family needs instead of enterprise growth leads some economists to reject these entrepreneurs as lacking in business acumen. In contrast, credit is widely dispensed to small farmers so that they can increase their productivity; and no donor expects every farmer to grow from one hectare to five or ten. This double standard for enterprises versus agriculture is compounded by a double standard for micro-enterprises run by women and those by men.

The nutritional content of street foods were dismissed because the extent and variety were unknown. The study has also identified other types of prepared food services thus far largely unstudied. These "invisible street foods" include informal restaurants, catering, contract meal arrangements, and community kitchens. To solve the problem of feeding the magna cities of the future, research on these activities and women's involvement in them are essential.

The strong role of women street food vendors in those countries where they sell alone was expected. What the current study has added is the importance of women in joint family ventures even in such patriarchal societies as Bangladesh. Analysis of the case studies not presented in this chapter illustrates women's decision-making roles which flow from her economic activity. These findings are consistent with recent research which emphasizes the relationship between women's work and the nutritional status of her children (Senauer 1990).

Women's involvement in the street food trade relates to the family system that is embedded in the culture and history of the society. Within the constraints of society, women make different patriarchal bargains in order to support the family, or their children, economically. Even in the more classic patriarchal systems, poverty overrides propriety; women must work, and men not only accept but often assist their wives in their trade.

The fact that in all the kinship systems represented in the study women stayed within the family came as a surprise. We had expected that more of the independent women sellers would be heads of households *without males present*. In fact, even wives of drunkards continued to support them. It would seem that the patriarchal bargain is more flexible and less onerous than predicted. Thus, the importance of women's economic roles in the family questions the applicability and perhaps the definition of patriarchy itself.

The street food study provides primary data that can be used to improve development programs for the urban poor; it speaks to intra-household bargains not well understood by scholars or practitioners; it forces a new look at the economic importance of micro-enterprise in providing income and services to urban populations. More studies of survival strategies of the poor are needed if global equity is to become a reality.

Notes

1. Today, it is not only the family, but also the state, that tries to influence these patriarchal bargains by enforcing conformity to the ideal of womanhood (Papanek 1991).

2. A review of the debates and case studies funded by or in response to the ILO initiatives may be found in Bromley (1978). The ILO summarized the findings of nine country studies it funded in Setheraman (1981). Richardson (1984) summarizes subsequent literature on the informal sector and notes the shift in the focus of the debate to practical analysis once the permanent existence of the informal sector had been acknowledged. In the same special issue of the *Regional Development Dialogue*, Moser (1984) presents a new slant on the theoretical debate in the field by illustrating how the use of different concepts and methodologies can produce differing results.

3. Neo-Marxists have proposed the articulation theory to explain the persistence of pre-capitalist modes of production within a dominant capitalist

system; this concept replaces Marxist dualism which predicts antagonism between old and new economic formations. Kusterer (1990) reviews this shift and applies the articulation theory to household production. Liberal economists have proclaimed the informal sector as "dynamic entrepreneurs" (House 1984) who are outside the formal sector primarily because they are inhibited by cumbersome governmental registration, regulations, and restrictions (deSoto 1987).

4. Recent studies of old and new informal forms in both the industrialized and the developing countries may be found in *The Informal Economy* (Portes, Castells, and Benton 1989). A radical feminist view of the persistence of the informal sector is presented in *Women: The Last Colony* with chapters by the three authors: Mies, Bennholdt-Thomsen, and von Werlhof (1988).

5. In agricultural subsistence societies, women are farmers; tailoring generally is a male occupation. While landless women can be taught sewing skills in order to earn non-farm income, it takes time to produce consistently fine work. Further, because such work is regarded as housework, women seldom receive a reasonable return for their labor. Mies' study (1982) of lacemaking in southern India has been widely quoted to show exploitation of these women both by their husbands and by the economic system.

6. All of these outcomes have occurred. The "tricyclos" owners in Santo Domingo rented their vehicles to workers at high rates; loans allowed the workers to purchase the vehicles with the expectation that the increased income would improve their living standards; but many simply turned around and rented out the vehicles themselves. In Los Angeles, loans to street vendors have in the past been used to set up hamburger stands even though outside cooking was being banned by clear air regulations; leaders of the loan program now oppose such loans. In Bangladesh, women used small loans to buy up rice at the end of the harvest and sell it later at higher prices, imitating the traditional role of moneylenders whose hold on the poor women was supposed to be reduced by the loan program.

7. Provincial towns were selected so that the entire urban area could be mapped in order to show where street vendors were located. Previous studies of vendors had assumed vendors primarily operated in downtown areas and in markets. Site selection, however, was also based on local interest and support. As a result, three cities in highly populated countries were too large to map in entirely; statistical samples were drawn to provide information outside of major commercial and market areas. See Table 7.1.

8. The first round of studies, funded by the United States Agency for International Development (USAID), included Senegal, Bangladesh, the Philippines, and Indonesia. These countries were selected because the USAID country mission was interested in the issues raised. The cities were chosen by the country director, the only expatriate involved in the study, who hired local researchers to collect data.

The second round of country studies were supported by the Ford Foundation, with grants directly to research groups in the countries that EPOC had identified to conduct the study. Cities were chosen by the local women who directed the projects; EPOC supplied a consultant to the project in order to maintain consistency of data collected to allow for global comparisons.

A third arrangement was entered into in Jamaica, where the study was funded by the International Development Research Council of Canada; EPOC helped launch the project but thereafter assisted only occasionally with methodology and analysis. Other research groups have subsequently utilized EPOC methodology in conducting their own studies.

9. Country research teams were all women with two exceptions: The Philippine study director was a man whose wife was associate director; in Bangladesh, male-female teams were used in deference to local cultural norms.

10. Agricultural demands also meant fewer customers, a fact that also must have contributed to the existence of fewer vendors.

11. Spalter-Roth (1988) writes: "Because they [women vendors] are on male turf, they are seen as visible targets by men on the streets, by shoplifters, by male vendors, and by the police."

References

Agarwal, Bina. 1985. "Women and Technological Change in Agriculture." In *Technology and Rural Women: Conceptual and Empirical Issues,* edited by Iftikhar Ahmed. London: George Allen and Unwin.

Ashe, Jeffrey, ed. 1985. *The Pisces II Experience.* Volume I: *Local Efforts in Micro-Enterprise Development;* Volume II: *Case Studies from Dominican Republic, Costa Rica, Kenya, & Egypt.* Washington, DC: USAID.

Banerjee, Nirmala, ed. 1991. *Indian Women in a Changing Industrial Scenario.* Sage: New Delhi.

Beneria, Lourdes. 1980. "Accounting for Women's Work." In *Women and Development: The Sexual Division of Labor in Rural Societies,* edited by Lourdes Beneria. New York: Praeger.

Beneria, Lourdes, and Martha Roldan. 1987. *The Crossroads of Class and Gender: Industrial Homework, Subcontracting, and Household Dynamics in Mexico City.* Chicago, IL: University of Chicago Press.

Bijlmer, Joep. 1991. "The Wholesomeness of Common People's Food in Indonesia," a report of the Bogor Streetfood Project, Bogor Agricultural University.

Boserup, Ester. 1970. *Woman's Role in Economic Development.* New York: St. Martin's Press.

———. 1990. "Economic Change and the Roles of Women." Pp. 14-24 in *Persistent Inequalities: Women and World Development,* edited by Irene Tinker. New York: Oxford University Press.

Boserup, Ester, and Christina Liljencrantz. 1975. *Integration of Women in Development: Why, When, How?* New York: UNDP.

Bromley, Ray, ed. 1978. *The Urban Informal Sector: Critical Perspectives.* Special issue *World Development* 6/9–10.

deSoto, Hernando. 1987. *El Otro Sendoro.* Buenos Aires: Sudamericana.

Dixon, Ruth. 1983. "Land, Labor, and Sex Composition of the Agricultural Labor Force: An International Comparison." *Development & Change* 14:347–372.

Dwyer, Daisy, and Judith Bruce, eds. 1988. *A Home Divided: Women and Income in the Third World.* Stanford, CA: Stanford University Press.

Grown, Caren A., ed. 1989. *Beyond Survival: Expanding Income-Earning Opportunities for Women in Developing Countries.* Special issue of *World Development* 17/7.

House, William J. 1984. "Nairobi's Informal Sector: Dynamic Entrepreneurs or Surplus Labor?" *Economic Development and Cultural Change* 32:277–302.

Hyden, Goran. 1980. *Beyond Ujamaa in Tanzania: Underdevelopment and an Uncaptured Peasantry.* Berkeley, CA: University of California Press.

Kandiyoti, Deniz. 1985. *Women in Rural Production Systems: Problems and Policies.* Paris: UNESCO.

———. 1988. "Bargaining with Patriarchy." *Gender & Society* 2:274–290.

Kusterer, Ken. 1990. "The Imminent Demise of Patriarchy." Pp. 239–255 in *Persistent Inequalities: Women and World Development,* edited by Irene Tinker. New York: Oxford University Press.

Mies, Maria. 1982. *The Lacemakers of Narsapur: Indian Housewives Produce for the World Market.* London: Zed Press.

Mies, Maria, Veronika Bennholdt-Thomsen, and Claudia von Werlhof. 1988. *Women: The Last Colony.* London: Zed Press.

Moser, Caroline. 1984. "The Informal Sector Reworked: Viability and Vulnerability in Urban Development." *Regional Development Dialogue* 5:3–40.

Otero, Maria. 1990. *A Handful of Rice: Savings Mobilization by Micro-Enterprise Programs and Perspectives for the Future.* Monograph Series 3. Washington, DC: Accion International.

Papanek, Hanna. 1991. "The Ideal Woman and the Ideal Society: Control and Autonomy in the Construction of Gender," paper presented at a seminar on Identity Politics and Women. WIDER, Helsinki.

Portes, Alejandro, Manuel Castells, and Lauren A. Benton, eds. 1989. *The Informal Economy: Studies in Advanced and Less Development Countries.* Baltimore, MD: Johns Hopkins Press.

Richardson, Harry. 1984. "The Role of the Urban Informal Sector: An Overview." *Regional Development Dialogue* 5:3–40.

Senauer, Benjamin. 1990. "The Impact of the Value of Women's Time on Food and Nutrition." Pp. 150–161 in *Persistent Inequalities: Women and World Development,* edited by Irene Tinker. New York: Oxford University Press.

Setheraman, S. V., ed. 1981. *The Informal Sector in Developing Countries: Employment, Poverty and Environment.* Geneva: ILO.

Singh, Andrea Menefee, and Anita Kelles-Viitanen, eds. 1987. *Invisible Hands: Women in Home-Based Production.* Sage: New Delhi.

Sirola, Paula Marie. 1991. "Economic Survival Alternatives for Urban Immigrants: Informal Sector Strategies in Los Angeles," paper presented at the XVII Pacific Science Congress. Honolulu.

Spalter-Roth, Roberta. 1988. "Vending on the Streets: City Policy, Gentrification, and Public Patriarchy." Pp. 272–294 in *Women and the Politics of Empowerment*, edited by Ann Bookman and Sandra Morgen. Philadelphia, PA: Temple University Press.

Stoler, Ann. 1977. "Class Structure and Female Autonomy in Rural Java." *Signs* 3:74–89.

Sullerot, Evelyne. 1971. *Women, Society, & Change*. NY: McGraw-Hill.

Tinker, Irene. 1976. "The Adverse Impact of Development on Women." In *Women and World Development*, edited by Irene Tinker, Michelle Bo Bramsen, and Mayra Buvinic. New York: Praeger for the Overseas Development Council.

———. 1983. "Women in Development." In *Women in Washington: Advocates for Public Policy*, edited by Irene Tinker. Beverly Hills, CA: Sage.

———. 1987a. *Street Foods: Testing Assumptions about Informal Sector Activity by Women and Men*. Entire issue of *Current Sociology* 35/3.

———. 1987b. "The Human Economy of Micro-Entrepreneurs," address published in Proceedings, International Seminar on Women in Micro- and Small-Scale Enterprise Development, convened by the Canadian International Development Agency, October 26, 1987, Ottawa. Revision forthcoming in selected papers from the seminar.

———. 1989. "Credit for Poor Women: Necessary, But Not Always Sufficient for Change." *Marga* 10/2.

———. 1990. "A Context for the Field" and "The Making of a Field: Advocates, Practitioners, and Scholars." Pp. 3–13 and 27–53 in *Persistent Inequalities: Women and World Development*, edited by Irene Tinker. New York: Oxford University Press.

Wipper, Audrey. 1972. "The Roles of African Women: Past, Present, and Future." *Canadian Journal of African Studies* 6/2.

Chapter 8

Women, Political Activism, and the Struggle for Housing: The Case of Costa Rica

Montserrat Sagot

This chapter examines the participation of women in the struggle for adequate housing in Costa Rica, with particular emphasis on the women constituents of the Comite Patriotico Nacional (National Patriotic Committee or COPAN), the country's most effective housing movement organization. COPAN was founded in the late 1970s and has a membership of approximately 20,000. The majority of COPAN's constituents are women and their children who have already built three new communities by self-help. This chapter aims, then, to show how this substantial involvement of women in the housing movement has had crucial implications and consequences at three different levels: the government's housing policy, the layout and structure of social relations of the communities that are being built, and the women's personal and family lives. Furthermore, following what Chow and Berheide call the "system interdependence model," this chapter aims to demonstrate how women's particular social locations and multiple responsibilities across both the productive and reproductive spheres create the groundwork for political activism aimed at improving their living conditions.

Research Methods

I selected COPAN for this case study due to its efficacy, and the massive presence of women in its constituency. The study is based on years of volunteer work with COPAN and six months of intensive field work (from December 1988 to June 1989). During the field work, I conducted several interviews with government officials, including the Vice-Minister of Housing and Human Settlements, the Vice-Minister of Culture (in charge of all women-related government programs), and the Personal Advisor to the Minister of Housing and Human Settlements. Five women and eight men members of COPAN's Directorate and fifty-eight women from the housing committees were interviewed in depth. In addition, I attended meetings and activities at all levels, including COPAN's National Directorate meetings, housing committees and communal meetings, plus other types of activities such as social gatherings and demonstrations. I also worked as a volunteer with the community health committees and with a program for the prevention of domestic violence. Several group interviews and informal discussions with women constituents and COPAN's leaders were held. Finally, I kept a detailed and systematic field diary and an interview file throughout the period.

Women, Political Activism, and Social Movements

The traditional studies on social movements and political participation have obscured and in some cases denied the role and presence of women in urban and housing movements in the Third World. However, women have been centrally involved in them (Chant 1987; Moser 1987a; Vance 1987). Further, women have been and continue to be centrally involved in resistance movements in many workplaces and neighborhoods (Ackelsberg 1988; Navas 1987; CESIP 1986). That the presence of women and their key roles in social movements have not been fully studied is a product of the traditional view of social movements' activity and politics as pertaining to the "public world," that is, the masculine world (Schneider 1988). By seeing political activity as inherently masculine, the studies on social movements have neglected the fact that the organization of gender relations also gives shape to the processes of social change. Further, little attention has been paid to the fact that in a period of economic crisis, gender as well as class inequalities are likely to increase rather than decline (Barbieri and Oliveira 1991; Edgell and Duke 1983).

The failure to recognize these crucial facts and to see women as social actors has been reinforced by a failure to see communal activities as political (Schneider 1988). This is the result of a prevalent conception in Western political theory which has identified politics with the public realm, a world limited to men. The private realm, identified as the home or the close community, was assigned to women. The full effect of this ideological separation between public and private has limited both the agenda of politics and the range of likely participants by considering women's protest activities as lying outside the domains of properly construed politics (Ackelsberg 1988).

A common consequence of the separate-spheres model is the tendency to perceive women's concerns for their children and their socially ascribed roles within their families as the determinant of all their activities outside their homes. However, recent empirical research, which has searched for interconnections between production and reproduction, has found that women's experiences as community members and workers may affect their roles and responsibilities as much as the converse (Ackelsberg 1988; Bookman and Morgen 1988). Thus, applying the system interdependence model to the relationships between women's work, family, and politics, it can be argued that women's multiple roles and responsibilities across spheres shape their political and protest activities. Women, therefore, in their role as main providers for their families and as developers and sustainers of the networks of human relations inside the community, are potentially the primary builders of social movements that struggle for issues of daily subsistence and collective consumption.

Hence, social movements which, like the housing movement, deal with matters of daily subsistence and survival are the ones that can most easily "politicize" the so-called "private domain." Therefore, they can facilitate the transformation of women into conscious political actors. Furthermore, the new political subjects are increasingly using this type of social movement in their attempts to resist or change state policy. By the same token, and following the system interdependence model again, it can be argued that social movements mediate the relationship between new political actors and the state or the economy. In the light of these assumptions, the remainder of the chapter demonstrates how women as the main organizers of Costa Rica's housing movement have influenced government housing policy and have also been transformed into conscious political actors.

The Socio-Political Reality

Due to Costa Rica's democratic tradition and the presence of a welfare state, the economic crisis that affects the region has not provoked a serious political upheaval. However, an array of social problems have arisen as a direct consequence of the crisis. One of the most severe is the shortage of appropriate housing and related community services.

Since almost 50 percent of Costa Rican households are headed by women, they are the most affected by this. Furthermore, Costa Rica, like the rest of the Latin American countries, experiences a process of "feminization of poverty," which transforms women and their children into the main targets of the effects of economic crisis and lack of services.[1]

National statistics show that during the 1980s the country accumulated a deficit of 270,000 houses, affecting 62 percent of the total population (Valverde 1987). The shortage, particularly in the urban areas, is a direct consequence of the social and economic processes that characterized Costa Rica's capitalist development in the 1950s and 1960s. By that time, the country began to experience an accelerated process of property concentration, a dramatic reduction of the so-called agricultural frontier, and the first steps of the industrialization process. As a result, the rural population rapidly became impoverished and was forced out of the rural areas. This situation was also reinforced by the need for a larger urban labor force created by industrial development.

What historically had been a primarily rural and agrarian country began to face a rapid but uneven growth in the urban areas. By 1983, 40 percent of the poor families were already living in the urban areas (Sojo 1988). Urban expansion has led to severe social problems, such as a dramatic increase in the price of urban property, shortage of appropriate housing, and the creation of squatter settlements. This growth of squatter settlements in the urban areas has also become a major source of social conflict. From the unsatisfied needs and anger of the families living in these poor urban communities a strong movement struggling for housing arose in the country during the late 1970s.

COPAN: Its Creation, Strategies, and Influence on Housing Policy

Women's Needs as the Starting Point for Political Action

COPAN traces its origins back to the mid-seventies when the women members of a Trotskyite party, the Organizacion Socialista de Los Trabajadores (Socialist Worker's Organization or OST), founded the first feminist group in the country, El Movimiento de Liberacion de La Mujer (Women's Liberation Movement or MLM). The MLM began its work with women from the poor communities ("barrios") of San Jose, the nation's capital, around 1975. At that time, they went into these "barrios" to organize women to fight for their reproductive rights. While working around health and reproductive rights issues, the

MLM realized that the most important unsatisfied need among these women was housing and related community services.

Furthermore, they discovered that these women were very unhappy with the solutions offered by the government and were willing to organize into independent housing committees. In 1978, the OST and the MLM began organizing housing committees and looking for a suitable program that could be implemented to satisfy the low income population's needs. They discovered that the government, through the INVU (National Institute of Housing and Urbanization), had a proposal for a program called "Site and Services." Through this program the government would provide the land, basic infrastructure, and loans for people to build their own houses.

This program had widespread acceptance on the part of international agencies. Several national governments in the Third World also recognized that "self help" housing was a benefit to the city and to them, for it reduces the responsibility of the state to provide conventional housing for the large working class groups within the urban areas (Moser 1987a, p. 4). However, the OST and MLM realized that although the proposal existed, the government was not implementing it. The first housing committees were organized, then, with the goal of pushing the government to implement the Site and Services Program in an efficient, nonmanipulative manner on a large scale.

By 1981, both the OST and the MLM had been transformed into COPAN and the Centro Feminista de Informacion y Accion (CEFEMINA) respectively. By changing their names, the two organizations were acknowledging the shift in their political agenda. They had become organizations attempting to connect practices and everyday problems with political action; that is, grass-roots organizations with more short-term and practical goals: basically the pursuit of adequate housing for the poorest sectors and the general improvement of living conditions.

The main characteristic of these housing committees has been the massive presence of women and their children. The women from COPAN's committees are either urban working class or peasants who have migrated to the city. Among the fifty-eight women interviewed, thirty-eight (65 percent) of them did not have permanent outside jobs and the rest (35 percent) worked in the service sector or in factories. The data indicate, then, that many women heads of households are not able to earn even the minimum wage necessary to support their families. The ages of the women interviewed ranged from 20 to over 65, but thirty-three (57 percent) were between 30 and 50 years old. Although fifty-six of them had children, with an average of four, only thirty-one (53 percent) had a steady husband or partner at the time of the interview. The rest (47 percent) were single, divorced, or had been abandoned by their partners (fourteen of them) as a result of their involvement with the housing movement.

From the beginning of the struggle, women such as the ones described above attended meetings and organized themselves into the committees. Children also became visible members of the movement, for they had to come along to women's protest activities due to the lack of day-care facilities. When men attended, their participation was neither regular nor reliable. Sonia, who has been involved with COPAN for eight years, had this recollection about men's participation:

> We were always more women in the committees. The few men that came, came only to control their wives. They did not care about housing. They are always out, working, they don't feel the problem. We spend more time in the house, we see the problem closer. . . .

Ana, who has been involved for seven years with COPAN, also remembered the situation:

> My husband believed that God would provide, but I thought that it was necessary to struggle. Women are more hard-working and dedicated than men. . . .

These women were keenly aware that they are the ones who feel the need for appropriate housing most strongly. They recognized that their different position in the social structure made them act and think differently from men. Women not only spend more time in the house, even if they have an outside job and a husband or partner, they still have the main responsibility for all the activities related to social reproduction and for the satisfaction of their families' material and emotional needs. Thus, women are more likely to get involved in movements aimed at improving their living conditions.

The time and effort dedicated to political organizing, however, poses many problems for women. While the protest activities provide women with the opportunity to improve their daily lives and to break their domestic routines, they are also time-consuming and detrimental to women's income-generating activities. Gloria, a fifty-nine-year-old woman, explained how she managed her time:

> I used to get up at 4 A.M. to do the housework and prepare meals. I left the house at 7 A.M. for my job and after that, I spent the evening in meetings and activities. Sometimes I came home and

felt so tired that I went to bed without having eaten anything. The next day, I was so busy before I left that I used to forget that I had to eat.

Marta, a member of the oldest housing committee, describes her activities during the construction period:

> When we first got this land, sometimes we realized that it was already 12 midnight and we were still here working. The next day, I had to go to work and I was so tired that I could not function well. Some other times, I spent the whole weekend here, working. . . .

Thus, multiple commitments obligated these women to work for very long hours in different and exhausting activities. These women have a "triple day" by having a job in the paid labor market, a major responsibility at home, and a primary role in protest activities and community building.

However, they were forced to join the struggle by their harsh living conditions and as a consequence of the lack of solutions offered by the government. Elsa, who has participated in the struggle for ten years, remembered her experiences before her family finally obtained a house:

> We moved around. We were renting in different places, sometimes in a slum, sometimes in a better place, depending on our luck. Many times we ended up in places where the rain would come through the ceiling, with no floors, only mud, and filled with roaches and fleas. . . .

Eduvina, a member of the housing committees since 1981, had this recollection:

> I really needed a house, a decent place to live. I was renting a house close to a river, when a flood washed it away. You cannot live like that. . . .

These women, then, abandoned "proper" social roles and engaged in political action. They were not "politicized" before they became members of the housing movement and had never been an active part of an organization or party. As the economic crisis worsened the living conditions, they had to struggle harder for survival. Joining COPAN was, thus, part of their strategy for survival.

The Importance of Women's Ties in the Creation of COPAN

The majority of the women interviewed (90 percent) learned about the housing committees and decided to get involved through their network of friends and relatives. This fact points to the importance of women's networks and relationships in the creation of this organization. Researchers in the United States (Delgado 1986; Lawson and Barton 1980; Rubin 1976) and Latin America (Cordero and Gamboa 1990; Moser 1987b) also report that organization is commonly based on a network of social ties within a building or community, which women, whether employed outside the home or not, are more likely to form.

Women, due to their familiarity with their communities and neighbors, are more likely to make contacts and share a common understanding of their daily problems. Thus, they tend to be the ones who create and participate in organizations aimed at improving their daily lives. The social relations of reproduction, centered on the home and the community, the importance and density of women's ties, and their struggle for survival helped, then, to create the groundwork for successful mobilization.

However, the most important factor that explains COPAN's success is the solidarity developed among the constituency. The massive presence of women was crucial in the development of strong solidarity ties. Women's more dense network of social ties created a sense of common identity, shared fate, and a commitment to stay together. A COPAN founder and member of its leadership explains how the solidary relations developed within the organization:

> The goal of obtaining a house was transformed into an element of solidarity. We promised to stay together, not to abandon one another. Against the reality of life in which many people are abandoned to their fate, the organization provided them with an element of human solidarity, a place to share, a place to feel better. . . . The participation of women was very important in this process, they contributed with the emotional and subjective elements. . . .

According to Fireman and Gamson (1979), three factors constitute the base of solidarity: 1) the presence of friends and relatives, 2) the sharing of the same position in the social structure, and 3) the difficulty of leaving the group once a person is inside. Women's acknowledgement that they learned about the movement through their network of friends and relatives suggests that networks of related people formed COPAN. These people's existing relationships facilitated, then, the creation of solidarity ties within the organization. Further, all these women shared a similar position in the social structure. They were all relatives or friends, poor, and lived in the same barrios. Finally, the pre-existing network most likely made the option to leave the organization a very difficult one to exercise. Leaving the organization would have implied leaving friends and relatives behind.

In sum, although women's struggle for survival can explain COPAN's origins, its success and permanence on the political scene for over a decade cannot be explained only by using the utilitarian assumption that people stayed for their own self-interest. The element of solidarity and their feeling of shared fate are the crucial facts that explain COPAN's efficacy and success.

Strategy and Negotiation with the Government

COPAN has used a combination of legal and illegal forms of political action like land invasions, barricades closing major streets, pacifist demonstrations, and hunger strikes. The first period of the struggle (from 1979 until 1983) was characterized by the most confrontational forms of political action. During this period, which also corresponds to a peak in the country's popular movement due to the economic crisis, the government was very repressive toward popular protest. Elsa, who has participated in the movement for nine years, recalls:

> They called us communists and I did not understand why. All that we wanted was a house. They treated us so badly. The police used to come and arrest us, and they did not care who they were arresting and how. They did not care. They arrested pregnant women, old people, everybody. . . .

The period of confrontation marked the beginning of the process of women becoming leaders. During the early years of the movement, the few male members of the committees instantly became the leaders. However, when the struggle became harder and, therefore, more commitment was needed, women realized that the men had left them practically alone. According to some, "The morning of the barricades most of the men were ill." The women, then, began to assume more responsibilities in the organization and to occupy more leadership positions.

In 1984, after the worst confrontation with the police in which many constituents were injured, COPAN decided to use other forms of political action. On October 22nd, four women and five men went on a hunger strike demanding a rapid and efficient solution to the housing problem from the government. After eighteen days of the strike, which received vital international and local support from politicians, intellectuals, other popular organizations, and the Roman Catholic Church, the government accepted the demands and agreed to give the 1,450 most needy families on COPAN's priority list immediate help. This action marked the first major victory for COPAN and opened the doors for further negotiations with the government.

In 1985, COPAN made an agreement with Oscar Arias, then presidential candidate of the National Liberation Party, to support him in the February 1986 election if he would commit himself to the solution of the housing problem. One of Arias' most important campaign promises, then, was to build 80,000 housing units for low-income people. Housing was also included as a "strategic area of action" in the National Development Plan, and was defined as the "most important unsatisfied need" (Ministerio de Planificacion Nacional 1986).[2]

When Arias won, his promise to build 80,000 houses in four years forced a total reorganization of the government housing sector. Two new major institutions, the National Financing System for Housing and the Ministry of Housing and Human Settlements, were created in order to accomplish the goal (Valverde and Lara 1988). It is evident, then, that COPAN had an important influence on the definition of the Arias Administration priorities and policy. Moreover, it was only after this electoral agreement that COPAN was able to obtain enough resources to begin the construction of the new communities.

Thus, the women members of COPAN organized a movement profoundly based on their needs and were able to influence the government housing policy because of their belligerency and persistence. Only through COPAN were they capable of establishing contact with the policy-makers and of having some effect on the political decisions that affect their daily lives and well-being.

The New Communities: Women as Builders for Grass-roots Organizing

Finally, in 1986, COPAN's constituents began the process of building what they call the "new communities." The organization of the self-help construction project has required an enormous effort and lots of creativity. The major problem encountered was that although the people were ready and willing to start, the majority of them (mainly women) did not have construction skills. The solution they found was communal construction through joint building groups: The ones who had the skills taught and supervised the rest. The women very soon proved to be successful self-builders. All the women interviewed acknowledged having worked in the construction and done "everything." COPAN also developed a whole support system that included day-care centers, communal kitchens, and temporary shelters. The older women and disabled people could work in the support activities and that counted as hours of work toward the allocation of a house.

COPAN has been involved in three major construction projects that have produced 2,000 plots altogether. These include an upgrading project totally based on self-help, the Juan Pablo II community with 46 houses; projects in which the government totally urbanized the site and partially built the houses by providing a "wet core" (a toilet, a shower, a sink, and part of the walls and floors), as well as the Corina-Guapil community with more than 800 plots, which were finished by self-help. Finally, a community that has been totally designed and built by the people themselves, the Guarari community.

These communities can be seen as the concrete implementation of the government's policy. All the weaknesses and inherent problems of the new housing policies surfaced when the members of COPAN started applying for loans and building the plots. First, the majority of them still could not qualify for government loans. Families headed by women, the elderly, and those who did not earn a minimum wage did not even qualify for what is called the "Family Bonus," a loan of 440,000 Costa Rican colones (approximately U.S. $3,500) for housing construction. Second, COPAN wanted the land tenure and house ownership to be under the women's names even when husbands or companions were present. That would protect them against unstable or violent domestic situations and improve their objective position within the family's internal hierarchy. COPAN found, however, a very rigid mentality among government officials, who wanted the men to have the legal rights over the property so they could assume financial responsibility for the loans. Eligibility criteria for participating in these projects was designed in terms of the income of men and evidence of regular employment.

The right to design and build the houses and communities according to women's models and needs has also been part of a long struggle. The first communities totally designed and partially built by the government were laid out facing busy roads, did not have recreational areas, and did not respect the natural environment. This layout forces women to work in more isolated conditions and presents a danger for the children, since the risk of traffic accidents increases. Some basic services such as schools, public transportation, garbage collection, and pay phones were not provided. Government settlement planning did not allocate resources for childcare provisions in the communities on the assumption that women would stay home and take care of the children. As Ackelsberg (1988, p. 301) argues, this is a product of the translation of the public/private dichotomy into social policy and settlement planning. As a result, women do not have the freedom (from childcare responsibilities) to get involved in income-generating activities outside the community. Finally, the women complained that the kitchens were not big enough and that the sinks were too high, thus causing them back-pain.

These women have clearly learned how housing design and settlement layout affect their domestic labor and their daily lives in general. Through the actual implementation of the new policies, COPAN's women also understood that the government just wanted to build cheap houses and that the community and construction models developed by male officers did not take their needs into consideration.

Existing research suggests that women as a group bear the greater social costs of living in inadequate settlements (Peterson, Wekerle, and Morley 1978). These problems are often exaggerated by poverty, especially among single mothers and the elderly (Chant 1987; Peterson et al. 1978). In sum, the Arias Administration's policy was designed only to stop the social belligerency shown by the housing movement; it did not consider the real needs of the majority of the people involved in the struggle, namely, women and their children. Further, the government was treating the problem as a welfare issue rather than a social justice and development issue.

COPAN has, then, continued organizing demonstrations, rallies, and two more hunger strikes (May 1988 and August 1989). These actions have forced the government to yield to some of its demands. Thus, by 1992 most of the original members of the committees have obtained their loans or are in the process of getting them. Furthermore, in 1990 a woman's right to land tenure and house ownership was ensured after President Arias signed the "Real Equality Bill" into law. The women members of COPAN were instrumental in making this legal change. The Real Equality Law states that women are to have the property rights over all houses funded with subsidized state resources. If a husband is present, the house is considered "family patrimony," meaning that all the family members own it collectively. Finally, COPAN gained the right to design and build the new communities according to its principles.

Based on all these years of experience, and after countless discussions at all levels of the organization, COPAN developed three principles. First, each inhabitant must participate from the beginning in construction work through the communal self-help program, and each family must accumulate a minimum of 900 hours of work. The second concept is the idea that they are building whole communities, not individual houses. COPAN's members consider the house as not only a place to sleep, but a place to live. Recreation is then promoted as a means to foster better human communication. Further, the communities are designed to prevent traffic accidents by situating the houses with the front doors facing recreational areas closed off to traffic. The third principle is the preservation of environmental resources.

The new communities built by COPAN already constitute a complex structure of new organizational forms and social relations. In each community people have formed different groups for the organization of communal life. These groups include committees for the prevention of domestic violence, committees for the improvement of basic services, health committees, etc. Moreover, two of the communities have their own health centers basically for women and children. After all these years of communal organization and decision-making, issues such as child abuse and domestic violence against women are not seen as private issues anymore, but as communal matters.[3]

Although more men have become involved (particularly in construction work) now that the communities are being built, it is still the women who overwhelmingly participate in community activities. Just as they assume full responsibility for the activities related to social reproduction, women see the improvement of their families' living conditions through participation in communal activities as their responsibility. In this case, their efforts have paid off. By living in a better community and an adequate house, women have improved their daily lives and families' well-being. They now have access to different communal services and the social environment of the new communities is more appropriate for raising children and safer for women.

Thus, the substantial participation of women has had a strong impact in the way these communities are organized. Women's issues have become an important focus of attention and action, and specific women's needs and ideas have been the starting point for the development of construction and designing principles. As Sonia, a woman leader, says: "The new communities have a woman's soul."

Women, the Family, and Personal Transformation

Participation in this organization gave women the opportunity to create important bonds with other women and opened the doors for discussing and sharing common problems. Women began to recognize the lack of adequate housing as a social problem, rather than an individual problem that could be solved through individual actions. Cecilia, who has participated in the housing committees for eight years, expressed her understanding of the situation:

If you are alone nobody pays attention to you. I had tried for years to get a house all by myself and I couldn't. It was only through the struggle with all the other people that they paid attention to us. We were so many, we were on the streets for years; so, finally, they had to listen to us.

During all these years, however, the women have also faced serious problems in relation to their involvement with COPAN. First, they had to win the right just to go to meetings and to become members of the housing committees. Most of the women interviewed (76 percent) faced problems with their husbands, partners, or relatives who did not approve of their participation; some were actually abandoned. Then they had to face the opposition of some male members of the committees who did not want the women to become leaders and organizers. This became a major issue of discussion at all the organization's levels, from the Directorate to the base committees. As a woman member of the Directorate explained it:

We the women had to "infiltrate" COPAN. We had an organization whose members were mostly women, and only very few of us were occupying leadership positions. We had long discussions about that, and although the male members were very understanding, it was not a matter of "understand"; it was a matter of the power structure within COPAN which was reflecting the power structure of society at large. Since the women very quickly began to assume more responsibilities, they became leaders and now most of the main leaders are women.

However, while it is true that women play key roles in COPAN's organizational structure, and that some of them are actually in power positions (particularly the Directorate's members), men have retained important leadership positions.

An important factor in the process of empowerment for these women has been their participation in construction work. Through the formation of the joint building groups, COPAN tried to reduce the nature of inequality between women and men, and succeeded. According to the women's recollections, there were no differences between the tasks assigned to women and those assigned to men. After that, women saw themselves as capable of doing anything and in control of their lives. However, the time and effort dedicated to the construction work can also be seen as detrimental to them. Now the women were not only responsible for most of the housework and sometimes for outside jobs, but also for the heavy work of building the houses.

Furthermore, while some of their ideas about the role of women in society have changed and they now believe that women have a crucial role to play in community development and even in the country's destiny, their subordinate position inside the home has, in most cases, remained unchanged. They are still responsible for all the housework.

Despite all the problems, these women recognized that their participation in the movement has completely changed their lives and their perceptions about themselves. Most of them recall feeling worthless, useless, and isolated before. Further, most of them described themselves as shy and quiet before they became involved in the movement. Now they not only have recovered their own worth, but they perceive themselves as outspoken and capable of facing any difficult situation. The interviewees who still live with husbands or partners have won the right to go to meetings, to participate in community activities, and even to make some of their own decisions regarding their personal lives, which has changed their sense of self and competence.

The concrete result of their long struggle—a house that they own—has also changed their objective position within their families. This not only protects the women against unstable or violent situations, but also, by becoming property owners, gives them the ability to apply for other loans in order to start small or home businesses. This, in turn, gives them more independence, improves their families' living conditions, and enables them to make some of their own decisions about their lives and futures. These women have demonstrated their effectiveness in managing their daily lives to ensure family survival. In the process, they have also improved their objective position within the family's hierarchy, which has therefore contributed to their process of empowerment.

Conclusion

The social relations of reproduction, centered on the home, and women's struggle for survival created the groundwork for the development of the Costa Rican housing movement. This movement has had a strong impact on shaping the country's social struggles by incorporating new forms of political action and new social subjects into the political arena. The housing movement has also had a strong impact on the government's social policies, and of course, on the women participants themselves. Although it can be argued that these women's involvement has only been an extension of their traditional roles inside the "domestic domain," that participation has also changed them. Changing their perceptions about themselves, their attitudes, and some of their roles were important steps in their empowerment. Clearly, these women's multiple roles and responsibilities across the public and domestic spheres have shaped their history of political action and their process of empowerment. Thus, these poor women's marginal position in the paid labor force and their centrality to the family have set the stage for their protest activities aimed at improving their daily lives.

In the process these women recognized that issues previously considered as individual are, in fact, social problems, the solution of which requires collective action. Hence, through community activism, those women have "politicized" the private domain and have become "visible" by engaging in political action. So, although community activism has often been neglected as political action, the experiences of these women and this organization show how this type of activism can have an important impact not only on the people's lives, but also on social policy and the country's political destiny.

The women members of COPAN, with their commitment, discipline, and high levels of organization, have also created a gender-conscious movement. This can be seen through the ways the communities are physically designed and through the important focus on specific women's issues. By organizing themselves into the housing committees, they have made connections between their lives and those of other women, between the issues that affect their families and those that affect other families, and between their access to basic resources and state policy.

However, dilemmas do exist since the gender and class structures have not been modified. These dilemmas are demonstrated by the fact that males have retained many leadership positions within the organization and that women's subordinate position inside the home remains, in most cases, unchanged. Even though these women have been transformed by their political participation and their needs and ideas had an important influence on social policy and communal organization, the gender structure has not been openly changed by the housing movement.

In sum, while some levels of gender consciousness have been achieved, particularly by the women leaders, and some steps toward women's empowerment have been taken, the prevailing conditions in the Costa Rican society have not allowed the gender issues to move beyond the individual level. Women's subordinate position inside the home and in the economic sector are still major constraints. This demonstrates that more structural processes of social and cultural change are needed in order to transform gender issues into political issues.

Notes

1. It is estimated that throughout the Third World more than 50 percent of the households are headed by women (Moser 1987a). In some of the communities that I studied, particularly the Juan Pablo II, that figure went up to 75 percent.

2. The Arias Administration ended May 1990. There is still some debate about the number of houses that were actually built during the four-year period. According to official statistics the government accomplished the goal of 80,000. However, statistics revealed in 1990 showed that only 26,000 of those houses were low-income (Molina 1990). The rest were middle-class housing.

3. An example: When a woman leader who was being abused by her husband spoke up, the community assembly threatened the man with throwing him out of the community if he did not stop. Since the abuse continued, the woman decided to separate from him. She not only had the community's support, but some of the men watched over her house for several weeks in order to protect her against his return.

References

Ackelsberg, Marta. 1988. "Communities Resistance and Women's Activism." Pp. 297–313 in *Women and the Politics of Empowerment*, edited by A. Bookman and S. Morgen. Philadelphia, PA: Temple University Press.

Barbieri, Teresita, and Orlandina de Oliveira. 1991. "La Presencia Politica de las Mujeres." Pp. 9–23 in *Presencia Politica de Las Mujeres*, edited by R. Menjivar. San Jose, Costa Rica: FLACSO.

CESIP (Centro de Estudios Sociales y Publicaciones). 1986. "Feminism and the Grassroots Movement of Poor Women." Pp. 99–103 in *Women, Struggles and Strategies: Third World Perspectives*, produced by Isis International Women's Information and Communication Service. Rome, Italy: Isis Internacional.

Chant, Sylvia. 1987. "Domestic Labor, Decision-Making, and Dwelling Construction: The Experience of Women in Queretaro, Mexico." Pp. 33–54 in *Women, Human Settlements and Housing*, edited by C. Moser and L. Peake. London: Tavistock.

Cordero, Allen, and Nuria Gamboa. 1990. *La Sobrevivencia de los mas Pobres*. San Jose, Costa Rica: Porvenir.

Delgado, Gary. 1986. *Organizing the Movement: The Roots and Growth of ACORN*. Philadelphia, PA: Temple University Press.

Edgell, Stephen, and Vic Duke. 1983. "Gender and Social Policy." *Journal of Social Policy* 12:357–378.

Fireman, Bruce, and William Gamson. 1979. "Utilitarian Logic in the Resource Mobilization Perspective." Pp. 18–42 in *The Dynamics Social Movements*, edited by M. Zald and J. D. McCarthy. Cambridge, MA: Winthrop Publishers.

Lawson, Ronald, and Stephen Barton. 1980. "Sex Roles in Social Movements: A Case Study of the Tenant Movement in New York City." *Signs* 6(2).

Machado, Leda. 1987. "The Problems for Woman-Headed Households in a Low-Income Housing Programme in Brazil." Pp. 55–69 in *Women, Human Settlements and Housing*, edited by C. Moser and L. Peake. London: Tavistock.

Ministerio de Planificacion Nacional. 1986. *Plan Nacional de Desarrollo*. San Jose, Costa Rica: Imprenta Nacional.

Molina, Eugenia. 1990. *Repercusiones Politico-Organizativas del Acuerdo Politico entre los Frentes de Vivienda y el Estado Durante la Administracion Arias Sanchez*. Unpublished M.A. Thesis, Maestria Centroamericana en Sociologia, Universidad de Costa Rica.

Morgen, Sandra, and Ann Bookman. 1988. "Rethinking Women and Politics." Pp. 3–32 in *Women and the Politics of Empowerment*, edited by A. Bookman and S. Morgen. Philadelphia, PA: Temple University Press.

Moser, Caroline. 1987a. "Women, Human Settlements, and Housing: a Conceptual Framework for Analysis and Policy-Making." Pp. 12–32 in *Women, Human Settlements and Housing*, edited by C. Moser and L. Peake. London: Tavistock.

————. 1987b. "Mobilization is Women's Work: Struggles For Infrastructure in Guayaquil, Ecuador." Pp. 166–194 in *Women, Human Settlements and Housing*, edited by C. Moser and L. Peake. London: Tavistock.

Navas, Maria Candelaria. 1985. "Los Movimientos Femeninos en Centroamerica: 1970–1983." Pp. 200–237 in *Movimientos Populares en Centroamerica*, edited by D. Camacho and R. Menjivar. San Jose, Costa Rica: EDUCA (Editorial Universitaria de Centroamerica).

Peterson, Rebecca, Gerda R. Wekerle, and David Morley. 1978. "Women and Environments: An Overview of an Emerging Field." *Environment and Behavior* 10:511–535.

Rovira, Jorge. 1982. *Estado y Politica Economica en Costa Rica*. San Jose, Costa Rica: Editorial Porvenir.

Rubin, Lillian B. 1976. *Worlds of Pain*. New York: Basic Books.

Sacks, Karen B. 1988. "Gender and Grassroots Leadership." Pp. 77–96 in *Women and the Politics of Empowerment*, edited by A. Bookman and S. Morgen. Philadelphia, PA: Temple University Press.

Schneider, Beth. 1988. "Political Generations and the Contemporary Women's Movement." *Sociological Inquiry* 58:4–21.

Sojo, Ana. 1988. *Morfologia de la Politica Estatal en Costa Rica y Crisis Economica*. San Jose, Costa Rica: Instituto de Investigaciones Economicas, UCR.

Tuchmann, Gaye. 1981. "Contradictions in an Ideology: The Nineteenth Century Doctrine of Separate Spheres." *Quarterly Journal of Ideology* 5:5–10.

Valverde, Jose Manuel. 1987. *Elementos para la Comprension de la Politica Estatal de Vivienda en Costa Rica*. Unpublished M.A. Thesis, Maestria Centroamericana en Sociologia, Universidad de Costa Rica.

Valverde, Jose Manuel, and Silvia Lara. 1988. *La Politica de Vivienda de la Administracion Arias Sanchez*. San Jose, Costa Rica: CEPAS.

Vance, Irene. 1987. "More than Bricks and Mortar: Women's Participation in Self-Help Housing in Managua, Nicaragua." Pp. 139–165 in *Women, Human Settlements and Housing*, edited by C. Moser and L. Peake. London: Tavistock.

Vargas-Valente, Virginia. 1986. "El Aporte de la Rebeldia de las Mujeres." *Revista Paraguaya de Sociologia* 23:145–152.

❧ Chapter 9 ❧

Fertility, Selective Recruitment, and the Maquila Labor Force

Susan Tiano

Since its inception in 1965, the "maquiladora" or maquila program has grown to become Mexico's second largest source of foreign exchange and a key employment source for Mexican workers. Maquila firms, most of which are subsidiaries of transnational corporations (TNCs), employ a predominantly young female work force to assemble clothing, electronics components, and other products for export to other nations. Although the female proportion of the maquila work force has declined somewhat in recent years, the number of women workers has grown steadily, quadrupling from about 45,275 in 1975 to 171,603 in early 1988 (Sklair 1989, p. 167).

The consequences of the maquila program for women and families have been the focus of considerable controversy. Some have championed the program for providing stable jobs and steady wages to help women and their families survive Mexico's economic crisis, while others have condemned it for exploiting women within poorly paying, dead-end jobs, or for contributing to family disintegration by employing wives and daughters rather than men, the traditional breadwinners (Tiano 1987a). A number of studies have refined this debate by documenting women workers' demographic characteristics, house-

An earlier version of this paper was presented at the annual meetings of the American Sociological Association, Washington, DC, August, 1990. I am grateful to Claudia Isaac for her insightful comments on prior drafts.

hold structures, and working conditions (e.g., Carrillo and Hernandez 1985; Fernandez Kelly 1983; Pena 1987; Tiano 1987a); however, few have explored whether maquila employment affects the family by altering women's fertility patterns.

This omission is noteworthy given the obvious relevance of the question to public policy. Despite some recent advances toward reducing the high fertility that underlies her rapid population growth, Mexico continues to rank among the world's fastest-growing countries. Mexico has also lagged behind other Latin American nations in providing employment opportunities for women: In 1980, only 27 percent of the adult female population was economically active, a low rate even by Latin American standards (Brannon and Lucker 1989, p. 46). If, as many social scientists have maintained, women's employment is an important determinant of their fertility, then Mexico's weak performance in facilitating women's entrance into the labor force may combine with other factors, such as the influence of the Catholic Church, to limit Mexico's ability to curb population growth. Policies and programs that expand women's employment opportunities may both benefit women by increasing their access to economic resources, and serve the nation by reducing population increase. Within this context, the maquila program might contribute to Mexico's efforts to reduce overpopulation.

This chapter explores the links between maquila employment and fertility, considering both the influence of maquila jobs on women's childbearing and the effect of maquilas' selective recruitment practices on women workers' fertility levels. It is based on data collected during 1983 and 1984 from 194 women in Mexicali, Baja California. The sample includes 66 electronics assemblers, 58 apparel assemblers, and a comparison group of 70 women working as maids, waitresses, cashiers, and clerks, and in other service jobs. This sample is limited to women in the formal industrial and service sectors; it excludes full-time houseworkers as well as women generating income through "informal" activities (Arizpe 1977). This sample limitation precludes a thoroughgoing analysis of the relationship between labor force participation and fertility. Nevertheless, it permits an exploratory discussion comparing women in two sectors of the maquila industry and women in the formal service sector.

Production, Reproduction, and Household Survival Strategies

The field of women in development has focused much discussion on the links between women's productive and reproductive roles (Nash

1983; Tinker 1976). Public production refers to the creation of goods and services for market exchange. Domestic reproduction includes bearing, nurturing, and caring for children, and providing services that ensure the day-to-day maintenance of family members. Although production and reproduction occur in both the household and the public sphere (Lamphere 1987), my focus is on public production as it is shaped by state policy and the condition of the economy, and domestic reproduction as it reflects family structure and gender roles and relationships.

Fertility-related behaviors are integral to women's reproductive roles. Despite their biological basis, they are primarily social activities reflecting reproductive relations within the household. They respond to structural influences emanating from both the capitalist and domestic modes of production; yet they are not pre-determined in the sense that individual choices have no part to play in the outcome. Having a child is a component of a "household survival strategy" which family members develop and negotiate to help the household adapt to its economic and social environment. The anticipated viability of a household's strategy—and hence the decision to bear a child—depends on the household's composition and life-cycle stage, its members' ability to generate income and allocate reproductive tasks, and the potential mother's bargaining power vis-a-vis other household members.

During the early days of Europe's industrial revolution, having many children was an adaptive response to the household's need for multiple wage earners. This pattern changed with continuing industrialization, however, as the capitalist system's demand for an educated labor force led families to employ child-centered adaptive strategies. As the financial cost of children rose, families began to have fewer children, expending more time and resources on each one. Similar trends have been documented for Mexico (Rothstein 1982) and China (Chow and Chen, in this volume), where economic changes and governmental policies are leading families to limit their number of offspring and employ increasingly child-centered strategies. These reproductive strategies reflect relations of production within the public sphere.

Conversely, relations of reproduction within the household and the larger society shape women's productive roles (Beechey 1978; Beneria and Sen 1981). The gender-based division of labor in capitalist society shapes the terms under which women participate in the labor force. The ideology that women are primarily wives and mothers, and that their wages merely supplement male breadwinners' contributions, becomes a justification for confining women to low-status, poorly paid jobs within gender-segregated labor markets (Beechey 1978). Regardless of their domestic status, women are seen as actual or potential wives and mothers whose duty is to their families rather than their employers (Thorne 1982). Women's waged work is often considered a temporary pastime to occupy them until they find a husband and become full-time houseworkers. This ideology has shaped Mexican women's labor force participation rates, which peak between the ages of 20 and 25, and decline with advancing age (Tiano 1987b). Women typically leave the work force by age 30 to raise their families; although they often continue to contribute household income, they typically generate these funds in the informal sector. They select informal tasks both because they are compatible with domestic duties and because discriminatory hiring practices limit older women's job opportunities (Arizpe 1977).

Within this context, women's participation in the maquila labor force comes into clearer focus. TNC firms have employed a predominantly female labor force not just in Mexico, but throughout the Third World (Deyo 1984; Lim 1983; Ong 1987). The preference for women reflects their presumed dexterity, docility, and willingness to work for low wages, while the selection of young women reflects the notion that their more limited domestic responsibilities make them more dedicated employees (Fuentes and Ehrenreich 1983; Safa 1986a). Women assemblers are expected to work only until they assume full-time domestic roles (Mitter 1986, p. 49; Safa 1983, p. 99). Although this expectation has clear ideological undertones, it has some factual basis: Maquila workers' average age is twenty-five years or younger (Carrillo and Hernandez 1985; Seligson and Williams 1981).

Not all women assemblers are young, however. Rather, their age profiles vary across industrial sectors in a way that reflects an industry's links to the international economy (Fernandez Kelly 1983). Only some maquilas, such as those within the electronics industry, are TNC subsidiaries; others, such as most firms within the apparel industry, are Mexican-owned subcontracting operations. The technologically sophisticated and globally powerful electronics industry offers better working conditions than the apparel industry, whose labor process and productive technologies have changed little during the 20th Century. Apparel assembly jobs tend to be less stable, more prone to recruitment abuses, and more strenuous than jobs in the electronics sector (Fernandez Kelly 1983, pp. 111–112). The disparity in working conditions gives electronics firms a recruitment advantage over apparel firms. The intense competition for electronics jobs has enabled TNC firms to hire the "most desirable" women workers—young, single, secondary-school graduates (Fernandez Kelly 1983, p. 51; Safa 1986b, p. 67). Apparel firms tend to employ older, less educated women who are often partnered or single household heads (Fernandez Kelly 1983, p. 51; Stoddard 1987, p. 61). These contrasts in house-hold composition and life-cycle stage may lead to the different fertility patterns between electronics and apparel assemblers.

Although fertility has not been a key focus of empirical work on the maquila labor force, some studies have documented women work-ers' fertility along with other characteristics such as age, marital status, and household composition. These studies concur that maquila work-ers typically have fewer children than the norm for Mexican women generally (Carrillo and Hernandez 1985; Fernandez Kelly 1983; Selig-son and Williams 1981). Researchers offer different explanations for this pattern. Some argue that maquila workers' relatively low fertility is a result of paid employment, which presumably augments their independence and empowers them to control their biological repro-duction (Seligson and Williams 1981). Others claim that women assemblers' low fertility reflects the selective recruitment practices of firms which avoid the costs of maternity leaves and childcare facilities by hiring young, unmarried women (Carrillo and Hernandez 1985; Fernandez Kelly 1983).

This debate suggests the need for studying the dynamics under-lying the negative association between maquila employment and fer-tility. Is there a direct causal connection between them, or do other factors affect the relationship?

The Fertility-Maquila Employment Relationship: Three Possible Models

Figure 9.1 models three possible relationships between maquila employment and fertility. Model I, in which the causal flow is from employment to low fertility, is consistent with data from various soci-eties (Blumberg 1976; Harrison 1979; Rosen 1982). Women who have spent most of their lives in the workforce tend to have fewer children than life-long houseworkers or informal sector workers. This view assumes that women's status, which reflects their access to productive roles and resources, affects their ability to choose their reproductive activities (Blumberg 1976; Charlton 1984). Steady waged employment offers women an economic alternative to early marriage and childbear-ing. Moreover, the demands of waged work and motherhood may con-flict, particularly since women bear primary responsibility for child-rearing. Women who want or need to remain in the labor force, or to reenter once their children are older, may thus facilitate this choice by having fewer children. Again, a woman's income may reduce her household's need for wage-earning children, leading to a household strategy centered upon devoting family resources to a small number of

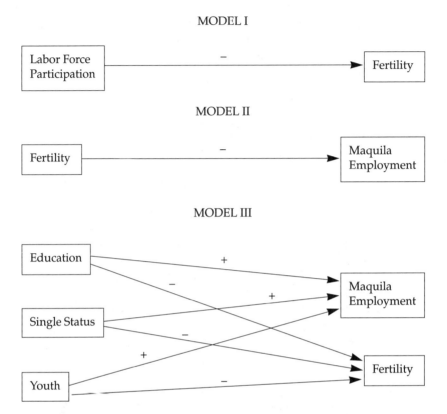

Figure 9.1   Three Models of the Maquila Employment-Fertility Relationship

children. Thus, having few children may be a beneficial adaptive strategy if the employed mother's income is essential for family survival, and the demands of raising a large family would interfere with her wage-earning abilities.

In Model II, the causal flow is from low fertility to maquila employment. The underlying rationale concerns the selective hiring of childless women for maquila jobs. The excess of labor available has enabled employers to be highly selective, hiring only those workers they deem most suitable (Baird and McCaughan 1979). This is especially the case in the electronics industry, where competition for jobs has been particularly intense. In my interviews with Mexicali maquila managers, many stated that they favored childless women because motherhood interferes with optimal job performance, contributes to higher rates of absenteeism and distracts women from their work. Managers of both electronics and apparel firms expressed this preference, but because apparel firms' applicant pools were more limited, they were not as able to implement these selective practices (Tiano 1987a). Hiring childless women also helps employers avoid maternity and childcare costs (Carrillo and Hernandez 1985, p. 116; Fernandez Kelly 1983, p. 51). This suggests, consistent with Model II, that low fertility increases a woman's access to maquila jobs, particularly in the electronics industry.

Model III also illustrates a selective recruitment effect, but this time the selection criteria are education, youth, and single status. According to this explanation, highly educated, young, single women are both most readily hired for maquila jobs, and most apt to have low fertility. This model does not rule out the possibility of a direct causal link between fertility and maquila employment. However, it focuses on the possibility that maquila employment and lower fertility appear together not because they directly affect each other but because they are both results of the same set of causes.

The links between education, youth, single status, and maquila employment are well-established empirically (Carrillo and Hernandez 1985, p. 119; Fernandez Kelly 1983, p. 52; Seligson and Williams 1981, p. 42; Tiano 1987a, pp. 85–86). The Mexicali managers I interviewed said they preferred young workers with no previous work experience because they were easier to train, and favored single women because male partners often made demands that distracted wives from their jobs and contributed to their absenteeism and frequent resignations (Tiano 1987a, p. 84).

Education, youth, and single status also tend to limit fertility (Seligson and Williams 1981, pp. 38, 40). The links between fertility, age, and marital status are clear: Young women have had fewer years in which to bear children, and they are also less apt to be in stable unions predisposing them toward motherhood. Education is assumed to empower women, giving them more control over their fertility by increasing their household bargaining power. Education may also increase women's access to family planning information and technologies (Harrison 1979, p. 248). Thus, young, single, educated women both have lower fertility levels, and have a better chance of maquila recruitment.

Different theoretical assumptions underlie the three models. Model I, depicting fertility as a dependent variable, illustrates propositions from modernization theory and its feminist variant, developmentalism (Elliott 1977; Tiano 1984). The central argument is that participation in the formal labor force generally, and in large-scale, complex organizations in particular, increases women's status and gives them more control over their lives, including their fertility-related behaviors

(Charlton 1984; Tinker 1976). Thus women's participation in the productive sphere transforms their reproductive behaviors, leading them to value small families and empowering them to implement their choices, either individually or in concert with other family members.

Models II and III, which both view maquila employment as a dependent variable, are drawn from the socialist-feminist literature on the new international division of labor (Nash and Fernandez Kelly 1983). The underlying argument is that TNCs employ preferential recruitment standards based on patriarchal ideologies defining women primarily as wives and mothers. Third World women are in a particularly vulnerable position on the international labor market: Many must somehow earn an income to support themselves and their families, but their job opportunities are limited. These constraints lead to intense competition for assembly jobs and force women who are hired to work under terms dictated by their employers. Thus, TNC employment does little to make women more independent, or to increase their household bargaining power. If assembly workers have low fertility, this reflects not their autonomy or their personal choices, but the fact that low fertility is a pre-condition for TNC employment. In this case, women's reproductive roles condition their access to the productive sphere.

Although these alternative theories imply contrasting assumptions about how capitalist industrialization transforms women's productive and reproductive roles, the propositions derived from them need not be mutually exclusive. Though low fertility may increase a woman's access to maquila jobs, once employed her experiences may transform her life in ways that shape her childbearing. Data from the Mexicali sample permit an exploratory evaluation of these models.

Findings

Table 9.1 presents average fertility levels for electronics, garment, and service workers according to their age groups. As would be expected, fertility levels vary directly with age, increasing from fewer than one child apiece for women under 24, to more than three children apiece among women 35 and older. Garment assemblers and service workers reveal the same relationship between age and fertility as the sample as a whole; electronics workers also conform to this pattern, with the exception of the 30 to 34 year olds and women 40 or over, whose small numbers may account for the discrepancy. Consistent with expectation, electronics workers have fewer children than apparel assemblers. The finding that women in all three occupations have fewer children than

Table 9.1   Average Number of Children by Age and Occupation

	Age						
	15–19	20–24	25–29	30–34	35–39	40 +	Total
Electronics Assemblers:							
Mean	.10	.22	2.60	.60	4.20	2.50	.74
Number	31	18	5	5	5	2	66
Apparel Assemblers:							
Mean	.17	.60	1.82	2.40	3.50	3.56	1.66
Number	12	15	11	5	6	9	58
Service Workers:							
Mean	.11	.32	1.30	2.20	3.50	3.17	1.31
Number	9	22	20	5	8	6	70
Total Sample:							
Mean	.12	.36	1.64	1.73	3.68	3.29	1.22
Number	52	55	36	15	19	17	194
Mexicali Population*:							
Mean	.1	.9	2.1	3.4	4.9	6.1	2.7

*Data from X Censo General de Poblacion y Vivienda, 1980, Estado de Baja California, Volumen I, Tomo 2, 1983, Cuadro 13.

Mexicali women generally supports Model I, which holds that labor force participation reduces fertility.

These data tell us little about how women's employment histories might have shaped their fertility patterns. If waged work reduces fertility, then we might expect this influence to be especially pronounced among women with relatively lengthy employment histories. To explore this question, the mean number of children for women in the various age groups can be considered relative to the age at which they joined the labor force. Table 9.2 presents the results of this comparison. Women who did not join the work force until 30 or older, and thus devoted their early years to domestic or informal sector roles, had more children than those who spent much or all of this time working for wages. This finding lends further support to Model I. It is likely

Table 9.2   Average Number of Children by Present Age and Age at
First Job

Age at First Job	Present Age						
	16–19	20–24	25–29	30–34	35–39	40 +	Total
7–14:							
Mean	.00	.33	1.25	1.33	3.20	3.00	1.47
Number	6	6	8	3	5	6	34
15–19:							
Mean	.13	.32	1.59	1.43	2.40	2.33	.68
Number	45	41	22	7	5	3	123
20–24:							
Mean	—	.63	1.75	2.00	5.00	2.00	2.00
Number	0	8	4	2	4	2	20
25–29:							
Mean	—	—	3.50	1.00	—	3.00	2.75
Number	0	0	2	1	0	1	4
30–39:							
Mean	—	—	—	3.50	4.40	4.80	4.42
Number	0	0	0	2	5	5	12
Total Sample:							
Mean	.12	.35	1.64	1.73	3.68	3.90	1.22
Number	52	55	39	15	19	17	194

that these women took jobs in order to support households with several dependent children. Women over 35 who began working while very young also have fairly high fertility. Although they have fewer children than those who entered wage work in later life, they have more children than women who first took jobs between 15 and 19 (the most common time of first employment for women in the sample). Intense financial need likely forced these women into the labor force while still very young, probably at the expense of their education. The schooling levels of these eleven women confirm this suspicion: Seven had between zero and six years of primary school, and none had finished the three years of secondary school. These educational levels are low compared to the rest of the sample, over half of whom had secondary school educations or beyond. These women's relatively low educations may have counteracted the fertility-reducing effect of their labor force participation. This hypothesized effect of education suggests that employment is not the only influence on women's fertility.

Although the dynamics depicted in Model I help explain the complex reality surrounding fertility-related behaviors, they clearly do not tell the whole story.

Formulating a more complete picture of the forces affecting fertility requires a statistical technique such as multiple regression that measures the separate and combined effects of several possible influences. The dependent variable for the regression analysis is number of children. The independent variables include age, a continuous variable ranging from sixteen to fifty-two; marital status, a dichotomous measure contrasting single women (scored as one) with women who are married, in consensual unions, divorced, separated, or widowed (scored as zero); and age at first job, a continuous measure ranging from seven to thirty-nine. To account for the contrast in types of schooling, education is measured in continuous categories, rather than years of school; the scores range from zero (no schooling) to twelve (finished three years of preparatory school plus some additional commercial training). Table 9.3 summarizes the results of this analysis. The symbols "+" and "-" indicate positive and negative effects, while asterisks (*) indicate statistically significant effects—those strong enough to suggest that they are not simply due to random variation. Tables A-1 and A-2 in the Appendix provide more detailed information, with the former presenting the correlation coefficients for the variables, and the latter showing the multiple regression results.

The results in Table 9.3 show that each predictor has a significant effect on fertility over and above the effects of the others. Fertility increases with age, and decreases with both education and single status, consistent with the predictions of Model III. Also, fertility levels are

Table 9.3 Summary of Effects of Present Age, Single Status, Education, and Age at First Job on Fertility

| | *Independent Variables* | | | |
	Present Age	*Single Status*	*Education*	*Age at First Job*
Dependent Variable:				
Number of	**	**	*	**
Children	+	-	-	+

+ Positive Effect
- Negative Effect
* Significant, p< .05
** Significant, p< .01

higher among women who entered the labor force at older ages, as Model I would predict. Together, the four independent variables account for 60 percent of the variation in fertility among women in the sample.

To explore the effects of fertility on maquila employment, as well as to evaluate the predictions of Model III that youth, education, and single status increase a woman's access to maquila jobs, I performed a series of multiple regression analyses, treating each employment type as a dependent variable, and number of children, youth, education, single status, and age at first job as independent variables. I constructed the dependent variables by contrasting respondents in each employment category with women in the other two. Table 9.4 summarizes the results of these analyses. Table A-3 in the Appendix provides a more complete description of these results. The correlations presented in Table A-1 portray different reproductive and life-cycle profiles for women in the three occupational sectors. The electronics workers are the most likely to be young, childless, well-educated, to have begun working at younger ages, and to be recent entrants into the labor force. Being single is positively related to electronics employment, but the relationship is not significant. With this exception, the emerging profile closely matches the typical electronics worker

Table 9.4 Summary of Effects of Fertility, Present Age, Single Status, Education, and Age at First Job on Type of Employment

	Independent Variables				
	Number of Children	*Present Age*	*Single Status*	*Education*	*Age at First Job*
Dependent Variables:					
Electronics	**	*			
Employment	−	−	−	+	−
Apparel	**		**	**	
Employment	+	−	+	−	−
Service		**		**	
Employment	+	+	−	+	+

 + Positive Effect
 − Negative Effect
 * Significant, p< .05
** Significant, p< .01

depicted in the empirical literature, suggesting preferential hiring according to the prevalent image of the "ideal worker." Garment assemblers tend to be older, to have children, to be less educated, and to have spent more time in the labor force, than electronics and service workers. Finally, compared to maquila workers, service workers tend to be older, to have more children, to be better educated, and to have entered the labor force at older ages; they are also less likely to be single. In short, the typical profile for garment assemblers is much like that of service workers: Both tend to be older women with children. However, service workers' higher educational attainment offers employment alternatives to garment assembly.

The effects portrayed in Table 9.4 permit evaluating the importance of fertility relative to the other independent variables that affect a woman's employment in a given sector. Both low fertility and youth are significant predictors of electronics employment; education, marital status, and age at first job have no effect after the regression equation statistically controls for fertility and youth. Interestingly, although single status correlates positively with electronics employment, it has a negative, though insignificant, effect when the influence of the other predictors is controlled. These findings suggest that low fertility and youth, rather than single status or education, increase a woman's chances of electronics recruitment. This finding is consistent with Model II.

Fertility has a different influence on participation in the garment industry: The apparel industry provides jobs for single mothers who must earn a wage to support themselves and their offspring. Limited educational attainment may compound the disadvantage of single motherhood, making it difficult for these women to find employment outside of the apparel sector. Neither youth nor previous labor force experience counteract the employment disadvantage posed by fertility and limited educational levels.

These findings suggest straightforward conclusions about the role of fertility and other factors in the maquila recruitment process. Low fertility and youth, the key determinants of electronics employment, each have independent effects over and above the impact of the other. Childless women are preferred over mothers regardless of their age, while young women are favored over older women regardless of their fertility levels. Young women also tend to have few or no children. Further, although young, childless women are more apt to be single and relatively better-educated than older mothers, marital status and education are not in themselves important predictors of electronics employment. TNC firms might desire an unpartnered, highly educated labor force, but they appear more willing to relax these requirements than their standards concerning age and fertility. This conclusion supports Model II, which holds that low fertility facilitates entrance into the maquila industry, but runs contrary to Model III's emphasis on the importance of single status and relatively high education for gaining access to maquila jobs.

Low fertility is not a prerequisite for apparel sector employment. Rather, apparel maquilas tend to recruit mothers, as well as women who are single and relatively uneducated. These women occupy a particularly vulnerable position on the northern Mexican labor market, departing from the "ideal" worker in terms of both their educational attainment and their reproductive status. Even their tendency to be single, which typically gives women a recruitment advantage, is unlikely to elevate the labor market status of women who are also mothers, for single mothers are a stigmatized category in northern Mexico. The composition of the work force in the apparel industry appears to reflect its global marginality and the relative inadequacy of its working conditions. These data provide no way of judging whether the demand for sewing skills outweighs the importance of education, youth, and low fertility, or whether apparel firms' applicant pools are so limited that employers cannot employ stringent recruitment criteria. Clearly, however, childlessness is not a precondition for apparel employment. Model II is less appropriate to describing recruitment into the apparel sector than the electronics sector. And contrary to Model III, factors related to low fertility, such as youth and educational attainment, are not associated with employment in apparel firms. These contrasting patterns demonstrate the need for theoretical models accounting for the heterogeneity among different sectors of the maquila labor force.

Discussion and Policy Implications

These findings confirm the pattern of low fertility observed in previous studies of the maquila workforce, and demonstrate, moreover, that women in formal service jobs have fewer children than the Mexicali norm. Thus formal labor force participation decreases fertility regardless of where women are employed. Also, women who have spent much of their adult lives working for wages have fewer children than women who entered the workforce at a more advanced age. These findings support the developmentalist hypothesis depicted in Model I: Women's productive activities affect their fertility-related choices. There is no way to determine from these data whether the fertility-reducing effects of waged employment reflect women's decision-making autonomy, as the developmentalist hypothesis would predict, or whether they derive from other household-level dynamics over which the employed woman has little influence, as socialist-feminist perspectives would have it. Further research focusing on household-level decision-making processes and adaptive strategies is necessary to provide a fuller account of the links between employment and fertility.

Just as a woman may limit her childbearing to facilitate employment, she may also opt to have many children in order to compensate for her limited employment opportunities and ensure her financial security in later life. If she assumes that her employment options are likely to dwindle as she ages, she is apt to bear several or more children who can contribute to her support. Border region women are well aware that older women face pronounced employment barriers. Hence, their choice to pursue a high fertility strategy is often a rational response to their objective circumstances. Such considerations suggest that the fertility-reducing effects of paid employment can only be achieved in a context which guarantees women job security throughout a major portion of their life cycle. Employment within the maquila industry—where jobs are typically short-lived and older women face employment barriers—may not have stable, long-lasting negative effects on women's fertility levels.

This interpretation is consistent with the finding that maquila workers' low fertility is as much a reflection of the industry's selective recruitment practices as an effect of women's economic activity. Part of the explanation for women assemblers' low fertility levels is that TNC firms more readily hire childless women. Low fertility is not the only criterion for electronics recruitment: Young workers have an advantage over their more mature counterparts. Youth may counteract the disadvantage of motherhood, enabling them to secure electronics jobs even though they have children. However, an older mother may find it difficult to gain access to the electronics sector, regardless of her education or other factors which could contribute to her on-the-job competence.

This finding is consistent with the selective recruitment argument depicted in Model II and with the socialist-feminist thesis that reproductive roles and relations condition women's participation in the productive sphere. Fertility, a key dimension of women's reproductive roles, influences their employment opportunities. Selective recruitment practices favoring childless women are one mechanism through which low fertility affects women's access to electronics jobs. Hiring standards that discriminate against employed mothers marginalize them from firms at the center of capitalist production.

Unlike TNC electronics maquilas, apparel firms do not recruit a primarily childless labor force. The composition of their workforce reflects the relative undesirability of apparel assembly jobs, which are often the last resort for single mothers with few other job options. The selective recruitment effect depicted in Model II is thus much less appropriate to describing firms within the internationally peripheral apparel industry. Yet these data are consistent with the central insight conveyed in Model II, that women's fertility levels affect their employment patterns. Having children increases the likelihood of participation in the apparel sector. Were the model to be modified to indicate the positive effects of fertility on apparel sector employment, it would be an adequate representation of this trend. In this case the intervening mechanism would be the mirror image of the selective hiring practices that give preference to childless women. The shadow side of the selective recruitment dynamic is the discrimination against employed mothers which limits their access to TNC jobs, thereby relegating them to the least appealing jobs within a marginal branch of the maquila industry.

The conclusion that TNC subsidiaries employ selective recruitment criteria favoring childless women runs counter to much of the literature on complex organizations, which are assumed to employ universal recruitment standards emphasizing education, past experience, and other achievement-oriented criteria directly relevant to effective job performance (Hoselitz 1970; Weber 1969). An emphasis on universal criteria over more parochial standards centering on women's reproductive status could make TNCs a vehicle of progressive change in Mexico. Such employment policies could help rationalize the labor market by replacing patriarchal hiring practices with more egalitarian ones.

These findings suggest, to the contrary, that TNC's recruitment standards reflect and reinforce the patriarchal status quo. Such practices could simply mirror the biases of maquila managers, most of whom are Mexican nationals reared within a cultural context defining women's roles in terms of home and family. However, the fact that TNC firms in export zones throughout the world employ a primarily young, childless female labor force for their assembly operations suggests that these selective recruitment practices are not confined to maquila managers or TNC firms operating in northern Mexico. Rather, they appear to stem from corporate policies that emanate from TNC headquarters to be implemented throughout their networks of subsidiaries. The goals of such practices, some critics claim, are to ensure a docile labor force by employing young women, and to avoid the costs of maternity benefits by hiring childless women (Fuentes and Ehrenreich 1983; Mitter 1986). If such selective recruitment practices reflect a globally prevalent corporate strategy, then it is not surprising that TNC electronics maquilas have not transcended the patriarchal ideologies that abound. Indeed, such policies would find fertile soil in northern Mexico, for they dovetail closely with the dominant cultural belief that wage work and motherhood are inconsistent.

Regardless of their source, these recruitment practices disadvantage employed mothers. The underlying patriarchal ideology assumes that women with children are in stable relationships with a male whose wages are sufficient to support them and their offspring. This assumption clearly misrepresents the situations of both single mothers who must provide for themselves and their children, and non-single women helping their families survive the economic crisis inaugurated by the peso devaluations of the late 1970s and early 1980s (see Cockroft 1983). The rising male unemployment rate and the inflation and wage ceilings that have limited popular buying power have forced growing numbers of women with stable relationships into the labor force to help support their families (Beneria and Roldan 1987). Within this context, recruitment practices that bar mothers from the labor force spell hardship for these families.

Ironically, such practices and the ideologies that underlie them reflect a conservative image of Mexican family life that is antithetical to Mexico's anti-natalist goals. Ideologies that define women exclusively in terms of their reproductive roles and undervalue their productive contributions through waged labor reinforce the objective conditions that contribute to their high fertility. By bolstering the traditional gender division of labor, these ideologies bar women from roles that could increase their well-being as well as provide the resources and incentives conducive to fewer children. They also encourage women to believe that personal fulfillment and social prestige are best achieved through having numerous children.

Recruitment practices that discriminate against women with children reinforce these dynamics by excluding them from jobs that could help them break this pattern. The result is a vicious circle wherein having children, one consequence of women's confinement to the domestic sphere, precludes their ability to enter waged employment, thereby further ensconcing them within the domestic roles and relationships that are likely to lead them to have more children. Not only do these practices work to women's economic disadvantage, but they contribute to Mexico's burgeoning population growth.

State policies designed to help women balance the competing demands of their maternal and job-related responsibilities may compound this dilemma by fueling employment discrimination against employed mothers. Mexican law requires employers to provide maternity leaves for pregnant workers, and to help bear the costs of government-sponsored childcare centers for female employees. However, when firms attempt to avoid the costs of these programs by selectively recruiting childless women, these well-intended policies redound to employed mothers' detriment.

The state could attempt to prevent this unintended consequence by outlawing employment discrimination on the basis of women's reproductive status. In placing women's welfare at the center of public policy, such a law would send a clear message about the propriety of paid employment for wives and mothers, thus helping relax cultural norms proscribing their extradomestic work. Despite its symbolic value, however, such a law would likely be unenforceable, for willful discrimination is difficult to verify. Further, such legislation could upset the delicate balance of regulation and incentives which the state must maintain in order to encourage further TNC investment (Sklair 1989). The Mexican state is not alone in this dilemma. All governments promoting export-led industrialization face the risk that regulating recruitment practices or mandating companies to provide maternal leaves or childcare might cause TNCs to move to other export zones with fewer regulations (Yi in this volume). Yet governments that resolve this contradiction by abandoning women's interests in favor of encouraging TNC investment are likely to face unanticipated negative consequences stemming from women's marginalization from productive roles and resources, of which their continuing high fertility is but one example.

Another possible option for Mexican state policy is to provide the fiscal conditions for further maquila investment in the hopes that the industry's continued expansion will shrink the surplus female labor pool. The reduced availability of young, childless, relatively educated women could lead maquilas to cast their nets more widely. A recent Juarez-based study (Brannon and Lucker 1989) suggests that such dynamics are beginning to change the composition of the maquila workforce. The rapid growth of the maquila program in the post-1982 period has reduced the supply of what industry officials euphemistically label, "maquila-grade" labor—young, childless, secondary school graduates—leading companies to hire more older mothers. Were such a trend to continue, more older women and more married and single mothers might find their way into TNC electronics firms.

Such a trend does not, however, hold much promise as a long-term solution to employment discrimination against women with children. On the one hand, maquila managers could merely recruit more men for assembly jobs, an option which many are currently pursuing (Brannon and Lucker 1989; Sklair 1989). On the other hand, the migration stream from the Mexican interior, which is disproportionately young and female (see Tiano 1987b), is apt to replenish the ranks of the surplus female labor pool with "maquila-grade" women workers. That maquila managers in Juarez are recruiting more young female migrants for their assembly operations (Brannon and Lucker 1989) suggests that many employers are willing to subordinate their preference for long-term Juarez residents in order to maximize the number of young, childless women employees.

These considerations suggest that while the maquila industry may play a useful role in providing jobs for women, it is not likely to offer a viable long-term solution to the dilemmas faced by the state in its efforts to curb Mexico's explosive population growth. The crux of the issue is the contradiction between the interests of the state to limit fertility, and the interests of Mexican women to guarantee their own financial security throughout their life cycles. Unless the state is able to formulate policies that can simultaneously expand women's employment opportunities and erode the employment barriers faced by older women and mothers, many women will continue to pursue high-fertility strategies in an attempt to ensure their economic well-being.

The central contradiction that has limited the efficacy of the state's family planning programs is that they have continued to define women exclusively as wives and mothers. The ideological thrust of Mexico's anti-natalist campaign blends appeals to limit childbearing with injunctions to devote oneself to full-time domestic roles: The "good" mother has only a few children upon whom she lavishes her time and energy. Women are entreated to pursue such a child-centered strategy as a way of maximizing their children's opportunities for economic success (see Rothstein 1982). However, women are well aware that education cannot guarantee a stable livelihood in a crisis-riddled economy; hence, few are willing to risk their economic security on the income-generating capacities of a few grown children. Therefore, many have resisted the state's family planning efforts, preferring instead to continue with the high-fertility strategies that have afforded some material security for their mothers and grandmothers.

The most obvious solution to this policy dilemma would be to embed the state's family planning programs within a broader policy effort designed to erode the obstacles to women's employment. Assuring women of adequately remunerated jobs throughout a major portion of their life cycles would help remove the spectre of economic insecurity which motivates them to bear numerous children. The state's continued support of the maquila industry could supplement these efforts, particularly if it could induce TNCs to raise wages, improve working conditions, and guarantee job stability for their workforce. However, the state would be ill-advised to place the maquila industry at the center of its employment-generating effort, for it cannot guarantee the long-term stability of the maquila program or the firms that comprise it.

To summarize, the maquila industry may help Mexico curb her population growth somewhat. Yet its role must not be exaggerated, for much of the low fertility observed among maquila workers is merely an artifact of the recruitment process. Moreover, the popular conception of the industry as unstable, and of firms within it as "runaway shops" prone to geographical relocation, suggests that few women are likely to view maquila jobs as offering the kind of life-long job security that would lead them to adopt a low-fertility survival strategy. This problem may resolve itself during the 1990s if maquilas prove to be stable figures within the northern Mexican economic landscape. Perhaps the most effective means for maximizing the fertility-reducing potential of maquila employment would be to increase wages and improve working conditions throughout the industry. Such reforms would increase the likelihood that maquila jobs could offer the material conditions conducive to women's augmented autonomy, and would strengthen the appeal of a household adaptive strategy combining maquila employment with low fertility. However, unless the program offers employment opportunities to women who deviate from the culturally legitimated "ideal" woman worker, these potential benefits are unlikely to be realized.

References

Arizpe, Lourdes. 1977. "Women in the Informal Labor Sector: The Case of Mexico City." Pp. 25–37 in *Women and National Development*, edited by Wellesley Editorial Committee. Chicago, IL: The University of Chicago Press.

Baird, Peter, and Ed McCaughan. 1979. *Beyond the Border*. New York: NACLA.

Beechey, Veronica. 1978. "Women and Production: A Critical Analysis of Some Sociological Theories of Women's Work." Pp. 155–197 in *Feminism and Materialism*, edited by A. Kuhn and A. Wolpe. London: Routledge and Kegan Paul.

Beneria, Lourdes, and Martha Roldan. 1987. *The Crossroads of Class and Gender: Industrial Homework, Subcontracting, and Household Dynamics in Mexico City*. Chicago, IL: University of Chicago Press.

Beneria, Lourdes, and Gita Sen. 1981. "Accumulation, Reproduction, and Women's Role in Economic Development: Boserup Revisited." *Signs* 7:279–298.

Blumberg, Rae Lesser. 1976. "Fairy Tales and Facts: Economy, Family, Fertility, and the Female." Pp. 12–21 in *Women and World Development*, edited by I. Tinker and M. B. Bramsen. Washington, DC: Overseas Development Council.

Brannon, Jeff, and G. William Lucker. 1989. "The Impact of Mexico's Economic

Crisis on the Demographic Composition of the Maquiladora Labor Force." *Journal of Borderlands Studies* IV:39–70.

Carrillo, Jorge, and Alberto Hernandez. 1985. *Mujeres Fronterizas en la Industria Maquiladora*. Mexico, D.F.: CEFNOMEX.

Charlton, Sue Ellen. 1984. *Women in Third World Development*. Boulder: Westview.

Cockroft, James. 1983. *Mexico: Class Formation, Capital Accumulation, and the State*. New York: Monthly Review Press.

Deyo, Frederic. 1984. "Export Manufacturing and Labor: The Asian Case." Pp. 267–288 in *Labor in the Capitalist World Economy*, edited by C. Berquist. Newbury Park, CA: Sage Publications.

Elliott, Carolyn. 1977. "Theories of Development: An Assessment." Pp. 1–8 in *Women and National Development*, edited by Wellesley Editorial Committee. Chicago, IL: University of Chicago Press.

Fernandez Kelly, M. Patricia. 1983. *For We Are Sold: I and My People*. Albany, NY: State University of New York Press.

Fuentes, Annette, and Barbara Ehrenreich. 1983. *Women in the Global Factory*. New York: South End Press.

Harrison, Paul. 1979. *Inside the Third World*. New York: Penguin Books.

Hills, Stuart. 1981. *Demystifying Social Deviance*. New York: St. Martin's Press.

Hoselitz, Bert. 1970. "Main Concepts in the Analysis of the Social Implications of Technical Change." Pp. 11–32 in *Industrialization and Society*, edited by B. Hoselitz and W. Moore. The Hague: Mouton.

Lamphere, Louise. 1987. *From Working Daughters to Working Mothers*. Ithaca, NY: Cornell University Press.

Lim, Linda. 1983. "Capitalism, Imperialism, and Patriarchy: The Dilemma of Third-World Women Workers in Multinational Factories." Pp. 70–91 in *Women, Men, and the International Division of Labor*, edited by J. Nash and M. P. Fernandez Kelly. Albany, NY: State University of New York Press.

Mitter, Swasti. 1986. *Common Fate, Common Bond*. London: Pluto Press.

Nash, June. 1983. "The Impact of the Changing Division of Labor on Different Sectors of the Labor Force." Pp. 70–91 in *Women, Men, and the International Division of Labor*, edited by J. Nash and M. P. Fernandez Kelly. Albany, NY: State University of New York Press.

Ong, Aihwa. 1987. *Spirits of Resistance and Capitalist Discipline: Factory Women in Malaysia*. Albany, NY: State University of New York Press.

Pena, Devon. 1987. "Tortuosidad: Shop Floor Struggles of Female Maquiladora Workers." Pp. 129–154 in *Women on the U.S.–Mexico Border: Responses to Change*, edited by V. Ruiz and S. Tiano. Boston: Allen and Unwin.

Rosen, Bernard. 1982. *The Industrial Connection: Achievement and the Family in Developing Societies*. Chicago, IL: Aldine.

Rothstein, Frances. 1982. *Three Different Worlds: Women, Men, and Children in an Industrializing Community*. Westport, CT: Greenwood Press.

Safa, Helen. 1983. "Women, Production, and Reproduction in Industrial Capitalism: A Comparison of Brazilian and U.S. Factory Workers." Pp. 95–116 in *Women, Men, and the International Divison of Labor*, edited by J.

Nash and M. P. Fernandez Kelly. Albany, NY: State University of New York Press.

———. 1986a. "Female Employment in the Puerto Rican Working Class." Pp. 84–105 in *Women and Change in Latin America*, edited by J. Nash and H. Safa. South Hadley, MA: Bergin and Garvey.

———. 1986b. "Runaway Shops and Female Employment: The Search for Cheap Labor." Pp. 58–71 in *Women's Work*, edited by E. Leacock and H. Safa. South Hadley, MA: Bergin and Garvey.

Seligson, Mitchell, and Edward Williams. 1981. *Maquiladoras and Migration: Workers in the Mexico–United States Border Industrialization Program.* Austin, TX: University of Texas Press.

Sklair, Leslie. 1989. *Assembling for Development: The Maquila Industry in Mexico and the United States.* Boston and London: Unwin Hyman.

Stoddard, Ellwyn. 1987. *Maquila: Assembly Plants in Northern Mexico.* El Paso, TX: Texas Western Press.

Thorne, Barrie. 1982. "Feminist Rethinking of the Family: An Overview." Pp. 1–24 in *Rethinking the Family*, edited by B. Thorne and M. Yalom. New York: Longman.

Tiano, Susan. 1984. "The Public-Private Dichotomy: Theoretical Perspectives on 'Women in Development'." *Social Science Journal* 21:11–28.

———. 1987a. "Maquiladoras in Mexicali: Integration or Exploitation?" Pp. 77–102 in *Women on the U.S.–Mexico Border: Responses to Change*, edited by V. Ruiz and S. Tiano. Boston: Allen and Unwin.

———. 1987b. "Women's Work and Unemployment in Northern Mexico." Pp. 17–39 in *Women on the U.S.–Mexico Border: Responses to Change*, edited by V. Ruiz and S. Tiano. Boston: Allen and Unwin.

Tinker, Irene. 1976. "The Adverse Impact of Development on Women." Pp. 22–43 in *Women and World Development*, edited by I. Tinker and M. B. Bramsen. Washington, DC: Overseas Development Council.

Weber, Max. 1969. "Bureaucratic Organizations." Pp. 27–31 in *Readings on Modern Organizations*, edited by A. Etzioni. Englewood Cliffs, NJ: Prentice-Hall.

Appendix: Bivariate Correlation Matrix and Multiple Regression Results

Table A-1 Correlation Matrix for Employment, Fertility, and Other Independent Variables

	Single Status	Education	Age	Age at First Job	Number of Children	Electronics Employment	Apparel Employment	Service Employment
Single	1.0	—	—	—	—	—	—	—
Education	.14*	1.0	—	—	—	—	—	—
Age	-.40**	-.43**	1.0	—	—	—	—	—
Age at First Job	-.27**	-.11	.37**	1.0	—	—	—	—
No. of Children	-.64**	-.31**	.58**	.26**	1.0	—	—	—
Electronics Employment	.10	.17**	-.27**	-.12*	-.29**	1.0	—	—
Apparel Employment	.04	-.37**	.16*	.02	.15*	-.47**	1.0	—
Service Employment	-.13*	.18*	.12*	.10	.14*	-.54**	-.49**	1.0

*   Significant, $p < .05$
** Significant, $p < .01$

Table A-2 Effects of Age, Single Status, Education, and Age at First Job on Fertility

| Independent Variables | Dependent Variable: Number of Children | | | |
	b	Se	Beta	t
Age	.09**	.01	.16**	7.9
Single Status	-.24**	.18	-.35**	-6.8
Education	-.05*	.03	-.09*	-1.7
Age at First Job	.05**	.02	.16**	3.3
(Constant)	-1.03	.50		-2.06

R-Square for Equation = .60

   b = Unstandardized regression coefficient
  Se = Standard error
Beta = Standardized regression coefficient
    t = t ratio
   *Significant, p< .05
  **Significant, p< .01

Table A-3 Effects of Age, Single Status, Education, Age at First Job, and Fertility on Type of Employment

						Independent Variables											
	Number of Children			Age			Single Status			Education			Age at First Job			R Square
	b	Se	t	b	Se	t	b	Se	t	b	Se	t	b	Se	t	for equation
Electronics Employment	-.26**	.11	-2.43	-.01*	.01	-1.29	-.21	.10	-1.25	.01	.01	.90	-.01	.01	-.49	.107
Apparel Employment	.18**	.10	1.84	-.01	.05	-.38	.20**	.09	2.21	-.06**	.01	-5.18	-.01	.01	-.16	.163
Service Employment	.08	.11	.70	.01**	.01	1.61	-.08	.10	-.80	.05**	.01	3.86	.01	.01	.62	.099

b = Unstandardized regression coefficient
Se = Standard error
t = t ratio
*Significant, p< .05, one tailed test
**Significant, p< .01

※ Chapter 10 ※

Childcare Arrangements of Employed Mothers in Taiwan

Chin-Chun Yi

Taiwan resembles many other countries in having witnessed a rapid increase in women's labor force participation over the past several decades. In 1965, 33.1 percent of Taiwanese women aged 15 and over were in the labor force, constituting 27.3 percent of the total labor supply. Corresponding figures in 1992 were 44.8 percent and 37.7 percent, respectively (Executive Yuan 1992). Married women's labor force participation reached 43.3 percent in 1992. Research suggests that female employment will continue to increase. More and more women will combine paid work with family roles, which include housework and childcare. Of the two family roles, childcare is generally considered the more significant one, not only because of the greater value assigned to people care than to house care, but also because more flexible standards are applied to housework.

Data used in this chapter are from the "Study of Childcare Problems among Married Employed Women," Research, Development, and Evaluation Committee, Executive Yuan, R.O.C., 1986. Investigators included Shu-Kuei Kao, Er-Ro Lai, Annie Lee, and the author. Statistical help from Dr. Ruey-Ling Chu and data analysis by Yuay-Ling Tsai are greatly appreciated. Comments on previous drafts from Drs. Karen O. Mason and Rachel Rosenfeld as well as from the two editors of this book and Elaine Stahl Leo are gratefully acknowledged. An earlier version of this chapter was completed while the author was a visiting scholar at the Carolina Population Center (CPC), University of North Carolina at Chapel Hill, where CPC staff members Lynn Igoe and Catheryn Brandon provided valuable assistance.

235

Traditional patriarchies, such as Taiwan, view childcare as a woman's individual problem rather than as a social issue. Since women are still responsible for the domestic sphere, childcare arrangements are a serious concern for employed mothers, one aggravated by a lack of supportive social policies, which until quite recently neglected employed mothers' needs in general. The research on which this paper reports examined the childcare arrangements of employed mothers in Taiwan in an effort to illuminate linkages between family and work as interdependent social institutions. The research also revealed the relationship of these two institutions with others, especially education and the state. How this macro-environment interacts with gender is an important sub-theme.

Taiwan has been an exemplary developing country, with a steady per-capita income increase from U.S. $2,344 in 1980 to U.S. $7,990 in 1990 (Executive Yuan 1990). The country's rapid economic growth has coincided with an unprecedented expansion of secondary education, especially for females (Ministry of Interior 1992). Foreign contacts on both the state and individual levels have also mushroomed over the last decade, leading to even higher expectations regarding living standards than development thus far has satisfied. Both husband and wife must be gainfully employed to meet these rising living standards and expectations.

Since systematic studies of similar topics have rarely focused on Taiwan, the research provided an overview of current childcare patterns in the country's urban families. Employed mothers were asked about the childcare arrangements they had made, including location, type of provider, and extent of parents' involvement in childcare. The research also examined various aspects of women's paid work, particularly structural (objective) job conditions and psychological (subjective) employment orientation. Analysis focused on the importance of these two factors for childcare arrangements in families with eldest children in different age categories. Findings regarding after-school care have significant policy implications for "latchkey children." Hence, this research contributes to our understanding of the interaction between family and work as well as gender and its macro-environment in Taiwan.

Employed Mothers and Childcare

Most childcare studies distinguish various caregiving locations (child's own home, another's home, and childcare centers) as well as caretaker type (kin, non-kin, and institutional). In the United States, family day-care is the second most frequently used arrangement after own-home care for preschoolers and school-age children alike (Emlen and Perry 1975; Floge 1985; Giele 1982; Hofferth and Phillips 1987; Moore and Sawhill 1984). Kin constitute a high proportion of caretakers for young children (Hofferth and Phillips 1987).

Childcare studies in the United States also reveal a tendency to change from kin to group or multiple-care arrangements as children age (Floge 1985). Children of different ages (e.g., three and under, three-to-six-year-old preschoolers, six-to-twelve-year-old primary schoolers, etc.) have different care patterns (Hofferth and Phillips 1987; Lehrer 1983), with institutional care gradually becoming more prominent as children grow older. Preschool children are still the major focus of most recent childcare studies in the United States (Floge 1989; Mason and Kuhlthau 1989; Presser 1989), but research reports have also included school-age children (Cain and Hofferth 1989; Rodman and Pratto 1987). Self-care arrangements become increasingly prevalent as children grow older. A family's socioeconomic status affects how soon children may be left to care for themselves.

In Taiwan, Liu (1985) found caretakers for children under age three to be (in descending order of frequency) babysitters, paternal grandmothers, maternal grandmothers, other relatives, and institutional care. Although hired babysitters are the single largest category of caretakers, paternal and maternal grandmothers combined outnumber hired sitters, making kin the most frequent caretakers of preschoolers in Taiwan. Another study indicated that for children through age twelve, grandmothers are the second most common caretakers after mothers and are the most frequently cited caregivers for children under five (Cornwell, Casper, and Chou 1990).

The present study sought to determine not only who the major care provider was, but where care took place and how much time parents themselves put into childcare. Answers to the latter questions provide a fuller picture of childcare arrangements in Taiwan.

Childcare responsibilities constrain women's participation in employment (Presser and Baldwin 1980), while women's employment, in turn, has important effects on their families. Different aspects of paid work, such as its type, nature, hours, and workload, are significant determinants of family lifestyle or quality of life (Kanter 1984). Work satisfaction (Honig 1984), premarital work experience (Avioli 1985), and other work factors (Hoffman and Nye 1975) are all important in affecting how women rear their children.

Work commitment which can be regarded as a subjective orientation (Safilios-Rothschild 1971) is one variable among those likely to affect women's childcare arrangements. Various measures of this concept usually include future plans or expectations concerning work outside the home, job satisfaction and devotion, and/or employment plans at different stages of the family life cycle (Bielby and Bielby 1984; Sobol 1975). Work motivation (Sobol 1975), employment experience before marriage, years of employment (Rexroat and Shehan 1984), and conflict between family and work roles (Voydanoff 1984) are all important factors to consider in studying work commitment.

In addition to work commitment, women's employment orientation may be indicated by how they manage conflict between work and family roles. Relevant Western studies show that the physical separation of home and work, time constraints, and job demands tend to limit women's performance in family roles (Voydanoff 1984). A survey of women in selected professions in Taiwan found that employed women frequently lower their occupational aspirations in response to conflict between family and occupational roles (Chen and Liao 1985). The same study indicated that women with greater workloads perceived greater role pressure. Thus, women's objective job conditions may closely relate to their subjective employment orientation. Women's attitudes about conflicts between family and employment as well as their subjective orientation toward employment will reflect their objective occupational conditions.

The present study compares women's objective job conditions and subjective work orientations and explores relationships among these variables. Previous childcare studies have devoted less attention to parents' time involvement in childcare than to the type and location of caregivers and the quality of care (Coverman and Sheley 1986; Floge 1985; Lehrer 1983; Mason 1987; Moore and Sawhill 1984; Presser 1989). A major focus of the present study was the extent of parents' time involvement in childcare. In addition, since previous findings document an important relationship between children's ages and childcare patterns, this study categorized various age levels and compared care patterns for children of different levels.

Methods

Sample

In 1986, the Research, Development, and Evaluation Committee of the Executive Yuan, Republic of China (R.O.C.), launched a study of childcare issues in Taiwan. The study sample was drawn in the Taipei Metropolitan Area from among employed women with a spouse present at the time of sample selection. The data presented in this chapter derive from the 796 respondents to that survey.

The sample was divided into three categories according to the age of the respondent's eldest child. Categories consisted of age three and under; three to six, attending kindergarten; and six to twelve, attending primary school. Sampling sources included all fourteen local health centers in Taipei, which have complete records of vaccination for children under age three, nine kindergartens, and eleven primary schools randomly drawn from sixteen administrative precincts in Taipei. In each primary school, one class from each grade was randomly chosen. Questionnaires were given to employed mothers whose eldest child was in that class. Similar procedures were followed in kindergartens and day-care centers. The survey was conducted between December 1985 and May 1986. Of the sample of 796 mothers, 298, 200, and 298 respectively fell into the three eldest-child age categories. The mean age of the sample mothers was 32.2, their years of education averaged 13.5, and their average monthly family income in 1986 was between U.S. $1,150 and $1,750. The major family type in the sample was a nuclear one (63.5 percent); the mean number of children was 1.7.

Major Variables

Respondents' Mother's Employment. Most of the mothers of the employed women surveyed (62.8 percent) had never held outside employment. This study focused on whether the respondents' mothers had been employed when the respondents were between the ages of six and twenty since mothers of that generation were virtually never employed outside the home while their children were under age six. This variable was included in an effort to determine whether their mothers' employment while they were growing up bore any relationship to their own childcare arrangements.

Employment Orientation. Two indicators were used to measure respondents' employment orientation:
   1. *Career commitment.* Eight ordinal-scale questions were designed to measure respondents' occupational orientation on a continuum from high career orientation to low job orientation.
   2. *Occupational priority.* Six items were constructed to measure respondents' general attitudes toward employed women's roles. These items sought to differentiate among gradations in giving highest priority respectively to paid work and to childcare.

Job Conditions. Three indicators were used to measure this concept:
   1. *Job requirements.* Seven items described various job require-

ments. For each requirement, two categories—more or less restrictive—were delineated. The higher the total job requirements score a respondent received, the more restrictive the job requirements she had.

2. *Job demands.* Psychological pressure and high demands on time are important dimensions of job conditions. Three related questions measured job demands, with a higher score representing perceptions of higher job pressure.

3. *The possibility of leave from paid work.* One way to examine linkages between women's employment and family roles is to focus on her job flexibility. Ease of taking leave from paid work when a child was sick was considered an indicator of job flexibility. Five responses were distinguished for each of three consecutive questions related to such leave: difficult (2.4 percent), fair (21.8 percent), fairly easy (29.2 percent), no such need present during last year (36.8 percent), and no requirement at all to take leave from work (9.7 percent).

Childcare Arrangements. The study focused on three aspects of childcare arrangements:

1. *Extent of parental time involvement in childcare.* This major dependent variable had five ordinal responses: division of labor between the respondent and her spouse only (no need to hire additional help), care provided by outside help during office hours only (parental care after work), care provided by outside help for six days a week (parental care only on weekends and holidays), outside help always present (no parental care necessary), or child old enough to take care of him/herself.

The responses above were collapsed into three major types: higher parental involvement in childcare, to describe couples who did not rely on outside help; medium parental involvement, referring to couples who received help from others during office hours only; and lower parental involvement, which represents parents who spent weekends only or even less time taking care of their children. For kindergarten and primary-school children, parental involvement in childcare was restricted to after-school hours only. Respondents with primary-school children reported as being able to care for themselves were placed in the lower parental involvement category.

2. *Care providers.* Specific characteristics of the sample necessitated treating the care providers variable differently according to eldest-child categories. For respondents with eldest children under age three, major care providers were classified as either individual (paternal kin, maternal kin, non-kin) or institutional providers. For respondents with eldest children in kindergarten or primary school, all of whom used at least this one form of institutional care (that is, school),

"care providers" designated additional care arrangements (paternal kin, maternal kin, or non-kin) during after school hours.

3. *Childcare location.* Childcare location was categorized as either in home or out of the home. For children under age three, home care referred to any care provided in the child's home including that provided by the child's mother if she worked at home. If the child was sent to a care provider's home or a care-providing institution, the case was placed in the out-of-home category.

Results

Childcare Arrangement Patterns for Children at Different Ages

The overall pattern of childcare arrangements for the sample is reported in Tables 10.1–10.3, which contain information on parents' time involvement, care providers, and care location by age of the eldest child. Among respondents whose eldest child was aged three or under, most had help during office hours (Table 10.1). Almost a third of these respondents also had help during non-working hours. Only a small proportion had no help and thus had the highest time involvement in childcare.

Among the medium and lower parental time involvement groups, the only ones with care providers, individual providers clearly outnumbered institutional or multiple care (institutional plus individual care) arrangements. Kin consistently constituted a higher proportion than non-kin among individual caretakers. Paternal kin played a more important childcare role than maternal kin in the medium parental time involvement group; relatives from either line were of similar importance in the childcare arrangements of couples in the lower time involvement group. Respondents with children under age three more often arranged childcare outside than inside the home. Even those using individual caretakers usually used persons outside of the child's home.

Findings for the youngest age category show that most mothers in the sample used caretakers, especially kin, for childcare; they also tended to send their small children to someone else's home. While kin comprised half of all caretakers, paternal kin were more likely to provide care in the child's home (25.7 percent out of 33.3 percent) while maternal kin constituted a greater proportion of those offering care outside the child's home (13.9 percent out of 23.9 percent). Since paternal grandparents in Taiwan tend to live with married sons and to assume childcare responsibilities (Cornwell et al. 1990), not surpris-

Table 10.1 Childcare Arrangements for Children Under Age 3 (N = 296)

Extent of Parental Time Involvement	Care Providers	Locations	
		Child's Home	Outside of Child's Home
Higher: 5.7 (17)	Couple Only	4.1 (12)	1.7 (5)
Medium: 65.2 (193)	Caretakers		
	Paternal Kin	14.5 (43)	4.7 (14)
	Maternal Kin	3.4 (10)	7.1 (21)
	Non-Kin:		
	Neighbors*	—	12.2 (36)
	Others	1.7 (5)	9.1 (27)
	TOTAL	19.6 (58)	33.1 (98)
	Institutional Care	—	9.5 (28)
	Multiple Care: Institutional Care Plus		
	Paternal Kin	0.7 (2)	1.0 (3)
	Maternal Kin	0.7 (2)	—
	Non-Kin	—	0.7 (2)
	TOTAL	1.4 (4)	1.7 (5)
Lower: 29.1 (86)	Total Help Available Except Weekends 17.6 (52)		
	Caretakers		
	Paternal Kin	1.4 (4)	3.7 (11)
	Maternal Kin	0.7 (2)	4.4 (13)
	Non-Kin	0.4 (1)	4.7 (14)
	TOTAL	2.4 (7)	12.8 (38)
	Institutional Care	—	2.4 (7)
	Total Help Available Every Day 11.5 (34)		
	Caretakers		
	Paternal Kin	3.7(11)	1.7 (5)
	Maternal Kin	2.0 (6)	2.4 (7)
	Non-Kin	—	1.7 (5)
	TOTAL	5.7 (17)	5.7 (17)

*Neighbors are specified here due to their substantial proportion among care takers outside the child's home. In other categories, neighbors numbered less than six and thus were combined with other non-kin caretakers.

ingly this set of grandparents predominated in care given in the child's home. If paternal relatives are not present in the home, maternal relatives outside of the home are used if available, because kin are still considered more reliable caregivers for small children. However, kin are not always available so, as Table 10.1 indicates, parents turn to neighbors and other arrangements.

For kindergarten children (see Table 10.2), the most common degree of parental time involvement is the higher rather than the medium or lower ones. Since children of this age spend a considerable amount of time in school and some kindergartens have flexible hours to match parental work schedules, additional help becomes less necessary. When parents did use help for their kindergartners, they used individual caretakers rather than another institution.

Kin constituted the major type of caretakers for kindergarten children after school hours in the medium and lower parental time involvement groups. In general, paternal kin again tended to be more involved in childcare than maternal kin. If additional help was used after school, however, the location was as likely to be out of the home as in the home.

Table 10.3 shows that parental time involvement in childcare for primary-school children was almost equally distributed among the higher, medium, and lower level groups. Grade in primary school did not seem to make an important difference in parental time involvement. If caretakers were used after school, relatively more primary-school children in the lower grades than in the intermediate or higher grades had caretakers. Obversely, more children in the higher grades in primary school than in the intermediate and lower grades care for themselves. In the case of those with help during non-working hours, the difference in using caretakers by children's grade in primary school was quite small.

After-school care providers for primary-school children were again more likely to be kin, especially paternal kin, than non-kin, regardless of grade in school. However, only a minority of respondents (15 percent) were using an arrangement outside their homes. Kin of one line or the other almost exclusively had the major responsibility for care inside the child's home.

Relationships Between Parental Time Involvement and Employment

This section first explores correlations among personal and family variables, work role indicators, and parental time involvement in childcare. Multiple regression analysis is then used to determine the

Table 10.2   After-School Childcare Arrangements for Kindergarten Children (N = 198)

Extent of Parental Time Involvement	*Care Providers by Child's School Schedule*	*Locations*	
		Child's Home	*Outside of Child's Home*
Higher:	Full Day	57.6 (114)	—
61.6 (122)	Half Day	4.0 (8)	—
Medium:			
28.8 (57)	Full Day		
	Paternal Kin	5.6 (11)	3.0 (6)
	Maternal Kin	1.5 (3)	5.1 (10)
	Non-Kin	1.0 (2)	5.1 (10)
	TOTAL	8.1 (16)	13.2 (26)
	Half Day		
	Paternal Kin	3.5 (7)	1.0 (2)
	Maternal Kin	1.0 (2)	1.5 (3)
	Non-Kin	—	0.5 (1)
	TOTAL	4.5 (9)	3.0 (6)
Lower:			
9.6 (19)	Full Day		
	Paternal Kin	1.5 (3)	1.0 (2)
	Maternal Kin	1.5 (3)	1.0 (2)
	Non-Kin	0.5 (1)	1.0 (2)
	TOTAL	3.5 (7)	3.0 (6)
	Half Day		
	Paternal Kin	1.5 (3)	0.5 (1)
	Maternal Kin	—	0.5 (1)
	Non-Kin	0.5 (1)	—
	TOTAL	2.0 (4)	1.0 (2)

relative importance of these variables in accounting for parental time involvement in childcare. Comparisons among patterns for the three different eldest child age groups are then presented.

Table 10.3 After-School Childcare Arrangements for Primary-School Children (N = 295)

Extent of Parental Time Involvement	Care Providers by School Grade	Locations	
		Child's Home	Outside of Child's Home
Higher: 34.9 (103)	Lower Grades	10.8 (32)	—
	Intermediate Grades	12.5 (37)	—
	Higher Grades	11.5 (34)	—
Medium: 32.6 (96)	Lower Grades		
	Paternal Kin	4.7 (14)	2.0 (6)
	Maternal Kin	2.7 (8)	1.7 (5)
	Non-Kin	0.3 (1)	4.4 (13)
	Intermediate Grades		
	Paternal Kin	5.1 (15)	1.4 (4)
	Maternal Kin	2.0 (6)	1.7 (5)
	Non-Kin	0.3 (1)	—
	Higher Grades		
	Paternal Kin	2.7 (8)	1.4 (4)
	Maternal Kin	1.4 (4)	—
	Non-Kin	0.3 (1)	0.3 (1)
Lower: 32.5 (96)	Lower Grades		
	Paternal Kin	2.0 (6)	—
Parents have help 10.5 (31)	Maternal Kin	0.7 (2)	0.3 (1)
	Non-Kin	0.3 (1)	—
	Intermediate Grades		
	Paternal Kin	1.4 (4)	0.3 (1)
	Maternal Kin	0.3 (1)	0.3 (1)
	Non-Kin	0.7 (2)	—
	Higher Grades		
	Paternal Kin	2.0 (6)	0.3 (1)
	Maternal Kin	0.7 (2)	1.0 (3)
Child cares for self 22.0 (65)	Lower Grades	3.4 (10)	—
	Intermediate Grades	8.1 (24)	—
	Higher Grades	10.5 (31)	—

Table 10.4 shows that for respondents with children age three and under, the higher their education, occupational prestige, family income, and job demands, and the less restrictive the job requirements, the less time they and their spouses spent in childcare. The level of time involvement by parents of kindergarten children was associated with the mother's job experience before marriage and with the restrictiveness of her current job requirements. If the mother had job experience before marriage and had a relatively more restrictive job at the time of the study, she and her spouse spent less time in childcare.

For mothers whose eldest child was in primary school, job experience before marriage, less restrictive job requirements at the time of the study, and difficulty in taking leave from this job were all significantly correlated with lower parental time involvement in childcare. Appar-

Table 10.4   Zero-Order Correlations with Parental Involvement[+] in Childcare

Variables	Under Age 3	Kindergarten	Primary School
Personal and Family			
Respondent's Age	-0.0360	-0.0635	-0.0011
Years of Education	0.1314*	0.0657	0.0060
Occupational Prestige	0.1287*	-0.0746	-0.0674
Family Income	0.1786***	0.0692	-0.0437
Number of Children	0.0442	0.0429	-0.0425
Younger Siblings Present	0.0309	0.0147	-0.0496
Respondent's Employment	0.0117	0.0531	-0.0162
Premarital Employment	0.0435	0.1276*	0.0971*
Employment Orientation			
Career Commitment	0.0740	0.0373	-0.0201
Occupational Priority	-0.0449	0.0872	-0.0120
Job Conditions			
Job Demands	0.1776***	-0.0013	-0.0784
Job Requirements	-0.1103	0.1777**	-0.0979*
Possibility of Leave (if child sick)	-0.0638	-0.0157	-0.2108***

  * $p < 0.05$
 ** $p < 0.01$
*** $p < 0.001$
  [+] Time involvement in childcare: 1) higher; 2) medium; 3) lower

ently the easier it is to leave work when a child is sick, the more likely couples are to spend time caring for their primary-school children.

Both employment orientation indicators, career commitment and occupational priority, yielded low and insignificant correlations. On the other hand, the three job condition indicators—job demands, requirements, and leavetaking ease—were all associated with child-care patterns in the three different eldest-child age categories. Thus the hypothesized relationship between mother's employment situation and parents' time involvement in childcare seems to be supported with regard to job conditions but not with regard to employment orientation. Nevertheless, an indicator of employment orientation—occupational priority—was included in the multivariate analysis in an effort to determine the theoretical importance of this dimension of employment to parents' time involvement in childcare.

Table 10.5 shows that the total amount of variance in parents' childcare involvement explained by selected independent variables for each age group, although not high, is significant. For mothers whose eldest child is three or under, the higher their family income and their job demands and the less restrictive their job, the less time they and their spouses spent on childcare. Since children at these ages need the most extensive care, higher family income allows greater reliance on care providers, which entails more costs.

However, seemingly contradictory findings regarding job conditions appear. Higher job demands (as expected) and less restrictive job requirements (unexpected) both contribute to parents' low involvement in childcare. One possible explanation is that the degree of job restrictiveness does not change the intensive need of very young children for care. Consequently, mothers of such children are likely to seek help regardless of their current job requirements, as is reflected in the higher proportion (29.1 percent) of those who have help for at least six days a week (Table 10.1). Greater job demands simply increase the need for childcare help. These data imply not only that parents with younger children have greater childcare needs, but also that mothers' job conditions are significant factors explaining their time involvement in childcare.

For mothers with an eldest child in kindergarten, the higher their education, the lower their occupational prestige, and the more restrictive their job requirements, the less likely they and their husbands were to spend time on childcare. A comparison among these three significant correlations shows that job requirements are most important in accounting for parental time involvement in childcare.

Table 10.5 Multiple Regression Analysis of Selected Independent Variables on Parental Involvement[+] in Childcare

Variables	Under Age 3		Kindergarten		Primary School	
	b	Beta	b	Beta	b	Beta
Education	.0048	.0241	.0501	.2006*	.0089	.0355
Occupational Prestige	.0017	.0297	-.0128	-.1907*	-.0084	-.1021
Family Income	.0704	.1493*	.0476	.0940	-.0247	-.0441
Occupational Priority	-.0634	-.0978	.0676	.0906	.0219	.0228
Job Demands	.1066	.1473*	-.0205	-.0249	-.0444	-.0436
Job Requirements	-.0848	-.1232*	.2024	.2426**	-.0640	-.0665
Job Leave Flexibility (if child is sick)	-.0197	-.0347	-.0242	-.0367	-.1672	-.2002
R²		.0881**		.0887*		.0600*

* p< .05
** p< .01
+ Time involvement in childcare: 1) higher; 2) medium; 3) lower

Conclusion

This chapter explores two research issues: first, patterns of childcare arrangements for children in three different age categories; and second, relationships among different dimensions of mothers' employment and parental time involvement in childcare. The same study found that mothers took the major responsibility (ranging from 59 percent to 96 percent) for performing a list of eleven specific childcare tasks (e.g., preparing food, straightening rooms, playing with and tutoring children). This is quite different from the finding reported on Mainland China that the dominant pattern of the household division of labor is equality (see Chow and Chen in this volume). However, the present study's finding is consistent with those of other Taiwanese studies which indicate that women shoulder the major burden in the household division of labor (Wong 1987; Yi and Tsai 1989). Hence, the parent whose time involvement in childcare is examined here is most probably the mother.

The results show that for children aged three or younger, childcare help during office hours, kin as major care providers, and an out of home care arrangement were the most prevalent childcare patterns. The dominant practice was not to provide care for kindergarten children after school, but if caretakers were arranged, kin were the most common providers. For primary-school children, no specific care pattern was the most common; kin remained the most important care providers if care was used; and the child's home was the usual location of the childcare.

This overall pattern of childcare arrangements shows that while children at different ages may receive care from similar sources (e.g., paternal kin), their age affects both the degree of parents' (mothers') time involvement and the location of the care. Their age indicates not only their degree of maturity but also whether they attend school. Once children enter kindergarten or primary school, childcare involves arranging for care primarily for after-school hours, with the need for additional care varying according to compatibility of school hours with parents' job hours. In other words, the findings suggest that children of different ages have different childcare needs and that, perhaps even more importantly, families in general have developed similar childcare arrangements for children of similar ages.

This research also shows that objective job conditions, not subjective work orientations, are directly related to childcare arrangements. Higher job demands, job restrictions (longer weekly work hours, inflexible work shifts, shift rotations, frequent night shifts, and irregular holidays), and greater difficulty taking leave from paid work all contribute to mothers' lower time involvement in caring for their children, especially school-aged children. If job conditions are compatible with childcare needs, mothers are likely to spend more time in caring for their children themselves.

Since job conditions refer to more specific demands, regulations, or requirements of employment, these data imply that the linkage between women's employment and their time spent on childcare is more likely to be related to physical constraints present in their jobs. Despite the general belief that mothers' subjective attitudes toward their employment affect childcare arrangements, this study finds that they are not actually significantly related.

Therefore, assuming that childcare arrangements will continue to be an important issue with the increasing number of dual-earner families in Taiwan, future policymakers must be concerned with improving general job conditions so as to facilitate better childcare arrangements. To attain this goal, at least three measures related to objective job situations should receive priority:

1. *A longer period of parental leave should be allowed following the arrival of a new child (biological or adopted) with the option for either father or mother to take this leave.* The present postnatal paid-leave benefit in Taiwan is 45 days, and only mothers are allowed to take this leave. Traditionally, new mothers are expected to stay home and rest during the first month after giving birth. The belief that it will be difficult to continue breastfeeding after the mothers' return to work has apparently discouraged that practice among employed women in Taiwan, who breastfeed for a much shorter period than non-employed women do. Bottle feeding allows other caretakers to substitute for the mother as soon after birth as deemed necessary. Longer maternity (or preferably parental) leave during this critical stage of family development would enable parents to become more involved in their children's care.

Parental leave would not only benefit children and families but would potentially also have important implications for bringing about gender equality in Taiwan. Studies have shown that childrearing falls behind economic needs in Taiwanese fathers' priorities concerning their responsibilities toward their families (Yi 1987). More participation by fathers in childrearing would have positive consequences for gender equality. Studies in many countries have documented childcare as one area in the household division of labor in which fathers tend to contribute more. Thus this area appears to have particular potential for progress toward a more egalitarian division of labor in the home. Longer and gender-neutral parental leave is a critical first step toward greater marital equality.

Furthermore, access to parental leave by fathers is the fundamental key to changing the traditional Chinese concept of an exclusive mother-child bond. Although male involvement in childcare remains secondary to female involvement even in highly developed countries (Amato 1989), a substantial number of young, urban Taiwanese males are sharing childcare responsibilities. Enabling males to take an active role in childcare through a formal channel, such as parental leave, would allow them to recognize the need to balance work and family and eventually would produce a positive effect on gender equality.

2. *Daycare programs should be established at or near work sites.* Findings of this study confirm that employed mothers with small children require extensive childcare help. The experience of developed countries indicates that childcare convenient to parents' work site is an important component of a high-quality childcare program. With government support, employers must recognize the importance of parent-child interaction and make accommodations accordingly.

In the present study, 86.1 percent of the mothers said that no on-site childcare facility existed at their workplace; 67 percent stated that they would use such a facility if it did. If establishment of childcare centers at or near parents' work sites with professionally trained caretakers and programs of reliable quality was mandatory, the availability of such resources would become a significant consideration not only in childcare arrangements but also in parents' employment decisions.

Taiwan is in the process of completing the demographic transition that accompanies economic development (Chen et al. 1986). With a birthrate decrease from 27.2 percent in 1970 to 15.6 percent in 1991 and a relatively stable average death rate of 4.8 for the last twenty years, an aging population has become an urgent problem in Taiwan (Ministry of Interior 1992; Tu and Chen 1988). Population age structure changes imply changes in economic growth, employment, and educational opportunities, as well as household composition. The likely reduction in extended family resources as nuclear families become more prevalent will increase the demand for non-kin forms of childcare.

With higher education and an increase in the tertiary service sector, the proportion of dual-earner families will increase in the future. Taiwan's future generations will prosper to the extent that the quality as well as quantity of childcare are attended to now. Childcare is clearly an issue of critical importance not only for individuals and families but also for the economy and gender relations. More day-care programs near work sites would facilitate better relationships among these various social institutions.

3. *Flexible work hour options should be widely instituted to accommodate parental childcare responsibilities.* The finding of this study that most parents with restrictive job requirements are spending less time caring for their kindergarten children clearly reveals the necessity of employ-

ment schedules compatible with children's school hours. Most office hours in urban Taiwan are from 9 a.m. to 5:30 p.m., while school generally starts at 8 a.m. and ends at 4:30 p.m. The discontinuity between employment and school schedules creates a tremendous hardship for parents and children. Although additional help can be arranged for after school, as children become relatively more independent, parents see less need for such arrangements. The problem of latchkey children, especially those of primary-school age, has aroused much public concern in Taiwan as in other more advanced industrial countries. Children would not need to be left to their own devices before parents arrive home if flexible work hours were an option for parents.

In addition, policy-makers need to consider allowing sick leave to care for a sick child at home as well as so-called contact days, both practices in Sweden (see Acker's chapter elsewhere in this volume). More comprehensive childcare arrangements that closely relate to parents' labor force participation will benefit all.

Finally, a society should value and support women's contributions not only in the labor force but also at home. Childcare arrangements are certainly one of the most pressing needs for most employed mothers and dual-earner families. Societies such as Taiwan, in which family policy is still not well formulated, must seize the opportunity to recognize childcare as among the most significant issues affecting the well-being of all and to take positive steps to meet childcare needs.

References

Amato, Paul. 1989. "Who Cares for Children in Public Places? Naturalistic Observation of Male and Female Caretakers." *Journal of Marriage and the Family* 51:981–990.

Avioli, Paula Smith. 1985. "The Labor-Force Participation of Married Mothers of Infants." *Journal of Marriage and the Family* 47:739–745.

Bielby, Denise Del Vento, and William T. Bielby. 1984. "Work Commitment, Sex-Role Attitudes, and Women's Employment." *American Sociological Review* 49:234–247.

Cain, Virginia S., and Sandra Hofferth. 1989. "Parental Choice of Self-Care for School-Age Children." *Journal of Marriage and the Family* 51:65–77.

Chen, Kuanjeng, Temu Wang, and Wenling Chen. 1986. "Causes and Consequences of Population Change in Taiwan." *Journal of Population Studies* 9:1–23.

Chen, Wei-yuan, and Lung-Li Liao. 1985. *The Changing Women in Taiwan*. Taipei: Ta-Yang Publishing Company.

Cornwell, Gretchen T., Lynne M. Casper, and Bi-Er Chou. 1990. "Work, Family, and Child Care in Taiwan." Paper presented at the American Sociological Association meetings. Washington, DC.

Coverman, Shelley, and Joseph Sheley. 1986. "Change in Men's Housework and Child-Care Time, 1965–1975." *Journal of Marriage and the Family* 48:413–422.

Emlen, Arthur C., and Joseph B. Perry, Jr. 1975. "Child-Care Arrangements." Pp. 102–105 in *Working Mothers*, edited by Lois W. Hoffman and F. Ivan Nye. San Francisco: Jossey-Bass.

Executive Yuan. 1990. *Report on National Income, Taiwan Area, R.O.C.* Taiwan, Republic of China: Directorate-General of Budget, Accounting, and Statistics.

———. 1992. *Monthly Bulletin of Manpower Statistics, Taiwan Area, R.O.C.* Taiwan, Republic of China: Directorate-General of Budget, Accounting, and Statistics.

Floge, Liliane. 1985. "The Dynamics of Child-Care Use and Some Implications for Women's Employment." *Journal of Marriage and the Family* 47:143–154.

———. 1989. "Changing Household Structure, Child-Care Availability, and Employment among Mothers of Preschool Children." *Journal of Marriage and the Family* 51:51–63.

Giele, Janet Z. 1982. "Women's Work and Family Roles." Pp. 115–150 in *Women in the Middle Years: Current Knowledge and Directions for Research and Policy*, edited by J. Z. Giele. New York: John Wiley.

Hofferth, Sandra L., and Deborah A. Phillips. 1987. "Child Care in the United States, 1970 to 1995." *Journal of Marriage and the Family* 49:559–571.

Hoffman, Lois W., and F. Ivan Nye. 1975. *Working Mothers: An Evaluative Review of the Consequences for Wife, Husband, and Child.* San Francisco: Jossey-Bass.

Honig, Alice Sterling. 1984. "Child Care Options and Decisions: Facts and Figuring for Families." Pp. 89–111 in *Women in the Workplace: Effects on Families*, edited by K. M. Borman, D. Quarm, and S. Gideonse. Norwood, NJ: Ablex.

Kanter, Rosabeth Moss. 1984. "Jobs and Families: Impact of Working Roles on Family Life." Pp. 111–118 in *Work and Family: Changing Roles of Men and Women*, edited by Patricia Voydanoff. Palo Alto, CA: Mayfield.

Lehrer, Evelyn. 1983. "Determinants of Child Care Mode Choice: An Economic Perspective." *Social Science Research* 12:69–80.

Liu, Ke-Pin. 1985. "Child Care Problems in the Changing Society." *China Tribune* 229(4):10–13.

Mason, Karen O. 1987. "The Perceived Impact of Child Care Costs on Women's Labor Supply and Fertility." Research Report No. 87–110. Population Studies Center, University of Michigan, Ann Arbor.

Mason, Karen O., and Karen Kuhlthau. 1989. "Determinants of Childcare Ideals among Mothers of Preschool-Aged Children." *Journal of Marriage and the Family* 51:593–603.

Ministry of Interior. 1992. *1991 Taiwan-Fukien Demographic Fact Book*. Taiwan, Republic of China.

Moore, Kristen A., and Isabel V. Sawhill. 1984. "Implications of Women's Employment for Home and Family Life." Pp. 153–171 in *Work and Family: Changing Roles of Men and Women*, edited by Patricia Voydanoff. Palo Alto, CA: Mayfield.

Presser, H. B. 1989. "Some Economic Complexities of Child Care Provided by Grandmothers." *Journal of Marriage and the Family* 51:581–91.

Presser, H. B., and W. Baldwin. 1980. "Child Care Constraints on Employment: Prevalence Correlates, and Bearing on the Work and Fertility Nexus." *American Journal of Sociology* 85:1202–1213.

Rexroat, C., and C. Shehan. 1984. "Expected versus Actual Work Roles of Women." *American Sociological Review* 49:349–358.

Rodman, Hyman, and David J. Pratto. 1987. "Child's Age and Mother's Employment in Relation to Greater Use of Self-Care Arrangements for Children." *Journal of Marriage and the Family* 49:573–578.

Safilios-Rothschild, C. 1971. "Towards the Conceptualization and Measurement of Work Commitment." *Human Relations* 24:489–493.

Sobol, M. G. 1975. "Commitment to Work." Pp. 63–80 in *Working Mothers: An Evaluative Review of the Consequences for Wife, Husband, and Child*, edited by L. W. Hoffman and F. I. Nye. San Francisco: Jossey-Bass.

Tu, Edward, and Kuanjeng Chen. 1988. "The Effects of Fertility Adjustment and International Migration in the Future Populations in Taiwan." *Journal of Social Sciences and Philosophy* 1:77–98. (Sun Yat-Sen Institute for Social Sciences and Philosophy, Academia Sinica, Taipei, Taiwan, R.O.C.)

Voydanoff, Patricia, ed. 1984. *Work and Family: Changing Roles of Men and Women*. Palo Alto, CA: Mayfield.

Wong, Mei-Huei. 1987. "The Relationship Among Household Division of Labor, Sex Role Attitudes, Social Support, and Marital Satisfaction: A Study of Married Employed Women." Unpublished M.A. Thesis. Chinese Culture University.

Yi, Chin-Chun. 1987. "A Preliminary Analysis of Conjugal Power and Marital Adjustment." Report submitted to the National Science Council in Taiwan, Project Number: NSC 76–0301–H001–34B.

Yi, Chin-Chen, and Yuay-ling Tsai. 1989. "An Analysis of Marital Power in Taipei Metropolitan Area: An Example of Familial Decision-Making." In *Social Phenomena in Taiwan*, edited by C. C. Yi and C. Chu. Taipei: Sun Yat-Sen Institute for Social Sciences and Philosophy, Academia Sinica Monograph Series (25).

Part III

Conclusion

Chapter 11

Perpetuating Gender Inequality: The Role of Families, Economies, and States

Catherine White Berheide
and
Esther Ngan-ling Chow

The analyses of women's experiences included in this book reveal the variety of ways in which private patriarchy (in families) combines with public patriarchy (in economies and states) to create a system of domination which subordinates women. They detail how gender is constructed under specific political, economic, and cultural circumstances. Together these studies uncover significant similarities as well as important differences in how state policies affect gender and household relations in the context of dramatically uneven development.

The chapters highlight how structural circumstances in particular countries, ranging from less industrialized ones such as Malawi, to newly industrialized ones such as Mexico, to advanced industrialized ones such as Sweden, are associated with specific policies. Kick (1987) classifies one of the two First World nations covered in the book as in the core (Sweden) and the other as in the semi-core (Australia) of the world system. The Third World countries include a capitalist semi-core country (Taiwan), a socialist semi-core one (People's Republic of China), and others whose locations within the semi-periphery (Tunisia, Guatemala, Philippines, Indonesia, Thailand, Egypt, Costa

Rica, and Mexico) and within the periphery (Malawi, Bangladesh, Nigeria, and Senegal) vary. Comparing such a broad array of societies paints a complex picture of the role of families, economies, and states in perpetuating gender inequality.

This concluding chapter begins by identifying some key findings concerning women's subordination. Next, it considers common themes which cut across the widely varying political and economic contexts of the studies. The themes illuminate some causes and consequences of policies for women and families in societies at different stages in the process of economic development. In short, this chapter explores how the interaction of economic development, state policies, and household structures perpetuates gender inequality.

The Relationships among Families, Economies, and States

The introductory chapter indicates that this book contains research addressing a series of questions: How do particular political economies around the world transform gender and household relations? How do state policies seek to deal with these political economic realities? How do women and their households both initiate and respond to state policies? What are the implications of women's and households' survival strategies for policy?

The chapters' answers to these questions reveal that the issues women face in particular countries are closely connected to where the country falls in the hierarchy of states in the world system. Enloe (1989) captures this global dimension of women's problems when she recasts the feminist slogan "the personal is political" to "the personal is international." As world systems theorists from Wallerstein (1974) to Borg (1992) note, the division of labor among countries affects gender as well as class stratification within each.

Dramatically uneven economic development throughout the world since the 1960s has intensified the impoverishment of some countries, such as Malawi and Bangladesh, where women struggle to meet basic needs. In the most industrialized countries, like Australia and Sweden, economic restructuring threatens the gains women have made. In yet other countries, such as Guatemala and Mexico, the influx of multinational corporations (MNCs) has led to the incorporation of women into the international division of labor in ways that harness women's productive and reproductive labor in the interests of states and of world capitalism.

In this book, Tiano argues that the interests of states and MNCs can differ in ways that constrain women's lives. She finds that MNCs such as electronics maquilas in Mexico use selective recruitment practices which bar mothers from their labor forces because they assume that women bear greater responsibility than men for maintaining everyday family life. The preference of electronics maquilas for childless women as workers removes an incentive for mothers to keep their fertility low. Therefore, the recruitment practices of the maquilas actually encourage higher fertility among women with children, an outcome which runs counter to Mexico's population policy. Such practices reinforce the traditional gender division of labor, limit mothers' ability to improve their well-being and that of their children, and foster further childbearing.

By tradition, childbearing and childrearing *are* women's responsibilities. Women continue to shoulder a disproportionate share of the burden of fertility, family planning, and childcare even in industrialized countries such as Sweden (see Wright, Shire, Hwang, Dolan, and Baxter 1992 for example). Acker's analysis indicates that global restructuring has shaken Sweden's commitment to the welfare of women and children, leading to cutbacks in support for the public care sector. In her postscript, she makes a grave prediction for the future of the welfare state in Sweden. Similarly, the move toward capitalist economies and democratic political systems in Eastern Europe is eroding state programs which allow women to combine work and family, thereby reducing women's status. Newly industrializing countries, such as Taiwan and Mexico, have never had such programs. As women in these countries enter the industrial labor force, they face new dilemmas in meeting their traditional family responsibilities. For example, Yi finds that job requirements constrain women's childcare arrangements in Taiwan. The need for policies that facilitate combining waged work with family responsibilities tests the concern of this and other capitalist patriarchies for the welfare of women and children.

In the People's Republic of China, a socialist state where theoretically the influence of both capitalism and patriarchy are at a minimum, women bear the major burden for family planning. Chow and Chen find no pronounced differences in family structure, gender ideology, and division of labor between only-child and multiple-child families in Beijing. While job requirements lead many Chinese couples to share domestic labor and childcare equally, women still carry more of the responsibility for household work and childcare.

Blumberg's chapter posits that a woman's degree of "say so" in domestic and fertility decisions as well as in economic ones reflects her economic power. In her study of Guatemala, resources under women's direct control enhance their decision-making power within the family. Specifically, where development projects erode women's independent control of economic resources (as occurs in one of the villages), their dependence on their husbands increases while their status, input into family decisions, and even freedom to attend development project meetings all decrease.

Like Blumberg and several others, Tinker also focuses on intra-household dynamics in the context of economic development. As she explores gender differences in involvement in street food trade, she too notes the importance of women's control over their income. Tinker's research demonstrates how critical street food trade is to the survival of many urban poor families. Yet development programs commonly classify street food vendors as informal sector micro-enterprises and often dismiss them as an insignificant form of economic activity, thereby limiting women's access to critical resources.

The study of small-holder farmers in Malawi by Berheide and Segal finds female heads of households have less access than male heads of households to the resources that development projects provide, including information, advice, and credit. Because state policy discourages rural to urban migration, most people remain on the land. Labor, land, livestock, job opportunities, agricultural extension services, and farm club membership are not as available to female heads of households. Over time, small-holder households headed by men are likely to experience upward mobility into the semi-proletarian or petty commodity classes, whereas those headed by women are more likely to remain peasants, struggling to grow enough food to feed their families.

Sagot's chapter indicates that women struggle to provide for their families in ways that may escape the attention of researchers, practitioners, policy-makers, and the public. To obtain housing for their families, women in Costa Rica engage in activities ranging from construction to community activism. Her study finds that housing problems require collective action to resolve; therefore, women formed an organization demanding housing and thus transformed themselves into political actors promoting social change. By politicizing the private domain and by engaging in visible political action, they eventually had a significant effect on the Costa Rican government's housing policy. While many of the studies in this book take a top-down approach by analyzing how state policy affects women, Sagot's takes a bottom-up approach by examining how women affect policy.

The efforts of Costa Rican women to make housing, seemingly a private problem, into a public issue by venturing into the political arena (which traditionally excludes them) empowers them (Bookman and Morgen 1988). Just as C. Wright Mills reveals how private troubles relate to public issues and feminists note that "the personal is political," women's practical (i.e., providing basic needs) and strategic (i.e., achieving gender equality) interests are intertwined. To the degree that women gain the political power to make their personal struggles with everyday survival into public issues, they meet both their practical and strategic needs. If women in Taiwan can transform childcare from an individual problem to a social problem, they will increase their political power while addressing a practical interest. Women in Costa Rica have already demonstrated how working to solve their practical housing needs has led to (strategic) political gains.

Similarly, one of Baldock's findings is that Australian women's community work also empowers them. As women become aware of the value of their unpaid caring labor for the provision of social welfare, they demand rights as volunteers, meaningful work assignments, and training to facilitate their entrance into paid jobs. Economic restructuring in Australia and other countries often takes the form of privatization, implying that states are no longer responsible for delivering social goods such as health care, which may best be delivered collectively. As a result, women individually and collectively become responsible for delivering these goods in one way or another, as Baldock, Yi, and Sagot show. As Eastern European states withdraw support for women's employment, women now do (as volunteers and family members) what they previously did for pay. In short, policy changes at the macro-level, which often have negative effects on women and families, become catalysts for women's activism.

These studies, especially Baldock's and Sagot's, confirm the observation by Kandiyoti (1988) and by Acosta-Belen and Bose (1990, p. 312) that "women are not passive victims in this process; instead, they are developing creative ways in which to resist the new forms of subordination." They contradict the portrayal of women, especially Third World women, as helpless victims, including when done to justify the need for charity or development programs. Despite this book's emphasis on how macro-structural forces affect micro-structural interactions in families, the studies in it also reveal women challenging situations that are detrimental to themselves and/or to their families.

Across widely varying political and economic contexts, policies adopted to aid women prove to be mixed blessings. In Tunisia, Charrad examines how adoption of a new Code of Personal Status redefines the rights of women. While transforming gender relations and family life, this code also reinforces gender inequality. Women may look to the state for support in moving out from under family control and in laying claim to the resources that development generates. However, several of the chapters, including those by Acker, Charrad, and Chow and Chen, show that policy originally intended to benefit women brings disadvantages at the same time.

In Tunisia (a developing country), Sweden (an industrialized country), and the People's Republic of China (a socialist country), patriarchy responds to women-centered and women-sensitive policy reforms by asserting itself in new ways. For example, the Chinese patriarchal system has managed to survive under socialism by taking on new forms. Chow and Chen conclude that the Chinese communist state, as a socialist patriarchy, may in fact widen gender inequality as it subordinates women's interests to economic development by implementing the one-child policy.

The public patriarchy of states and, as Tiano's analysis indicates, of corporations too, has taken the place of the private patriarchy of the family in controlling women's reproductive lives. Berheide and Segal (1990) find that the population policies of many countries attempt to manipulate women's fertility to achieve national goals. States often use women as pawns as they pursue goals which reflect their need to manage economic and political crises rather than any desire to improve the lives of women and families or even to increase the level of economic development. As the chapters by Baldock and by Chow and Chen demonstrate, policy reforms, whether women-centered, women-sensitive, or women-peripheral, that use women as pawns perpetuate patriarchy.

The specifics of how states handle family issues from food and housing to fertility, childcare, and divorce once they become political issues vary according to structural and historical circumstances. However, as a gendered institution, the state often dismisses such nurturing responsibilities as outside of its domain, leaving families to fend for themselves. From the least industrialized countries of the South included in this volume to the most industrialized ones of the North, specific policies on these critical family issues are usually consistent with overall state directions which rarely give high priority to the needs of women and children.

Common Themes in Studying Women, Families, and Policies

A number of common themes emerge, both theoretically and empirically, from the disparate studies in this book as well as from feminist and Third World scholarship on families, economic development, and the state. Placing women at the center of the analysis of state policy reveals the first common theme: that the interests of women and children differ from those of men throughout the world. Blumberg argues that major development paradigms (e.g., modernization, dependency, and world system) have ignored the internal economy of the household, treating it as monolithic. Scholars in this volume regard the political economy of the family as an important topic because families distribute resources, including power and income, unequally according to gender and generation.

Attempting to understand the roots of women's oppression, the authors in this book consider the household or the family as the unit of analysis because they argue that its patriarchal structure controls not only the domestic labor involved in household production but also women's access to and control of their production in the labor market. Blumberg finds that a women-peripheral change that leads to men receiving payment for export crops which women produced hurts women's practical gender interests, especially their ability to meet their basic needs and those of their children. Her results as well as those from Tinker and from Berheide and Segal concur with many other studies (e.g., Gladwin 1991; World Bank 1989) which document that development policies targeted to men can cut off women's income sources and have a harmful effect on the well-being of women and children. These and other analyses of the political economy of the family reveal gender differentiated control of household economic resources in terms of access and allocation (Chow 1990; Dwyer and Bruce 1988; Rakowski 1991).

When women are able to exert greater control over economic resources, especially their earnings, they allocate more resources to children's needs and the well-being of the household than men do. They also develop more self-esteem and become empowered. As Blumberg's chapter demonstrates, women need direct control of the economic resources their labor produces to increase their self-worth, enhance their social position, and improve their family's well-being. Coltrane's (1992) analysis of 93 non-industrial societies provides further support for Blumberg's hypotheses. He finds that men treat women with more respect, expect less deference from them, and display less dominance over them when women have more control over both their property and the products of their labor.

The second common theme that emerges from the studies is that the well-being of women and their households varies according to the structural conditions that prevail in societies at particular points in time. For example, Berheide and Segal argue that the particular features of Malawi's women-peripheral policies concerning rural to urban migration, traditional land usage rights, agricultural production for export, and economic development generally give female heads of households some access to land but deny the majority of them sufficient access to employment opportunities, farm clubs, and extension services. Baldock provides a very different example in analyzing how a decline in the economic situation in Australia leads to women-peripheral changes in welfare policies which shift more of the burden for the well-being of families onto women. Acker expresses concern that moves toward greater privatization and fewer social welfare programs may produce a similar result in Sweden by relying increasingly on women to do more unpaid or low-paid caring labor.

Meeting women's practical interests by increasing their access to resources such as land, employment, income, education, housing, and health is a necessary condition for bringing about any dramatic changes in their welfare globally. However, the goal of improving women's well-being fundamentally challenges the very logic of a capitalist economy and national development. One of the distinctive characteristics of the development process is its gendered nature. It has different effects on men and women, even though they are both producers. Improving the well-being of women and families requires changing economic, political, and other social structures in ways which lead to the elimination of gender inequality.

The third common theme is that the macro-structures of domination (i.e., private patriarchy in families and public patriarchy in economies and states) have a dialectical relationship with the micro-interactions in households, with a meso- (or intermediate-) level mediating between the two. The studies in this book contain both theories and empirical evidence describing the connections between macro-structural patterns of hierarchical organization and micro-interactions of social life (Lengermann and Niebrugge-Brantley 1988). A meso-level links macro-political and economic processes with micro-level family processes. As Sagot's chapter illustrates, organizations, including community groups and social movements such as COPAN and CEFEMINA, intervene between women and the state. These chapters document the critical importance at the meso-level of MNCs (Blumberg and Tiano), legal systems (Charrad), and grass-roots organizations (Sagot) for women's struggles for their families' survival and for gender equality.

While men and women exert unequal influence on the state, women's groups can create political pressure on the state to formulate policies that improve social conditions. Acosta-Belen and Bose (1990, p. 310) argue that "women use their responsibilities as mothers and domestic workers, not only to enter the formal and informal economy, but as the basis for political demands." Baldock's and Sagot's chapters illustrate this point vividly in countries with very different political economies.

Specifically, Sagot's chapter demonstrates that women can create grass-roots organizations capable of influencing state policy. Her chapter describes how women cooperated with each other to build houses and to lobby the state for a more favorable housing policy. These women's political activities focused on their practical gender interests, that is, on basic family needs.

Similarly, Baldock finds that in Australia groups of women are fighting to achieve more control over the nature and conditions, including pay, of their volunteer work as the state pushes more responsibility for the provision of social welfare onto them. Deere and Leon (1987, pp. 262–263) document the importance of organizing rural women in Latin America to exert political pressure on states, whether capitalist or socialist, to make gender equality a high priority in formulating policy. In short, individual women working as part of women's groups or social movements can affect even these powerful macro-structural forces.

The fourth common theme is that these macro-structural forces devalue, if not completely ignore, women's work in the paid labor market, in the domestic sphere, and in the volunteer sector. The chapters in this book support the argument by Acosta-Belen and Bose (1990) that traditional development approaches tend to ignore women's economic contributions and assume that women are passive dependents working in reproductive roles in the private sphere. The chapters indicate that supporting one's household may mean wage labor, micro-entrepreneurship, household production, subsistence agriculture, or some combination of the four. They confirm Beneria's (1982, p. 135) assessment that women engage in a variety of activities to make a living rather than relying solely on paid employment. Thus women's daily survival strategies include much more than just wage labor.

As Tiano indicates, MNCs poorly compensate women's waged work. MNCs moving to Third World countries perceive women as cheap, docile, obedient, and easily replaced workers who are unlikely to engage in labor organizing or complain about poor working conditions (see also Fuentes and Ehrenreich 1983; Safa 1981). Development programs and others overlook the critical importance of women's unpaid labor in a variety of settings, including micro-enterprises (Tinker), cash crop production (Blumberg), and subsistence agriculture (Berheide and Segal). Their caring labor is devalued in the paid labor market (Acker), in the family (Yi, Charrad, and Chow and Chen), and in the volunteer sector (Baldock). This global pattern of failing to recognize the vital contributions of women's work, both paid and unpaid, reproduces gender inequality and threatens the welfare of families.

The fifth common theme is that the gendered nature of the interdependence between work and family is intimately connected to gender inequality. The chapters establish that the separation of work and family is part of an ideology that supports patriarchy. For women, work in the household and in the economy are not separate (Chow and Berheide 1988). For example, Yi analyzes the relationship between childcare responsibilities and women's objective job conditions in Taiwan. Her chapter and others demystify the popular notion that a split between private and public spheres justifies a gender-based division of labor.

Charlton, Everett, and Staudt (1989, pp. 2–3) suggest (and the studies in this volume confirm) that the state's ability to alter the boundaries between public and private has profound implications for women (see Acker, Baldock, Charrad, and Chow and Chen in this volume). These studies indicate that the effects of state policy spread beyond economic planning at the national level to influence the personal lives of individuals, especially women. For example, the chapters by Charrad and by Chow and Chen reveal how the state asserts its authority over previously private household matters, in particular divorce and fertility. They demonstrate that the public patriarchy of the state and of the economy control aspects of women's lives today which the private patriarchy of the family previously controlled. Walby (1990, p. 171) observes that as the private patriarchal form of the past has given way to a public one in the present "what has occurred is as much a change in the kind of patriarchal control as of degree," that is "the intensity of oppression" (Walby 1990, p. 174; see also Folbre 1987).

Even more advanced industrial economies like Australia and Sweden continue to divide productive and reproductive labor in a way that maintains the subordination of women. Acker notes that the women-centered policies in Sweden that facilitate the combination of work and family by both men and women also have some negative consequences for women and actually help to reproduce gender inequality. Charles (1992) suggests that these types of progressive social policies in Sweden and similar Western European countries partially account for their high levels of occupational sex segregation. Reskin (1988) argues that no matter what policy victories women achieve, elite men reshape the rules for allocating resources so that women are the relative losers. As Blumberg and other scholars in this volume explain, when women lose, children lose because women allocate a higher proportion of their resources to ensuring the welfare of their children than do men.

A sixth and related theme is the interdependence of families with other social institutions, especially economies and states. The chapters illustrate how diversity in household arrangements interacts with other social institutions to shape gender relations. For example, they differ under subsistence production as Berheide and Segal find in Malawi, under production in the informal economy as in the many countries with street food vendors that Tinker studied, and under production in the international division of labor as Blumberg's research in Guatemala and Tiano's in Mexico demonstrate. Studies in this volume as well as elsewhere (e.g., Croll, Davin, and Kane 1985; Mies 1986) provide examples of the continuing power of household structures to produce unequal outcomes for men and women. They illustrate how families link individuals, male and female, with changes in economies and states.

Recent feminist analyses, including those in this volume, reveal the gendered nature not only of the institutions of production and reproduction, but also of distribution (Acker 1988). As Staudt and Jaquette (1983) note, decisions about the allocation of society's resources and the ways in which states implement those decisions affect the lives of women and families. Flora (1992) indicates that current scholarship analyzing structural adjustment reveals the dramatic effects state policies have on women and families. In particular, the programs of structural adjustment states adopt in response to International Monetary Fund (IMF) mandates to reduce public expenditures have almost always cut into the kinds of basic infrastructure programs that address women's practical needs (food, education, health care, and housing).

The seventh common theme is that modernization and industrialization tend to intensify gender inequality. As the studies in this book and elsewhere (e.g., Bernard 1987; Ward 1990) indicate, the interaction of patriarchy with the development process, rather than women's lack of centrality to or participation in economic activities, increases male dominance and places women in subordinate positions at each level of the class, race, and gender systems of stratification. Since Boserup's pathbreaking work in 1970 established empirically the important part women play in agricultural production, a growing body of research, including the chapters by Blumberg, Berheide and Segal, and Tinker, has documented the negative consequences of economic development for women, as it deprives women of their traditional roles in production leading to economic crises and a loss of status.

Similarly, the penetration of capitalist industrial interests into subsistence economies from Guatemala to Malawi marginalizes women as they lose control over productive resources in the development process (see also Charlton 1984; Nash and Fernandez Kelly 1983). The globalization of the economy in the last two decades has resulted in the massive incorporation of women into blue-collar and service jobs, especially in the Third World. The proletarianization of women, even under conditions of exploitation in MNCs, subordinates women within the global economy while giving them some resources with which to resist subordination within their families. Work in the industrial economy empowers women by allowing them to acquire achieved status outside of their families through income-generating activities. As Blumberg and Tiano find, the wage economy offers some degree of personal autonomy and financial independence (see also Lim 1983; Wolf 1988). Public patriarchy thus reduces private patriarchy's control over women's lives.

An eighth and related theme is that the economic forces of industrialization and world capitalist accumulation interact with existing patriarchal systems in families and states in ways that often increase gender (as well as class and racial) inequality. Tensions between the interests of states and of MNCs tend to widen gender inequality at both the macro- and micro-levels in societies throughout the world. Acosta-Belen and Bose (1990, p. 304) note that "although local governments of developing countries try to promote male-dominated industries, which they see as providing more stable jobs and higher wages than those in which women workers predominate, the foreign labor needs of multinationals are being met primarily by women." According to Tiano, these differing interests can increase gender inequality. Thus patriarchy is only one of the structures forming the system of dominance which reproduces gender inequality. As capitalism and patriarchy interact in the development process, they shape gender relations inside as well as outside of the household, contributing to the gender differentiation of labor globally.

Patriarchy long pre-dates capitalism, with men dominating women within the household where gender forms the basis for the division of labor (Hartmann 1976; Sokoloff 1980). This collection of cross-cultural research joins others (e.g., Afshar 1987; Beneria and Stimpson 1987; Jelin 1991; Ward 1990) in reaffirming the connection between labor force participation and the household division of labor by gender. While recognizing that capitalist accumulation has a variety of effects on women, Beneria and Sen (1981) emphasize the sphere of reproduction, the structure of the household, and the patriarchal socialization process to which women are subject to explain the gender division of labor as well as women's subordination both in the marketplace and in the household. Patriarchy provides the capitalist system with an ideology to justify the existing socioeconomic relationships between men and women and offers a convenient hierarchical structure for the capitalist system to extend into the labor market and into the volunteer sector, thus further perpetuating or even widening gender inequality in different parts of the world. In return, world capitalism in terms of production, distribution, and accumulation provides a material basis for patriarchy in which men control women's work in the household and in the labor market because men are more likely than women to control the means of production.

Women do not seem to fare much better under socialism. Chow and Chen argue that socialist patriarchy does not differ substantially from capitalist patriarchy with regard to perpetuating male dominance. In both cases, state paternalism develops as control over women's lives is transferred from private patriarchy to public patriarchy. The power of the male-dominated state to make laws, shape ideology, and distribute resources replaces the power of the male-dominated family in reproducing gender inequality.

Together the chapters in this book reveal how private patriarchy, modes of production, and the state structure gender and household relations. Thus, the relationships among a set of patriarchal social institutions in both the private (the family) and the public (the economy and the state) spheres form a system of domination perpetuating gender inequality.

Families, Economic Development, and States: Some Implications

The introduction to this book synthesizes feminist and Third World critiques of research on families, economic development, and states to expand our understanding of the diversity of women's experiences globally. A global approach provides a powerful test of the assumptions, concepts, and propositions of family, development, and state theories in various sociocultural settings. Synthesizing the results from the studies in this book with the rich traditions from which they spring enables advocates, practitioners, and scholars to formulate more effective women-centered policies.

These studies point to the need for more gender-sensitive programs. They challenge a common belief among policy-makers and practitioners that general economic growth is a sufficient condition for improving women's lives. The studies suggest that practitioners and scholars must advocate a transformation of the development process so that it decreases rather than increases all forms of inequality. They demonstrate the need for programs addressing women's material well-being (e.g., access to credit) and their position relative to men (e.g., divorce law). They also demonstrate the necessity for programs which go beyond meeting women's basic needs (e.g., food and housing), which are often rooted in their traditional roles, to those meeting their strategic interests as well by strengthening their power in the family, the economy, and the state. Development and donor agency programs should support the empowerment of indigenous women, women's groups, and women's movements.

Women and development scholars (e.g., Sen and Grown 1987; Tinker 1990) frequently talk with state policy-makers, donor organizations, and other international development agencies, attempting to influence policies that affect women and their families. Unfortunately, state and international agencies that bear responsibility for formulating and implementing development policies employ few women in policy-making positions (Staudt 1990). Placing more women-sensitive people in such positions might improve the quality of decision-making and influence the existing system to allocate more resources for women, although Staudt (1990) and others question whether it will.

Resistance to incorporating knowledge by and about women into the policy formation process remains a barrier that both researchers and practitioners have to overcome. Policy needs to recognize the differences between women and men as well as among women by race, class, age, and culture. Women play a vital role in the process of national economic development, and failure to recognize their involvement seriously limits the effectiveness of programs as the chapters by Blumberg, Berheide and Segal, and Tinker demonstrate (see also Bonilla 1990).

We need more research on whether social policy reforms are a viable path to meet women's practical and strategic interests. Policy by its very applied nature is conservative because it works for social reform within the existing structure. While arguing for more women-centered or at least women-sensitive changes in policies, the chapters in this book (especially the first three) provide a cautionary note which warns that even these kinds of policies can have mixed results for women. Walby (1990, p. 201) observes that patriarchy responds to women's policy successes by changing "in form, incorporating some of the hard-won changes into new traps for women," an observation which the studies in this book confirm. Basic structural changes are necessary for uprooting gender inequality.

The research in this volume and elsewhere (e.g., Beneria and Sen 1981; Jaquette 1982; Roger 1983; Tinker 1990) points to the pressing need for micro-studies, shifting from critiques of capitalism and international dependence to critiques of patriarchy and patriarchal development strategies. Such research should analyze the relationship between formal and informal sectors to capture the full range of productive activities. It would continue the examination of the linkages between macro-level political-economic processes and micro-level interpersonal interaction, as well as examination of the meso-

(intermediate-) level of social organizations which we have identified as mediating between the other two levels. It would follow Sagot's lead and analyze the efficacy of women's groups for meeting their practical and strategic gender interests.

In addition to those contained in this book, case studies and comparative-historical analyses in different parts of the world are needed to identify the conditions (e.g., variations in political economies, or the relationship of religion to the state) under which certain types of state policies occur and to examine their effects on women, families, the definition of private and public spheres, and other structures involved in the social construction of gender. Increasingly, scholars, particularly in Third World studies, transcend the boundaries of specific fields to engage in comparative, historical, and structural studies of social institutions and their effects on gender relations. We need more such research, particularly on gender and the state and on the internationalization of gender politics.

Finally, we need more research on how structural adjustment programs designed to reduce debt by de-emphasizing basic needs, especially in the Third World, affect women and their families, paying careful attention to class differences. We need to know whether specific structural adjustment policies are altering gender- and class-based differences in resource accessibility, either by attenuating or by enhancing them. Existing research (Gladwin 1991; Sen and Grown 1987) already documents serious negative consequences for Third World women. Both Acker and Baldock suggest that economic restructuring bodes ill for women even in industrialized societies. Their research demonstrates the need to resist privatization when it creates more unpaid and/or poorly paid work for women, which is its usual outcome. When the reduction of debt becomes the primary goal of state policies, programs which support women's and children's welfare are typically eliminated before military spending is cut. Obversely, increasing militarization usually harms women and families by consuming resources that the state could direct toward them.

In conclusion, by making women the central focus of analysis to explicate their standpoint with regard to both objective conditions and their subjective experience (Smith 1979), the studies included in this book provide a richly textured understanding of how state policies affect the status of women, gender relations, and household structures during the process of economic development. They demonstrate that a combination of material and ideological circumstances (that is, of objective conditions and subjective meanings) shape women's experiences throughout the world. These studies also reveal that women respond to changing socioeconomic and family arrangements by

resisting adverse situations and seeking creative strategies for ensuring family survival. In this process, women empower themselves for
their personal well-being and for the collective good.

References

Acker, Joan. 1988. "Class, Gender and the Relations of Distribution." *Signs*
    13:473–479.
Acosta-Belen, Edna, and Christine E. Bose. 1990. "From Structural Subordina-
    tion to Empowerment: Women and Development in Third World Con-
    texts." *Gender & Society* 4:299–320.
Afshar, Haleh, ed. 1987. *Women, State, and Ideology: Studies from Africa and Asia.*
    Albany, NY: State University of New York.
Beneria, Lourdes. 1982. *Women and Development: The Sexual Division of Labor in
    Rural Societies.* New York: Praeger.
Beneria, Lourdes, and Martha Roldan. 1987. *The Crossroads of Class and Gender.*
    Chicago, IL: University of Chicago Press.
Beneria, Lourdes, and Gita Sen. 1981. "Accumulation, Reproduction and
    Women's Role in Economic Development: Boserup Revisited." *Signs*
    7:279–98.
Beneria, Lourdes, and Catharine R. Stimpson, eds. 1987. *Women, Households,
    and the Economy.* New Brunswick, NJ: Rutgers University Press.
Berheide, Catherine White, and Marcia Texler Segal. 1990. "A Feminist Per-
    spective on the Relationship between Fertility and Development in
    Malawi." Presented at the American Sociological Association meetings,
    Washington, DC.
Bernard, Jessie. 1987. *The Female World from a Global Perspective.* Bloomington,
    IN: Indiana University Press.
Blumberg, Rae Lesser. 1988. "Income Under Female Versus Male Control."
    Journal of Family Issues 9:51–84.
———. 1991. *Gender, Family, and Economy: The Triple Overlap.* Newbury Park,
    CA: Sage Publications.
Bonilla, Elssy. 1990. "Working Women in Latin America." *Economic and Social
    Progress in Latin America: 1990 Report.* Washington, DC: InterAmerican
    Development Bank.
Bookman, Ann, and Sandra Morgen, eds. 1988. *Women and the Politics of
    Empowerment.* Philadelphia, PA: Temple University.
Borg, Marian J. 1992. "Conflict Management in the Modern World-System."
    Sociological Forum 7:261–282.
Boserup, Ester. 1970. *Woman's Role in Economic Development.* London: George
    Allen and Unwin.
Charles, Maria. 1992. "Cross-National Variation in Occupational Sex Segrega-
    tion." *American Sociological Review* 57:483–502.

Charlton, Sue Ellen M. 1984. *Women in Third World Development*. Boulder, CO: Westview.

Charlton, Sue Ellen M., Jana Everett, and Kathleen Staudt, eds. 1989. *Women, the State, and Development*. Albany, NY: State University of New York.

Chow, Esther Ngan-ling. 1990. "The Gendered Process of Economic Development of High-Tech Industries: The Case of Taiwan." Presented at the XIIth World Congress of Sociology sponsored by the International Sociological Association, Madrid, Spain.

Chow, Esther Ngan-ling, and Catherine White Berheide. 1988. "The Interdependence of Family and Work: A Framework for Family Life Education, Policy, and Practice." *Family Relations* 37:23–28.

Coltrane, Scott. 1992. "The Micropolitics of Gender in Nonindustrial Societies." *Gender & Society* 6:86–107.

Croll, Elisabeth, Delia Davin, and Penny Kane, eds. 1985. *China's One Child Family Policy*. London: MacMillan.

Deere, Carmen Diana, and Magdalena Leon, eds. 1987. *Rural Women and State Policy: Feminist Perspectives on Latin American Agricultural Development*. Boulder, CO: Westview Press.

Dwyer, Daisy, and Judith Bruce, eds. 1988. *A Home Divided: Women and Income in the Third World*. Stanford, CA: Stanford University Press.

Enloe, Cynthia. 1989. *Bananas, Beaches, and Bases: Making Feminist Sense of International Politics*. Berkeley, CA: University of California Press.

Fernandez Kelly, M. Patricia. 1989. "Broadening the Scope: Gender and International Economic Development." *Sociological Forum* 4:611–635.

Flora, Cornelia Butler. 1992. "International Development Policies and Women." Presented at Sociologists for Women in Society meeting, Minneapolis, MN.

Folbre, Nancy. 1987. "The Pauperization of Motherhood: Patriarchy and Public Policy in the United States." In *Families and Work* edited by Naomi Gerstel and Harriet Engel Gross. Philadelphia, PA: Temple University Press.

Fuentes, Annette, and Barbara Ehrenreich. 1983. *Women in the Global Factory*. Boston: South End Press.

Gladwin, Christina, ed. 1991. *Structural Adjustment and African Women Farmers*. Gainesville, FL: University of Florida Press.

Hartmann, Heidi. 1976. "Capitalism, Patriarchy, and Job Segregation by Sex." *Signs* 1:137–169.

———. 1981. "The Family as the Locus of Gender, Class and Political Struggle: The Example of Housework." *Signs: Journal of Women in Culture and Society* 6:366–394.

Jaquette, Jane S. 1982. "Women and Modernization Theory: A Decade of Feminist Criticism." *World Politics* 34:267–284.

Jelin, Elizabeth, ed. 1991. *Family, Household and Gender Relations in Latin America*. London: Kegan Paul International.

Kandiyoti, Deniz. 1988. "Bargaining with Patriarchy." *Gender & Society* 2:274–289.

Kick, Edward L. 1987. "World-System Structure, National Development, and the Prospects for a Socialist World Order." Pp. 127–156 in *America's Changing Role in the World-System*, edited by Terry Boswell and Albert Bergesen. New York: Praeger.

Lengermann, Patricia Madoo, and Jill Niebrugge-Brantley. 1988. "Contemporary Feminist Theory." Pp. 400–443 in *Contemporary Sociological Theories*, edited by George Ritzer. New York: Alfred A. Knopf.

Lim, Linda Y. C. 1983. "Capitalism, Imperialism, and Patriarchy: The Dilemma of Third-World Women Workers in Multinational Factories." Pp. 70–91 in *Women, Men, and the International Division of Labor*, edited by June Nash and M. Patricia Fernandez Kelly. Albany, NY: State University of New York Press.

Mies, Maria. 1986. *Patriarchy and Accumulation on a World Scale*. London: Zed Books.

Nash, June, and M. Patricia Fernandez Kelly. 1983. *Women, Men, and the International Division of Labor*. Albany, NY: State University of New York Press.

Rakowski, Cathy A. 1991. "Gender, Family, and Economy in a Planned, Industrial City: The Working- and Lower Class Households of Ciudad Guayana." Pp. 149–172 in *Gender, Family, and Economy: The Triple Overlap*, edited by Rae Lesser Blumberg. Newbury Park, CA: Sage Publications.

Reskin, Barbara. 1988. "Bringing the Men Back in: Sex Differentiation and the Devaluation of Women's Work." *Gender & Society* 2:58–81.

Roger, Susan. 1983. "Efforts towards Women's Development in Tanzania: Gender Rhetoric vs. Gender Realities." Pp. 23–41 in *Women in Developing Countries: A Policy Focus*, edited by Kathleen Staudt and Jane Jaquette. New York: Haworth Press.

Safa, Helen. 1981. "Runaway Shops and Female Employment: The Search for Cheap Labour." *Signs: Journal of Women in Culture and Society* 7:418–34.

Sen, Gita, and Caren Grown. 1987. *Development Crises and Alternative Visions: Third World Women's Perspectives*. New York: Monthly Review Press.

Smith, Dorothy E. 1979. "A Sociology of Women." Pp. 135–187 in *The Prism of Sex: Essays in the Sociology of Knowledge*, edited by J. Sherman and E. Beck. Madison, WI: University of Wisconsin.

Sokoloff, Natalie J. 1980. *Between Money and Love: The Dialectics of Women's Home and Market Work*. New York: Praeger.

Staudt, Kathleen, ed. 1990. *Women, International Development and Politics: The Bureaucratic Mire*. Philadelphia, PA: Temple University Press.

Staudt, Kathleen, and Jane S. Jaquette. 1983. *Women in Developing Countries: A Policy Focus*. New York: Haworth.

Tinker, Irene. 1990. *Persistent Inequalities*. New York: Oxford University Press.

Walby, Sylvia. 1990. *Theorizing Patriarchy*. Cambridge, MA: Basil Blackwell.

Wallerstein, Immanuel. 1974. *The Modern World System, Vol. 1: Capitalist Agriculture and the Origins of the European World-Economy in the Sixteenth Century*. New York: Academic Press.

Ward, Kathryn, ed. 1990. *Women Workers and Global Restructuring*. Ithaca, NY: School of Industrial and Labor Relations, Cornell University Press.

Wolf, Diane L. 1988. "Female Autonomy, the Family, and Industrialization in Java." *Journal of Family Issues* 9:85–107.

World Bank. 1989. *Women in Development: Issues for Economic and Sector Analysis*. Washington, DC: The World Bank.

Wright, Erik Olin, Karen Shire, Shu-Ling Hwang, Maureen Dolan, and Janeen Baxter. 1992. "The Non-Effects of Class on the Gender Division of Labor in the Home: A Comparative Study of Sweden and the United States." *Gender & Society* 6:252–282.

About the Contributors

Joan Acker is a Professor of Sociology and former director of the Center for the Study of Women in Society at the University of Oregon. From 1987 to 1990 she was Visiting Research Professor at the Swedish Center for Working Life in Stockholm. She is the author of *Doing Comparable Worth: Gender, Class, and Pay Equity* and articles on women and class, feminist theory, gender and organizations, women's work in Sweden, and wage setting.

Cora Vellekoop Baldock is a Professor of Sociology at Murdoch University in Perth, Western Australia. Previous academic appointments were in sociology departments at the Australian National University; the City University of New York; San Diego State University; Canterbury University, New Zealand; and Leiden University. She is an alumna of Leiden University and holds a Ph.D. from Canterbury University. Her publications include: *Volunteers in Welfare* (1990), *Women, Social Welfare and the State* (co-edited with Bettina Cass, second edition, 1988), *Australia and Social Change Theory* (1978), and *Sociology in Australia and New Zealand* (co-authored with J. Lally, 1974). She is the past president of the Sociological Association of Australia and New Zealand.

Catherine White Berheide is an Associate Professor of Sociology at Skidmore College. She received her Ph.D. and M.A. in sociology from Northwestern University and her B.A. in sociology from Beloit College. She is co-author of *Women Today: An Interdisciplinary Approach to Women's Studies* and co-editor of a special issue of *Teaching Sociology* devoted to sex and gender. She has engaged in policy-oriented research focusing largely but not exclusively on pay equity as a consultant for the Center for Women in Government at the State University of New York at Albany since 1985. She has written extensively on issues related to women's work and to undergraduate education in sociology.

Her current research with Marcia Texler Segal analyzes the relationship between fertility and development in Malawi.

Rae Lesser Blumberg is a Professor of Sociology at the University of California, San Diego. Her research interests focus on theories of gender stratification and gender and development. Her publications include *Gender, Family, and Economy: The Triple Overlap, Making the Case for the Gender Variable: Women and the Wealth and Well-Being of Nations, Stratification: Socioeconomic and Sexual Inequality*, and "A General Theory of Gender Stratification" in *Sociological Theory* (1984). She has conducted field research on gender and development in over a dozen countries worldwide, most recently in Ecuador, Swaziland, Guatemala, Nigeria, and the Dominican Republic.

Mounira Charrad, a sociologist, is currently a Mellon Fellow at the University of Pittsburgh. Her research interests are in the areas of politics, law, gender, and culture. She is completing a book on the politics of family law in Tunisia, Algeria, and Morocco, to be published by the University of California Press. Born in Tunisia and trained in France and the United States, she has taught at Harvard, Brown, the University of California-San Diego, and the University of Pittsburgh.

Kevin Chen is a research associate in the Department of Psychiatry at Columbia University, conducting a study on the epidemiology of drug abuse among American adolescents and youth. He holds a B.A. in philosophy from Chinese People's University (1978), a M.A. in Sociology from Bejing University (1985), and a Ph.D. in Sociology from Pennsylvania State University (1991). He was the principal investigator in a project on the "Social Impact of One-Child Family Policy on Chinese Society." His doctoral dissertation, entitled *Political Alienation and Voting Turnout in the United States, 1960-1988*, is published by Mellen Research University Press (1992). He has also published articles on dating choices, social affiliation of the only child, and only-child families in the People's Republic of China.

Esther Ngan-ling Chow received a Ph.D. from the University of California at Los Angeles and is a Professor of Sociology at the American University in Washington, DC. She is a feminist scholar and community activist. Her research interests span gender, work and family, race and immigration, women in development, state and social policies, feminist theories and methodology, and organizational studies. Her research projects include the impact of industrialization, labor stratification, and state policies in Taiwan and in the People's Republic of China, and ethnic transformation of Washington, DC's Chinatown. She has published extensively on issues related to Chinese/Asian

American women and women of color. She recently co-edited (with Doris Wilkinson and Maxine Baca Zinn) a special issue on "race, class and gender" in *Gender & Society*.

Montserrat Sagot recently received a Ph.D. from the American University and is currently an Assistant Professor of Sociology at the University of Costa Rica. She is active in the Costa Rican women's movement and the research coordinator for CEFEMINA (Feminist Center for Information and Action), the oldest feminist organization in Costa Rica. Her main research interests are in social movements, political empowerment, women and development, and family violence. The major foci of her current work, both as a scholar and an activist, are on violence against women and women in development.

Marcia Texler Segal is Associate Vice Chancellor for Academic Affairs and Professor of Sociology at Indiana University Southeast. She earned her B.A. at Harpur College (SUNY–Binghamton), her M.A. at Columbia University, and her Ph.D. at Indiana University, Bloomington. She has been a visiting faculty member at Chancellor College of the University of Malawi. Her research centers on gender issues in American ethnic communities and on women and development, especially in sub-Saharan Africa. She also writes and speaks to academic and general audiences about feminist scholarship and about developing more inclusive curricula.

Susan Tiano is an Associate Professor of Sociology and Acting Director of Women's Studies at the University of New Mexico. She is the co-author, with Vicki Ruiz, of *Women on the U.S.-Mexico Border: Responses to Change*, and has published several articles on women in development, the new international division of labor, and the maquiladora labor force. She has recently completed a book manuscript entitled *Patriarchy on the Line: Labor, Gender, and Ideology in the Mexican Maquila Industry*, which is under review.

Irene Tinker is a Professor in the Department of City and Regional Planning and Chair of the Department of Women's Studies at the University of California, Berkeley. She earned a Ph.D. in comparative government and political theory at the London School of Economics. Her work identifies the differential impact of international development on women and men. She engages in policy-oriented scholarship and social activism. She served as the first Director of the Office of International Science at the American Association for the Advancement of Science and as Assistant Director of ACTION under President Carter. She was Founder-President of the Equity Policy Center, founded the International Center for Research on Women and the Society for International Development's Committee on Women in Development, and co-founded the Wellesley Center for Research on Women and the Washington Women's Network.

Chin-Chun Yi, Research Fellow at the Sun Yat-Sen Institute for Social Sciences and Philosophy, Academia Sinica, Taiwan (ROC), received her Ph.D. in Sociology from the University of Minnesota in 1981. Her research interests are mainly in the field of family sociology, urban sociology, and women's status. Her publications include family type preferences, marital power and marital adjustment, urban housing satisfaction, and urban community image, as well as sex role attitudes of employed women and childcare arrangements among employed mothers in Taiwan. Her recent project examines the institutional transformation of private universities in Taiwan, Japan, and the United States. She is also the principal investigator for the General Survey of Social Attitudes in Taiwan.

Index